PITTSBURGH THEOLOGICAL MONOGRAPH SERIES

General Editor
DIKRAN Y. HADIDIAN

7

INFORMAL GROUPS IN THE CHURCH
*Papers of the Second Cerdic Colloquium
Strasbourg, May 13-15, 1971*

INFORMAL GROUPS IN THE CHURCH

Papers of the Second Cerdic Colloquium Strasbourg, May 13-15, 1971

Edited by
RENE METZ AND JEAN SCHLICK

Translated by
MATTHEW J. O'CONNELL

PICKWICK PUBLICATIONS
An imprint of *Wipf and Stock Publishers*
199 West 8th Avenue • Eugene OR 97401

Originally published as
Les groupes informels dans l'Eglise,
(Hommes et Eglise, 2)
Strasbourg, Cerdic Publications, 1971.

Pickwick Publications
An imprint of Wipf and Stock Publishers
199 West 8th Avenue, Suite 3
Eugene, Oregon 97401

Informal Groups in the Church
Papers of the Second Cerdic Colloquium, Strasbourg, May 13-15, 1971
Edited by Metz, Rene and Schlick, Jean
Copyright©1975 Pickwick Publications
ISBN: 0-915138-08-5
Publication date 1/1/1975

TABLE OF CONTENTS

INTRODUCTION   vii

PART I: FACTS   1

   1. Sociology of Informal Groups: A Socio-
      logical Theory of Informal Groups as
      Preliminary to an Analysis of Ecclesi-
      astical Problems.
      By Jean Remy. 3

   2. The Internal Dynamics of Informal Groups.
      By Jean Séguy 35

   3. Sociological Prolegomena on Informal
      Groups: An Essay in Institutional
      Analysis.
      By René Lourau. 71

   4. The Politico-Religious Ideology of Informal
      Student Groups: An Essay in Interpreta-
      tion.
      By Danièle Léger. 111

   5. Group and Person: A Philosophical Reflection.
      By Maurice Nédoncelle 137

   6. Church Structures and the Informal Groups.
      By Georges Casalis. 159

PART II: HISTORY   181

   7. The Johannine Group and Apostolic Christianity.
      By Joseph Schmitt 183

   8. Informal Groups at the End of the Middle Ages:
      Rhenish Types.
      By Francis Rapp 197

9. Informal Groups in the Reformation:
    Rhenish Types.
    By Rudolphe Peter 215

10. Informal Religious Groups of European
    Origin in the United States during the
    First Half of the Nineteenth Century.
    By Julien Freund. 233

PART III: THEOLOGICAL REFLECTION

11. Informal Groups in the Church:
    A Protestant Viewpoint.
    By Roger Mehl 257

12. Informal Groups in the Church:
    An Orthodox Viewpoint.
    By J. D. Zizioulas. 275

13. Informal Groups in the Church:
    A Catholic Viewpoint.
    By Yves Congar. 299

CONCLUSION   329

14. By Way of Conclusion   329

    I. Remarks of Georges Casalis 329

    II. Concluding Remarks of Yves Congar. 332

NOTES   341

INTRODUCTION

The annual Strasbourg Colloquiums sponsored by Cerdic have as their general theme "Mankind and Church". The 1971 meeting (May 13-15) took for its subject the informal groups which are playing such a striking role in contemporary social change and which cannot but have an influence on the Church. The very diversity of terminology--base communities, spontaneous groups, study groups, and challenge groups--is enough to show the vital and shifting character of the phenomenon.

In analyzing facts, studying the New Testament and later history, and offering theological reflection within an ecumenical framework, we had no intention of trying to provide a miraculous answer to the challenges now being issued to the Church. What we did intend to do was to undertake a more than superficial study that would cut across disciplinary and confessional boundaries and give the Church and men generally a glimpse of the issues involved in the questions being raised by the informal groups.

The study of informal groups passes over quite naturally into a study of the theme "Politics and Faith", which will be the subject of the Third Cerdic Colloquium, May 4-6, 1972.

René Metz. Jean Schlick.

Strasbourg
August 4, 1971

PART I

Facts

CHAPTER 1

Sociology of Informal Groups
A Sociological Theory of Informal Groups
as Preliminary to an Analysis
of Ecclesiastical Problems

by

Jean Remy

The problem of informal groups is arising with new intensity within the contemporary Churches. Most often the informal groups take the form of small groups and are given various names: base community,[1] parallel community or underground community, marginal groups, wildcat groups, teams, etc. All these groups resemble one another at first sight: all are marked by spontaneity, lack of structure, limited size, and affective motivation. But do they all have the same meaning, or on the contrary do they have divergent and even opposed meanings? Moreover, do they not acquire a very special significance in the contemporary social context? There are questions we would like to bring before you in the following analysis.

In the kind of analysis practiced by religious sociology, we find frequent use made of such categories as sect and church, which Troeltsch proposed. Without denying the interest and relevance of the categories of classical sociology, we shall adopt a different starting point and situate the informal groups by reference to the various criteria used by sociologists to explain the social order and large scale change.

In proceeding along these lines we shall first of all view the informal group in light of the concept of organization and

shall discuss the problems raised by the size of the group. We
shall then move on to consider only small informal groups and
their relation to institutions. This analysis will prepare for
a third step in which these groups will be situated by their
relationship to the dominant culture: withdrawal, opposition,
attempt to create a counter-culture. Their impact will be
considered according as they are inserted into a social movement. This will bring us to our last point in which the influence of the small group will be evaluated into terms of the
ideal which guides it: harmony, conflict, or some combination
of the two.

These various analytic viewpoints will provide various
directions in which to evaluate an informal group. These in
turn will enable us to work out typologies in which groups are
characterized by the complexity of their component elements.
Such typological classification will be one of the problems which
we shall take up in our Conclusion.

I. Informal Groups and Organization

1. Organization and the inability to control informal groups

Organization supposes that a group makes explicit its objectives and the rights and duties of each member. The group must
also provide itself with a visible structure of authority and
determine the norms for the choice and continuity of authority.
The formal character of a group flows from its rational mastery
of the rules according to which it functions.

The need for such formalization depends upon various factors
and especially the size of the group. If very small groups can
nonetheless be highly formalized, then, all other things being

equal, greater size will mean greater need of formalization.
Formalization makes it possible to set up a universe in which
the various parties have some foreknowledge of the future, to
establish intermediaries for situations in which direct and
immediate contact between all members is not possible, and to
create corrective mechanisms when there is lacking that direct
and constant visibility which enables each person spontaneously
to correct himself.

On the other hand, whatever be the efforts at formalization
(which manifest a will to be master of the situation), the larger
the size of the group, the more it makes possible spontaneous
subgroupings not provided for in the regulations adopted by the
group as a whole.

The first meaning of an informal group is determined by the
context in which it originates. The group arises within a
societal life that is highly formalized, but the formation of
the group cannot be controlled or determined by any organizing
power. From the viewpoint of established authority, such a group
introduces a non-controllable factor, and this factor is all the
more disturbing since it can either support or oppose the existing formal structure. Those in authority can try to attach the
stigma of guilt to such spontaneous formations, for example by
outlawing all contacts between members that are not provided for
in the formal structures. We know the threats levelled against
particular friendships in some religious communities. Or those
in authority may allow each individual to react as he wished in
mind and conscience but prohibit like-minded individuals from
coming together to express their reactions openly. These are
some ways in which established authority tries to stigmatize
shared reactions not provided for in the regulations. However,
there are instances in which authority favors the formation of
such groups. One example, to which we shall return later on,
is Catholic Action.

Informal groups which do not depend on authority for their existence may originate simply in psychological reactions, that is, in the quest for deeper relationships formed according to norms other than those allowed for regulated relations. In this case the informal groups do not represent any great danger to the formal structures and may even strengthen them. Nonetheless, once established, such groups become the locus for autonomous exchanges with a low degree of visibility and thus provide a context within which a critical outlook can develop.

The impulse to form such groups may be intensified when the formal structures foster a great deal of inertia and are considered inadequate by the members for reasons which may be either intrinsic or extrinsic to the objectives of the organization. When such inertia and inadequacy are verified, the expectations of the members in relation to the organization are disappointed and the formal structures which used to seem acceptable now appear a burdensome constraint. Informal groups give such reactions a concrete form and allow them to spread. Such groups provide an independent base for criticism, the will to effect change, and even the capability of working out strategies. Once established, informal groups can either develop counter-objectives within the perspective of the organization's goals or take an entirely different direction and concern themselves with non-organizational goals. In some cases, the distance between the latter and the objectives of the organization is so great that the spontaneous groups lose all interest in the future of the organization and in changes that may take place in the "outfit". This last derogatory term is applied by the group to structures which had at one time been regarded as supportive. Now, in the eyes of the group, anything important is taking place elsewhere. Thus we find within the Catholic Church not a few people who intend to remain in the Church but not concern themselves with changing the Church's internal structures: churchmen (they sometimes say) are locked up in their own little problems, meaning ecclesiastical or even simply episcopal preoccupations. Such reactions imply that these people see the important problems as situated elsewhere and that the organization offers no significant help in resolving them. This kind of reaction is less frequent in countries where confessional pluralism reigns and where one's religious affiliation is a decisive criterion of social identity. This fact shows clearly how a person's reaction does not depend solely on problems within the organization (in this case, the Church) but on the whole social context, from which the meaning of one's religious affiliation derives in part.

Small informal groups must not be considered simply in themselves but in the ways in which they are related to organized social wholes.

In order better to understand the problem we have been proposing thus far, let us draw a comparison with another kind of connection between informal groups and established authority. Catholic Action began with small base groups in which Christians with something in common (a professional activity, for example) gathered together but also received a mandate from the bishops. Believers of good will were here attempting to bring their faith to bear upon their lives. The group as such was an advantageous place for militant action. Yet these spontaneous groups were also linked to the hierarchy and to some extent with each other. Other kinds of organization or political parties can also try to apply the techniques of "cell" formation, using the base community as foundation. This is especially important when the objective of the organization is to master various forms of cultural orientation in order to create certain kinds of reaction in daily life.

The linkage in which informal groups and centralized directives are brought into unity is very different from the

phenomena we were speaking of above. To the extent that these
phenomena become important in the life of the Church, informal
groups will undoubtedly acquire quite a different significance.
But the difference is not in the psychological area but in the
group's social and cultural impact. The difference will be
even further accentuated if the base groups, as such, possess
such cultural autonomy over against authority that they can
think it legitimate for them to become pressure groups and to
elaborate their own strategies to achieve their ends.

2. <u>Statistical groups and small-size informal groups</u>

If we think of an informal group as a group that functions
without explicitly codified rules and does not depend for its
existence on any initiative from authority, then it is possible
to have a large group that is very unformalized, at least in
the first of the two ways mentioned. The public is an example
of such a group; so are the many groups which are typical of
urbanized milieus and which some writers call statistical
groups. To clarify this last concept, let us take an audience
at a conference. (In many respects, the following analysis may
be applied to a congregation at Sunday Mass in a large city.)

Despite the lack of organizational structure in a statistical group, such a group does comprise a number of individuals
who are involved in communal interaction. However, each member
is not aware of influencing that action in its totality; his
presence or absence hardly changes things in any way. He feels
no responsibility for the proper functioning of the whole. Thus,
when it comes to the Sunday liturgy, the individual is not prevented from choosing a place of worship other than his own
parish by any feeling of responsibility to a particular congregation. This attitude is all the more frequent as the idea of

a community in which place of residence plays an important part is disappearing.

The statistical group, in its turn, also enjoys an autonomy in relation to the particular members who make it up. Part of the public can change without affecting the general situation; even the leader can be replaced. Modifications occur only when the dominant characteristics of the public undergo a change or when the one who presides over the gathering does not respect the rules to which the group gives its adhesion. The group as a whole is thus quite open, yet each member of it feels that he is confronted with an autonomous reality which he does not control or even understand. It is in this way that the sense of "they" arises, the feeling that is typical of publics, especially if they exist without any need of gathering them into one place. The fact of its non-visibility makes us feel all the more that our actions are controlled by an anonymous reality which it is hardly possible to know and, in a sense, we do not even seek to know.

In this situation the lack of formalization combined with largeness of size can give rise to a very ambiguous outlook on the part of the individual, for he is aware of an absolute minimum of control over the collectivity, yet has the feeling that he is autonomous in his own action. This ambiguity gives rise in turn to other tensions, especially in urban social life where the individual is part of many such statistical groups. He feels isolated, yet also feels that he can react autonomously. The possibility of autonomous action, when confronted with the statistical groups of which the individual is a part, gives rise to a proliferation of small groups in which the presence or absence of the individual does have an impact on the activity of the whole; this is to say that interpersonal relations become a key factor in the formation of the group.

The process often leads to forms of mutual trust that become progressively unconditional. In short, there comes into existence a universe dominated by interpersonal relations of direct communication; in other words, an atmosphere quite opposed to that which governs the organization of large-scale social activities. The desire to live in a personalized world can end in the privatization of all preoccupations. Many workers are more interested in their rod and reel club than in their union, and the reason is that the club is a small-scale affair while the union is a large-scale operation.

In view of these facts, sociologists are at times tempted to regard the psycho-sociological variable as the determining factor in the rise and functioning of informal groups. In this perspective, the proliferation of small groups would be essentially a problem for psycho-sociology. The meaning of the phenomenon would derive from the isolation of the individual in large cities and from the concomitant disappearance of inclusive communities; it would derive from the failure of the nuclear family which for many people and especially for the young is not rich enough in varied kinds of human relationships. We do not deny the influence of this variable, but neither would we make it the all-determining one. It is one principle of explanation, but must be related to others. Thus, for example, the priority which the worker gives to his fishing club ought not blind us to the important contexts in which his cultural preoccupations and social possibilities are shaped. The way in which small groups related to such contexts is an important key to understanding their social meaning. The type of relatedness can either increase or lessen the desire of the small group to intervene in some effective way in society. A golfing club made up of men who have charge of various activities in a city can be an important context for decision-making. A fishing club, on the contrary, can be an excuse for avoiding professional responsibilities.

Small-size informal groups can thus be characterized by
whether they expressly aim at external action (in union with
or independently of authority) or on the contrary seek to be
only a place where the quality of interpersonal relationships
is very high. We have looked at two contexts in which either
of these forms can arise. We would now like to show how the
relation to institutions cast further light on the significance of each form.

II. Small Groups and Institutionalization

1. Small size, spontaneity, and institutionalization

Organization and institutionalization are two concepts which
must be carefully distinguished. The former is connected with
the formalization of interactions between members and with
control of the formalization by authority. Institutionalization
has to do rather with the cultural sphere. It depends upon the
existence of stable and widely accepted norms on the basis of
which needs arise, behavior is shaped, and actions are evaluated.

A small group can be very spontaneous, that is, it can
function without any rules to explicitly state rights and duties.
At the same time it can be highly institutionalized, that is, it
can be a group in which spontaneous daily activity is simply the
expression and continuance of pre-given cultural models. These
models enable individuals to decide on appropriate action in
everyday life. Their effectiveness and persistence, however,
is not always connected with an organization which decides on
their orthodoxy. That is true of the family which carries a
heavy weight of important cultural models, yet is not a formalized group acting according to rules. The same is true, for

example, of a village where behavior is highly institutionalized, yet there may be no notable measure of organizational development. For this reason, too, a spontaneous group may be serving the social order and cultural continuity. Institutions and the cultural models they impose are felt to be burdensome only to the extent that a group wants, or feels itself caught up in, a break with the culture in question.

Opposition exists between such groups, which operate under a deeply internalized institutional control, and a total institution. Total institutions (the term is Goffman's[2]) are, for example, a mental hospital, a monastery, or a military school. The point here is not to assimilate to each other the very different meanings which inmates of such institutions live out in their very different experiences. Our analysis is situated at a different level and is concerned primarily with structural likenesses.

In each instance we are dealing with a place controlled by an authority who intends to organize daily life, including the use of time, so as to achieve an objective which is usually the reshaping of personality. In these cases, success and the internalization of cultural models depends on an explicit organizational structure which aims to control and evaluate the results. The impact is greatly increased when the outward organization is assisted by deeply internalized models of authority, as is the case, for example, in a monastery.

It would be a mistake, however, to think that all institutionalization depends in this way on an organization. In some societies religious patterns are highly institutionalized, yet are not transmitted by special organizations. We are reacting here against the over-close connection made, especially in some Catholic circles, between depth of institutionalization and development of organizational control. Such a connection is no more valid than the view which identifies institutionalized behavior with unspontaneous behavior.

Institutionalization, as we have been describing it, involves further consequences for organizations. When a group or a social role is strongly institutionalized, it is difficult for any organization to control the development of the group or the role. The development depends too much on complex and dispersed mechanisms. Thus, it is not enough, for example, to define a priest's role juridically. To the extent that that role is a profoundly institutionalized one, it evolves with the transformation of certain cultural patterns over which no organization has or can have control. The same is true, for example, of the role of woman; this role can be radically changed and in turn radically change the functioning of the family unity, without anyone being able to control the direction of change, not even the individual woman in question.

We have a different situation in the establishing of a football club. Even if the members must accept the rules of the game, the rules themselves are always seen to be a social construct which can be changed by a national or international league. The situation of the Church, however, is utterly unlike that. As sociologists we would reject the idea that the Church is a total institution which is opposed to civil society as to another total institution. Such a conception too readily supposes that the formal structures of Church and civil society can control the internal direction of each by developing a code that is primarily juridical in character.

2. The right to privacy and de-institutionalization

What we have been saying brings us to an analysis of the connection between informal groups and the process of de-institutionalization.

De-institutionalization supposes that the area of cultural and social autonomy within which each group organizes its activity has been widened. Such autonomy can either lead to the rise of a counter-institutionalization or become stablized and end in the co-existence of varying behaviors, each with its own specific legitimacy. Within the framework of this very succinct analysis we shall focus our attention on a concept in use in contemporary life: the right to privacy. This current concept seems to be one that legitimizes de-institutionalization. It is, moreover, playing an increasingly important role in organizing men's perception of society, including the Church.

The right to privacy as applied to man in society claims the possibility of organizing an activity as one pleases and, if need be, without giving it any great social visibility and without authority having any right of supervision. The claim does not necessarily imply an exercise of pure creativity. All that is needed is a context in which reference models are numerous. The concept of privacy activates and legitimizes, however, only if the public enjoys a cultural autonomy vis-à-vis established authority. Such autonomy takes an increasingly concrete form as the person asserts his right to self-determination. In California I met a young Jewish girl who was very proud of her religious affiliation and was attending Eastern religious groups where she had learned meditation techniques and met her fiancé, also Jewish. She wanted to be married according to these Eastern rites because it was from them that she had learned to pray, even while retaining her Jewish affiliation. In addition, she said that she used to go to Newman Hall, a Catholic organization, where she had discovered groups of socially committed people. In all this, she explained, there was no question of syncretism; it was simply that by uniting varied experiences she was constructing for herself an autonomous personality with numerous dimensions.

The right to privacy is readily claimed by individuals who are breaking with their culture. In the name of the right to privacy some claim the right to gather into communities and create a social fabric which will enable them to develop new cultural forms without being drawn back again into the dominant culture. They are in effect saying that in the measure that marriage implies the possibility of long-term anticipation such as the financial commitments involved in having children require, it regularly draws the person into the wage-earning system dominant in society; consequently it makes it possible for society to co-opt the individual. The right to privacy can thus give social legitimacy to a counter-culture in the making.

The development of socially "private" areas, without necessarily weakening the dominant orientation of society, is one characteristic of our contemporary situation. This paradoxical evolution probably arises from an integration of social life that is effected by technological and economic interdependences which force men into relationships despite the numerous forms of opposition in daily experience. The very varied collective instruments on which our social life depends force us to be interdependent, despite the lack of any explicit consensus at the ideological level or at the level of affective motivation. Here we have one approach for analyzing the significance of an industrial society that functions by means of collective instruments. Even modern-style urbanization gives rise to spatial indivisibilities which in turn provide collective advantages that are independent of any cultural communion. Such a situation favors social controls that are technological and economic in nature while making those of an ideological and political nature relatively difficult to use.

Political and ideological controls have been made even more difficult by the development of new means of communication, whether in the form of transportation or in the form of message-sending. These technologies mean an increase in the number of parallel networks which are not visible to those in authority. Thus there is a lessening of such control as is exercised over local life when people live together and engage in varied social activities within a world that is dominated by interpersonal relations. The transformation of which we speak does not, however, affect controls that are technological and economic in character.

These varied structural changes make possible the extension of "private" zones without thereby creating numerous possibilities of changing basic orientations. Moreover, the so-called private zones expand to the extent that they concern non-professional activities and are thus not subject to the exigencies of collective instruments and large scale.

For these various reasons the extension of the area of privacy raises more questions for the Church than it does for a large industrial corporation. And we can ask to what extent religious institutions which played a key role in grounding the social order are threatened with a loss of their importance in this respect. On the other hand, religious institutions might develop a privileged place for themselves in the so-called private areas; this could affect their formal organizational structure. In the light of this suggestion, one might inquire into the success of liturgies held in private surroundings, into the quest for reduced social visibility when it comes to the choice of places for worship; in private surroundings people sometimes take the liturgies that are celebrated in the places proper to religion in a particular culture, but use them in other ways which society does not put down as religious.

In this section of our paper, we have indicated how spontaneous groups can serve both institutionalization and de-institutionalization. Such an approach is valid for spontaneous groups directed at intervention in society as well for spontaneous groups that give prime importance to the quality of interpersonal relations.

III. Goal of the Group: Withdrawal, Opposition, Defense of the Existing Order

We shall now try to specify somewhat further the relation of the group to the social order by inquiring into the goal of the group. This goal may be explicitly understood or implicitly operative. In speaking of "goal" we want to put the stress on an objective, conscious or not, on the basis of which the group takes shape.

The concept of "goal" must not be confused with the concept of the purpose which the members of the group have in mind. Purpose relates expressly to conscious intentions. Goal, however, in the sense in which we use the word here, is primarily characterized not by the fact that it is consciously maintained but by its ability to polarize the reactions of the members of the group. We are dealing with a long-range objective in function of which the daily life of the group takes shape.

1. Withdrawal

Social groups may experience a special insecurity in some area, the economic for example, and find themselves in a situation which they regard as hopeless. In order to survive, they may then develop new forms of solidarity by turning in upon themselves. They withdraw. "Hot" communities[3] thus build up a security against the unforeseen. If there is illness in the family, people know the neighbors will take care of the children.

If they visit relatives, they know they will find there, if
need be, the various things they cannot take with them. The
intimacy of such communities can be such that the members deny
the importance of the family unit as something with a right to
autonomy. We can even find ourselves faced with manifestations
that we might perhaps call "sects", though the term must be
used with caution. At this point, the distinction from the
outside world is clear, whether the group sees the world as
aggressive and evil, in which case they must protect themselves
by withdrawing from it, or whether on the contrary the group
sees the world as an attractive place from which they are excluded and which they are, in a sense, preparing to enter. Do
we not have here the problem of the bidonvilles which surround
the large urban centers of South America, to take but one
example? These shantytowns give birth to various kinds of
religious sect, for here people live in insecurity but on the
borders of paradise: the nearby city is both the place they
fear and the place they would like to enter but from which they
feel excluded.

2. <u>Opposition</u> <u>and</u> <u>counter-system</u>

Small groups can also arise out of a negative interpretation
of the dominant society and a desire to oppose the latter if not
to set up a counter-system. This kind of reaction can arise
whether the group has an optimistic or a pessimistic view of
the outcome of the struggle it is forced to sustain. Such a
reaction is usually behind social movement. The later supposes
that more or less broad sectors of the population feel a dissatisfaction which renders them quite open to identification
with one or other cause. Take, for an example, the Flemish
movement in Belgium. This social movement has lasted for

several generations without involving any transmission of power within it; no organization can claim a monopoly of the movement. Numerous small groups can be born, fight with each other, and disappear, but the movement goes on. The movement does, however, suppose an interaction between some leaders and the mass of the people, through various forms of cultural sympathy.

The small groups of which we are now speaking have no formal links with one another. Yet they are caught up in a movement, the meaning and direction of which cannot be determined in advance. After the fact, when a social movement has been unfolding through time, it is possible to see that a certain internal logic has been at work: what some sociologists would call teleonomy without teleology. The meaning of the change can be discovered, but only after the fact. There is therefore relatively little possibility of organizations taking control of the movement; in any event, no single organization can claim a monopoly of the movement.

Such a situation is, however, quite risky for the individuals who are involved in it. This is why it is so important to have ways of creating a sense of security as well as an objective verification of valid grounds for the direction being taken. Among other means of securing these goals there are a set of external referential norms and the formation of groups with a great capacity for affective motivation.

The referential criteria needed in order to make the group's action visible and to maintain it may be such as are called "natural": the fact of being young or old, white or black, man or woman, a member of a particular ethnic group or an adherent of a particular religion. Such criteria are a very important factor in self-identification. They are all the stronger in that people cannot abandon them (since they are, in a sense, criteria that cannot be rejected).

In other cases, the criteria of identification are socially established. In our present context clothing, for example, can become highly important, as can the formation of a common language. The hippies created an identification by means of clothing and other signs, just at the moment when Catholic priests were rejecting identification through garb and when Vatican II had reduced in number the criteria for determining in-groups and out-groups in relation to the Church. An analysis of these opposite developments would probably tell us a good deal about the relative position of the two groups vis-à-vis the dynamics of contemporary culture.

A further factor in identification and security arises out of devotion to some intellectual master. Consider, for example, the role Marcuse has played in the student movement.

In the first stage of a social movement, intellectuals may play an important role, for they can guarantee the analysis a group needs if it is to accept the breaks and risks we have mentioned. The acceptance of these leaders is connected with a cultural sympathy which cannot be called in question by such criteria and arguments as proceed chiefly from rational logic. What is important is rather the leader's "charismatic" quality (in the Weberian sense). Thus the success, some years back, which Teilhard de Chardin enjoyed in some Catholic circles was not to be explained by any support from the organization. In fact, in extreme cases, theological critiques of the incoherence of Teilhard's thought had absolutely no impact on those who believed in him. The critiques did, however, serve to confirm the rejection of Teilhard by those who had no cultural sympathy with him. The term "sympathy" I regard as rather important, for it points to a situation where the rational is not in the ascendant and where the evaluative criteria being used are difficult to explicitate.

In addition to achieving this self-identification (in which the leader plays an important part), a social movement must also set up such systems as will make it possible for the members to live autonomous lives and, further, to achieve affective security. This need is especially felt when the effort is being made to form a counter-culture. A counter-culture supposes that the members move from a feeling of shame to a feeling of pride. They must therefore put off all sense of guilt with regard to the kinds of behavior which the dominant culture calls normal, and become proud of adopting other ways.

For this reason, some of the communities we find in California, for example, resemble in some respects the early monks: in the desert the latter built up systems of interaction which were sufficiently autonomous to give rise to a counter-culture.

For these various reasons such groups develop a milieu which is highly affective in character. This is why their language becomes like that of religious sects. They like to speak of loyalty, fidelity, or betrayal in relation to the group.[4]

Such groups can thus be turned in on themselves, that is, have no explicit aim of intervening in or exerting pressure on society, and yet can have an important collective impact to the extent that they develop new and contagious cultural models. This fact distinguishes these groups from others which form simply to develop the quality of their interpersonal relations, and thus contribute to the translation into daily life of highly institutionalized models.

3. Defense of the social order

As counter-systems become influential and threaten the dominant models, other groups form to defend these models. They cannot, however, employ the same kind of strategy as their opponents. The innovative groups can rely on the relatively contagious nature of the values they are promoting. The group which defends the social order feels, on the contrary, that its values are disappearing and tries to stabilize them, for example, by trying to exercise a control over more explicit norms or verbalized and rationally managed contents. Thus, within the Catholic Church, groups which aim to defend the Church's traditional sanctity will fight, as occasion offers, for the cassock, Mass in Latin, certain dogmatic formulas, a particular way of viewing the authority of the Pope, and so forth. The innovative group cannot, of course, follow such a strategy as this, for quite often, in the name of more or less obscurely felt new values, it must attack traditional formulations and existing concrete forms, without always being able to offer other norms and formulations in their place. This lack of concrete suggestions is something that is especially liable to happen in the first stage of social movement. From all this it follows that the divergent strategies followed by the opposing groups are not a matter of choice but are in good measure imposed by the structural possibilities available to each group according to its position in regard to change.

4. Position of the movement in the social structure

Whatever be the attitude of a social movement to the encompassing society, its long-term impact will depend on the time and place where it comes to birth within the social structure. The Little Brothers of Charles de Foucault, who aimed at a presence in popular milieus, have never drawn their recruits chiefly from these same milieus. The fact that they have recruited so successfully in the middle and even the upper middle classes suggests that some of these people see a social conflict which they find insupportable and which they endeavor to resolve in symbolic fashion on the level of interpersonal reconciliation. In such a situation small groups which aim at bearing witness through friendship could take on a special significance, quite different from that which they would have in another context. This significance is to some extent independent of what goes on in the awareness of the agents involved, but the independence is not total. For, insofar as these agents adopt a different analysis of the social situation, they will react in different ways. Consider the attitude of some doctors who want to see the introduction of socialized medicine and seek to get themselves established in a working-class milieu in order to stir people there to awareness and to a rejection of various kinds of exploitation in the field of health. Far from concealing their institutional role they seek to use it in order to attain their goals. Such an attitude presupposes a certain analysis of the social situation.

The origin and function of these doctors are not those of the working-class, but their action takes on a new meaning and modifies the social structure. We may also ask what kind of social solidarity makes such a reaction possible. In answering the question, it would be important to compare these kinds of action with that of ministers of the Church who want people to forget their institutional role so that their social involvement may be more effective. Through such reactions in the form of daily choices, we could try once again, from a sociological standpoint, to evaluate the Church's position in respect to social change.

Divergent relations to social structure thus gives very different significance to groups which at first sight seem endowed with similar characteristics. Insertion into the social structure partly determines the possibilities open to a social movement in regard to the changing of cultural priorities. Thus, informal groups on the periphery of the artistic world can contribute to the creation of new forms of expression and yet initially have as their public only circles that are deeply rooted in the established order.

Such groups find themselves in a situation in which production and appropriation are unconnected. Whatever be their desire to win other publics, it is only the existing public that is able to appropriate what the artist has to offer; sometimes only that public is able to spread abroad what the artist does, and this in virtue of that public's ability to create objects that achieve prestige, especially when these objects are novelties. This is the case, for example, with some firms which deal in culture intended for the people and used by the middle classes.

Interpretation in terms of social structure can be applied to the other approaches we have been presenting and especially to the claim of privacy. The areas legitimized as private can be differently defined according to the social milieu involved. So too, certain groups can use the private sphere to establish themselves as invisible pressure groups, whereas others seek there only to escape from non-interpersonal social relations.

IV. Harmonizing or Conflictual View of Society

At an earlier point we distinguished the small group that is motivated by a strong sense of militancy, from the small group that arises out of a desire for autonomy and of felt needs in the area of interpersonal relations. These two extreme types combine in various ways to produce intermediate types.

The meaning of the two types is to be determined by their links to the organization, on the one hand, and by their insertion into a social movement, on the other; moreover, the point at which they come into existence and take root within the social structure determines their overall impact. On the level of cultural analysis we have already asked some questions about institutionalization. We would like to pursue the cultural reference by means of the content of the images in which the society or the group thinks of itself. This type of interpretation is to some extent independent of those which have preceded.

1. The harmonizing vision

The harmonizing vision thinks of society in images in which the convergence of individual interests plays the dominant role. Disagreements only supply material and will be resolved through improved mutual understanding. In this vision, therefore, reconciliation in the area of personal relations is a direct and important goal. For those who see reality in the light of a harmonizing vision, the experience of the small group is a prototype valid for society as a whole. Thus if in the small group friendship makes it possible to transcend social differences and the other divergences between people, this conception is applied to society as a whole. Such a transposition is all the more easily accepted within Christianity because the latter already has an image of universal brotherhood. We must note, moreover, that an optical illusion prevents these small groups from seeing the selective character of their recruiting. Implicitly they like to think: "If only everyone thought as we do!"

2. Total opposition

Other groups may think of society in terms of the presence or absence of a solidarity of interests. This was a common attitude, for example, in the countries occupied by the Nazis. In this confrontation no compromise was acceptable, and every kind of collaboration was regarded as cowardice. We can remember the negative sense given the word "collaborator" during the Second World War.

This kind of either-or attitude is easily taken up in Christian circles when a conflict arises that is external to the community or nation. In modern societies areas for radical opposition are also seen by some groups to exist within a society and to be relatively permanent there. For these small groups, the solidarities proper to themselves are seen as totally opposed to the images they use for representing to themselves the larger society. This kind of opposition to what is outside has nothing to do with the presence or absence of personal relationships. It is said rather to be a more radical thing, that is, it continues to exist behind the veil thrown over it by correct interpersonal relations.

3. Areas of solidarity and opposition

Intermediate images can also arise. Then society is seen as a mixture of oppositions and solidarities. The oppositions may predominate at the moment but leave the hope that in the long run solidarity will gain the upper hand. In such groups, the various forms of opposition are easily viewed as the condition of a new creation. Thus some groups can be very critical of the Church and authority while continuing to feel themselves part of the Church and to consider the matter of schism to be an unreal and outdated problem.

Yet some conflicts are regarded as marginal and therefore to be eliminated, since they only distract attention from the important struggles. Here, once again, images of reconciliation can be used in order to surmount these conflicts; that is what is now taking place between the Christian confessions. New oppositions can then arise, but they are quite different from the traditional ones. For now various members of the Protestant and Catholic confessions have found a solidarity in outlook and reactions, and instead are opposed to a party within their own confessions. The image of reconciliation is used to eliminate conflicts between the confessions; it is hardly used to handle the new form of opposition.

As such images of partial solidarity become widespread, it is important to become clearly aware of those areas of opposition which have been legitimized and become socially stable and within which pluralism is accepted. Each group may interpret these areas differently and want to change the boundaries of them. The result can be numerous misunderstandings which point to cultural discontinuities.

From this point of view, social life implies encounters at two levels: on the one hand, the multiplication of small groups in which a process of selection leads to cultural homogeniety; on the other hand, places where divergent tendencies, none of which has a monopoly, may meet and confront each other. Some people would like to see this second kind of encounter become the business of those in authority in the Church. The latter should promote encounter and confrontation between persons and groups who are all committed but have made different choices.

Some pastoral councils are conceived according to this model. A council will be composed of various delegations, each of which reacts as a group to get across to others the milieu and direction they represent. During a session the delegations have the opportunity to caucus as distinct groups. The basic way in which the council functions is explicitly to confront points of view by allowing the spokesman for each delegation to express its opposition without disturbing the group's personal relationships with the members of the other groups. By depersonalizing conflicts and oppositions each person will, it is hoped, be led to distinguish carefully between opposition and the quality of personal relationships. To the extent that people within the Churches adopt the vision in which a new creation is bound up with numerous forms of opposition, it becomes very important to distinguish these two kinds of group: the one which is based on intense cultural communion and the one which aims at the confrontation and opposition of divergent tendencies.

V. Conclusion

1. Multidimensional analysis of informal groups

The preceding analysis has aimed to avoid a purely psycho-sociological interpretation of small groups. The interpretation we have offered is, on the contrary, correlative to a universe with several dimensions which are relatively independent of one another. It is possible to characterize an informal group either by interrelating its dimensions and constructing typologies, or by describing a particular group as a combination of complex characteristics. The former method allows a global view but becomes very complicated when one combines more than two interpretative viewpoints at a time. The second method allows more complicated combinations but loses the overall view. The two methods therefore complement each other and we shall introduce them both here.

a) <u>Presentation of a typological classification</u>

By way of example we shall propose a classification which combines two dimensions of analysis: the conflictual or harmonizing image of society, combined with the dimension of withdrawal or opposition or defense of the existing order. The following table is only one of a possible series.

<u>Combination of Image of Society with Group Goal</u>

	Conflictual Image	Harmonizing Image
withdrawal	sect	group concerned solely with the quality of interpersonal relationships and with the support it derives from these
opposition	"community" for promoting a counter-culture	a new culture deriving chiefly from the needs of the person; quality of interpersonal relationships as the supreme testimony
defense of the existing order	group defending the order against destroyers of the common good	various collaborations with authority in order to strengthen the foundations

b) **A particular group as combination of complex characteristics**

Another method is to present typical groups possessed of complex characteristics. For example, one might describe a group which sets a high value on interpersonal relations in the framework of the right to privacy, and has no intention of influencing society as a whole, of which it has a relatively harmonizing vision.

One could, on the contrary, describe a particular kind of pressure group as a small group which uses the right to privacy to develop areas of invisibility and thereby is able to influence organizations so as to make its own views prevail, its image of society being a semi-conflictual one.

These two basic situations could themselves be further subdivided according to their consequences: for example, according to the way the group is related to the social structure. Here, however, we simply want to show combinations of the two methods of classification.

c) **We must not lose sight of the overall dynamics**

Classification may cause us to stop at the characteristics of the small group considered in itself. Interpretation ought, however, keep in view the overall dynamics of the social situation. None of these groups can be so autonomous that it can be considered solely in itself and independently of its complex connections with society at large and its possible impact on the latter. We must bear in mind that these connections and this impact are independent of the group's awareness of them.

The same holds for analysis of the Church. Whatever be the modalities of its existence as a juridical entity, the Church cannot be assigned the autonomy proper to a complex society. It is not simply an autonomous society that intervenes in social life through treaty mechanisms. Rather, it is constituted in its own social reality and its possibilities of intervention by structures which comprehend the whole of society at large. Social and cultural dynamics depend in large measure on factors which are subject to no mastery. To grasp the significance of these small-size groups, especially if the intention is to situate them in relation to the organizations we call the Churches, requires an effort to uncover all these complex interconnections.

2. Some questions concerning the life of the Church

If we are to analyze the relation of small groups to the Church and to study the various consequences they may have for the Church, it is very important to ask certain questions about the Church. These questions will be taken up in later analyses.

a) To what extent is the institutionalization of religious behavior, a process that provides models which can be applied to the daily life of the Christian, to be distinguished from the action of a society that attempts to control the direction of behavior? In this religious sphere is the extension of institutionalization directly connected with organizational development? Before answering this question, it would be well to recall the limited possibilities open to an organization when it comes to controlling a culture.

b) Are the Christian Churches on the side of organization or on the side of social movement? The importance assigned to the formal transmission of powers is a key index in this respect. Both organization and social movement aim to create forms of collective solidarity and security. But each achieves its goal in different ways and with different purposes in mind. Usually it is through a social movement that groups are led to take the serious risks required if new values are to be fostered. It is clear that between these two social types there can be numerous combinational forms.

c) An organization will create quite different structures for itself depending on the objectives to be achieved and the possibilities of communication. This point is decisive in evaluating the distribution of initiatives. The latter may be centralized or delegated; if they are, then areas of autonomy become narrower and narrower as we reach the bottom of the pyramid. In other cases, the opposite cultural model may be in effect. We can evaluate the two types in different ways, depending on the objectives to which we give priority, and especially the importance we assign to innovation and renovation. In the Church, structures cannot be assigned a value independently of the objectives to be attained, unless we make the organizational structure the most important thing to be validated.

d) If we accept the innovative role of initiatives taken at the base of the pyramid, then the Church must multiply the situations in which various tendencies can confront each other so as to stimulate forms of opposition, for the latter, in this context, are being viewed as conditions for the emergence of something new. One preoccupation of those in authority will be to stir up reactions and to create the conditions which allow the confrontation of opposing views without aggressiveness. Such encounter situations must not make us forget the prior necessity of having base groups which rely on a process of selection that guarantees their internal solidarity even amid advanced kinds of cultural interchange.

e) When we speak of the influence of base groups as connected with new possibilities of communication within contemporary society and as likewise connected with the demands of of the person, who is relatively isolated and shares in a plurality of models of legitimation, the question arises: Will not such influence greatly modify the division of reality in the spheres regarded as public and private? If so, then will not the Churches move from a central place in the public sphere and take up their dwelling in the private sphere? To what extent will such a shift importantly affect the linkage between formal and informal structures?

In all the foregoing analyses, our intention has been simply to present a working tool, in the hope that it will make possible a more systematic and critical analysis of those facts of daily life in which we are all involved.

CHAPTER 2

The Internal Dynamics of Informal Groups

by

Jean Séguy

Introduction: Preliminary Questions

What does the term "informal groups" mean? Current and non-critical language uses various equivalent expressions: base communities, communal experiments, small gatherings or communities, underground or clandestine churches. These are but a specimen of a semantic inventiveness that undoubtedly points chiefly to the hesitation of observers as they try to come to grips with a very fluid phenomenon. But then, what institution--Church, party, perhaps even the police--does not have its "little groups" today? This apparent universality of "parallel groups"--more or less clandestine, usually small in size, in which social relations tend to be informal and un-programmed, and in which the goal is a sharing, whether of information or of various other material or ideological goods-- raises problems today for all organizations with their vested interests.

The researcher, too, must ask himself questions when he is bidden to focus his reflections on such an uncritical term as "informal groups", but his questions have to do rather with methodology. Is it possible to deal under a single heading both with "neighborhood communities" (sometimes also called "base communities") and with other groups made up, for example, wholly of priests who are engaging in some form of protest, or, again, with a lay community in which the priest plays a purely cultic role--and that a reduced and contested one--and in which the definition of belief and practice is determined by the membership as a whole which will accept nothing in these areas that has not first become the object of their explicit consensus? Despite the difficulty of thus joining quite different kinds of group, I think we need not completely reject--at least not for the moment and until we have more information--the uncritical terminology of everyday life. For we can discern one characteristic shared by all the "informal groups", and that is their remoteness, in varying degrees, from the traditional sources of regulation for "small groups" within the Churches. This remark seems to hold true even of the "neighborhood communities" that are organized along parish lines, to the extent at least that curial or episcopal regulation of them is exercised only in a relatively dialogical and, as it were, informal way; this seems to be true at least for the moment and with due allowance for exceptional cases. At the other end of the continuum of reference to the source of social regulation, we find some, perhaps rare, formations that are completely self-regulated; in other periods of history these would have been called, in non-sociological language, heretical or at least schismatic groups. Thus we move from the inside to the outside (or what is almost the outside); this presents some advantage for sociological analysis, even if the viewpoint be not shared by various other researchers.

In this communication I will therefore retain the term "informal groups". But what I shall have to say will apply to those groups situated near the extreme of self-regulation rather than to the "neighborhood groups". In general, the groups with which I shall be concerned profess radical ideas in most areas. We must note, however, that the phenomenon of informal groups can show up even in milieus that resist innovation. Little attention is usually paid to this aspect of the overall situation. Yet, though we shall not do it here, we should also pay attention to the groups or networks of groups that choose to regulate themselves, but in the name, as it were, of an ideal of maximal hierarchic regulation.[1]

The words "internal dynamics" in the title of this essay warrant some explanation. We do not take the words in the rather psycho-sociological sense of "group dynamics", but understand them as referring to a theory of the diachronic development of social groups, somewhat in the manner of Comte who opposes the static and the dynamic, or of H. Richard Niebuhr in his *The Social Sources of Denominationalism*.[2] You can see the difficulty of our undertaking to deal with contemporary informal groups. For the latter do not necessarily last long enough to lend themselves to this kind of analysis. It may even be asked whether we have sufficiently scientific studies of the phenomenon in question to allow the establishment of a sociological perspective. These two difficulties force us to stay on the theoretical level and to ask questions rather than to give answers concerning the informal groups. We shall, therefore, pursue our goal by offering methods of analysis and not by analyzing specific cases. One of these methods, however, the one proposed by Ralf Dahrendorf,[3] will make it possible to ask more relevant questions about the meaning of the emergence of the phenomenon which concerns us here.

The Excitement of Beginnings

The dynamics of religious bodies are the dynamics of any society. The beginnings are often anarchic and full of promises, oppositions of every kind, and informal enthusiasm; then comes a gradual putting in order, then institutionalization, and eventually, though the date cannot be foreseen, the disappearance. The excitement and vitality that marked the early days of Christianity has been well described by Engels in one of his essays on that period. The following extract will also suggest a number of questions about the manner in which dominant groups, or a group that had not been dominant earlier, later on appropriate and manipulate their own beginnings.

> We therefore see that the Christianity of that time, which was still unaware of itself, was as different as heaven from earth from the later dogmatically fixed universal religion of the Nicene Council; one cannot be recognized in the other. Here we have neither the dogma nor the morals of later Christianity but instead a feeling that one is struggling against the whole world and that the struggle will be a victorious one; an eagerness for the struggle and a certainty of victory which are totally lacking in Christians of today and which are to be found in our time only at the other pole of society, among the Socialists.
> In fact, the struggle against a world that at the beginning was superior in force, and at the same time against the innovators themselves, is common to the early Christians and the Socialists. Neither of these two great movements were made by leaders or prophets--although there are prophets enough among both of them-- they are mass movements, and mass movements are bound to be confused at the beginning; confused because the thinking of the masses at first moves among contradictions, lack of clarity and lack of cohesion, and also because of the role that prophets still play among them at the beginning. This confusion is to be seen in the formation of numerous sects which fight against one another with at least the same zeal as against the common external enemy. So it was with early Christianity, so it was in the beginning of the socialist movement, no matter how much that worried the well-meaning workers who preached unity where no unity was possible.[4]

This passage provides us with a number of ideas or terms that seem applicable to all crucial moments of fruitfulness and creativity.

Engels notes the simplicity of beliefs that were not yet fixed or universally accepted. He might have added that worship, too, was not yet regulated. He seems most struck, however, by a twofold opposition that marks early Christianity and early socialism as well: opposition between innovators and the outside world, and opposition among the innovators themselves on everything that did not form part of their quite minimal common front against the outside world. Intense eagerness, certainty of victory, uncertainty as to the role of authority, contradictions, confusion, lack of clarity and cohesion, and the impossibility of achieving unity--all these mark the emergence of the new reality. We have here the problem of social movement and its opposition to existing organizations.[5]

Engels' analysis seems valid for all periods when "imagination takes control". As for early Christianity, we must leave it to the exegetes to decide whether the picture is acceptable. We may note, however, that no one seems any longer to believe that early Christianity resembled the utopia portrayed in the Acts of the Apostles: "one heart and one mind". Yet all movements of radical challenge[6] are under the illusion that their innovations are a return to a paradisiac beginning when unanimity reigned. In fact "new beginnings" are always marked by anarchy. We can see this in the "apostolic life" movements of the Middle Ages, whether orthodox or heterodox, in the Protestant reforms, and, at the same period, in the radical reform[7] that took so many shapes, though not more than official reforms did. The same outburst shows in the varied religious life of the Cromwellian Commonwealth of seventeenth century England. Do the contemporary informal groups also show the "confusion" of which Engels speaks? It seems so, but the whole phenomenon has not yet been described in a sufficiently complete and dispassionate way.[8]

The Role of the Prophets

The reader will have observed, in the passage of Engels given above, a clear hostility toward the prophets who were active at the beginning of Christianity and socialism both: "Neither of these two great movements were made by leaders or prophets...they are mass movements." Yet prophetic leaders were there in both cases and played a role. Was it an important role? Yes, says Engels, but only in the perspective of the confusion that is characteristic of beginnings. That is, the prophets both reflect and create, in a dialectical process, the lack of coherence proper to mass movements in their initial stage. In Engels' terminology, prophets belong to the non-scientific, utopian stage, which Christianity never managed to get beyond.[9]

Engels seems both annoyed and attracted by the excitement that marked the early Christian and socialist communities; he seems to want to declare the masses right, yet also to lead them to a respect for order, the orderliness of an institution of which they are not yet aware. Here the later organization is attempting to claim for itself and simultaneously to neutralize the earlier social movement. That is the classical ploy of dominant religions as, like armies in battle array, they confront the creative freedom of their own beginnings. They must discredit the ancient values which diverge from those that replaced them at a later point, and must explain these later changes by arguing that charisms have meaning only in the first generation where no organization as yet exists. If you think differently, you are a heretic.

The interest of Engels' analysis is evident. It may not provide any methodological key but it does draw attention to a number of characteristic traits, some of which we have seen. The important thing to note is that the beginnings of a movement stand in contrast with later stages. The simplicity of beliefs and ethics, and the lack of formal organization give way, in a more or less lengthy process, to one or more organizational structures and to beliefs that are more elaborate and, in many respects, different from those of the beginning; a new ethic replaces the old. Above all, however, a social organism takes control of the relative freedom of the movement. We can leave aside the role of the masses in the early phase and note simply that at a later point the "wildcat" movement becomes organized and that the prophets are replaced by functionaries of a system. We shall see later on that Troeltsch and Weber provide almost the same analysis, except that they give a larger and less negative place to the prophets. All the analysts agree, however, on the glossing-over process that follows upon the change from movement to organization. The victorious party, or simply the later generations, reinterpret the original experience so as to justify and canonize the changes that took place later on. Engels tells us this indirectly and in self-defense as it were. But the phenomenon is always to be found accompanying the creation of a new orthodoxy, which must put the present generations in the wrong in two ways. On the one hand (this is not the case with Engels), picture of the far off past must be painted which will show up the deficiencies of the existing state of affairs as individuals experience it in their lives. On the other hand, this picture also portrays an ideal that cannot be realized, but it would require adherence to values

of individual initiative which the organization denounces as
contrary to the primitive message. The organization, of course,
also offers its members means of and models for action which
it regards as superior to those the original movement had at
its disposition. In consequence, people are henceforth to
admire but not imitate the picture of the beginnings, and to
find in it the justification for a later state of affairs which
is unlike the original. Thus the very admiration for that great
time of old will prevent its being brought to life again. The
organization which honors the prophets by idealizing them thereby makes them something extraordinary and neutralizes them.[10]

As we have seen, Engels does not like prophets, and his
tribute to their activity is ambiguous. We must go to Max
Weber to find neither tributes nor canonizations but a more
functional analysis of prophets.

In Weber's view the prophet is opposed to the priest and
to the magician (or sorcerer).[11] The latter two figures represent, at different levels, the fixed and codified tradition
that functions by way of institutionalization. Each has knowledge and techniques that are in large measure acquired. They
depend heavily on a more or less bureaucratic institution or a
traditional civilization. This means that their concern is the
preservation of the existing order, a social order that is assimilated to the cosmic order and thus to the divine order, even
if in practice the priest and the magician represent divergent
conceptions of the cosmic order. The two personages have in
common that all their energies are devoted to opposing social
change. The prophet appears in times of discontinuity. He is
the typical agent of the "breakthrough", the break with the
past and the introduction of novelty.

The justification for the prophet's power and authority
lies in charism, that is, in an appeal to the irrational. The

prophet speaks and is believed. It is true, of course, that not every one trusts him and that he may pay for his claims with his life, or at least suffer persecution for them. In any event, the credibility of his message, like his very appearance on the scene, are not unconnected with the general situation of the society in which he emerges. To think otherwise would be to jettison Weber in the interests of an idealism that has little sociological validity.[12]

In Weber's analysis the prophet is seen as the isolated individual who opposed the established powers. The divergence from Engels is clear, for the latter sees the prophets as abnormal epiphenomena of a mass movement. This is not the place to try to settle the conflict between the two viewpoints. It is more profitable to ask whether the prophet as seen by Weber is relevant to an analysis of contemporary informal groups. In raising this question we must be careful to avoid several possible illusions. We must note, to begin with, that in Weber's account sociology studies relations to values but not the normativity of the values themselves. In other words, he passes no judgment, favorable or unfavorable, on the attribution of the label "prophet" to an individual. Moreover, the sociologist must always be critical toward what people say and not accept their statements at face value. Many contemporary informal groups would probably tend to accept Engels' opinion of the prophets and say: no prophets, or everyone a prophet. The sociologist will not swallow this claim without finding out whether the facts correspond to the expressed norm and whether the implicit or explicit statement of fact hides a wish for what doesn't exist. Finally, we must realize that Weber's conception of the prophet does not necessarily correspond to the popular (some would say "sacred") image which people may commonly have, according to which the prophet is recognized only after the fact, when he is canonized. This latter understanding of the prophet arises with the emergence of an organization and is connected with a number of contingent events, with normative choices, and with the regulating of a group's collective memory by orthodoxy or felt needs (even unorganized) of orthodoxy. The collective memory can therefore eliminate the prophets who failed or transform their history;[13] it can also canonize persons who were not prophets in Weber's sense. From the latter's viewpoint a prophet is any individual whose message, attitudes, and authority do not rest on an inherited tradition or acquired techniques but on the summons to a first-hand experience that is not regulated by anything outside itself.[14]

If we hold to Weber's conception and avoid all verbal inflation, whether or not intended to strengthen the prophet's claim, it is possible to maintain that prophetic personages are more a part of the contemporary informal group phenomenon than is believed. In our time, however, the prophet may be a priest, inasmuch as priests can oppose clericalism and try to give higher status to the layman, for the conflict is often between priests and laymen on the one side and bishops on the other. This fact does not gainsay Weber's analysis, for in his view the priest does not represent a stratum in a hierarchy but a generalized adherence to an established system. We are of the opinion, in any case, that the atmosphere, practices, and ethos of many informal groups show charismatic traits, along the lines of which we have been speaking. On this point, we must wait for judgments provided by first-hand research. Such research will doubtless find that the more self-regulated an informal group is, the more charismatic it is and the more reliant on one or several prophetic persons. It may be that some groups are, for a time at least, made up entirely of prophets. But all this requires experimental verification.

From Prophetism to Institution: Sect or Church?

Engels would have it that the prophets were disturbing elements within early Christianity. According to the Marxist thinker, the masses, who are the important people in the situation, must organize to rid themselves of these troublemakers.[15] For Weber, on the contrary, the very dynamism of the prophetic preaching and the requirements for its transmission lead to the creation of an organization.

Between prophet and ecclesial community Weber has an intermediate stage.[16] The prophet's activity, his challenges and struggles, attract hearers. Among these some begin to follow the innovator, share his life, gather up his message, and broadcast it under his direction. Possibly they share his charism in whole or in part. Their relations with the prophet are informal or at least not very formal; they are related to each other as equals, even if one disciple is given a special role, and despite the tensions this special choice can sometimes engender.[17] The privileged links between the prophet and the band of disciples give structure to the circle.[18] The animosity directed at them by the established priesthood which they are challenging strengthens the intimacy and cohesion of the little group; this period will be remembered later on as a lost paradise.

The passing of the prophet, generally by death and often by a violent death, will confront the disciples with the question of the meaning of their mission. At the same time they will ask what the prophet meant to them. From this double questioning, a renewed, or possibly a new, conception of the message received will arise,[19] and the canonization of the lost leader. The ensuing preaching and the consequences of the ensuing proselytism will give rise to a new kind of group, the apostolic community. The latter continues to be charismatic, but in an increasingly differentiated fashion. For the transmission of the prophetic message establishes a tradition, and the need of communicating it in the real conditions of the surrounding society leads to the emergence of an orthodoxy and a hierarchy, at least in some rudimentary form. Preaching, catechism, sacraments, and priesthood gradually replace the direct links with the prophet or the divine. Cultic functionaries replace the disciples, whose disappearance plays a very decisive role in what Weber in a disillusioning phrase calls the "routinization of charism". At the term of the process "charisms of function" have replaced firsthand experience. The way is now open to the bureaucratization of the sacred, provided the community remains in existence a sufficiently long time. All the written histories of the Church bear witness to this phenomenon.

What about the present-day informal groups? Or rather what about these processes which the groups cannot escape, to the extent that they show prophetico-charismatic traits, to the extent, that is, that they represent, by-contrast to ecclesiastical ordinariness, an ecclesial extraordinariness? Does the average low age of the informal groups prevent Weber's analyses from applying to them? We think not. A confidential document recently received from a milieu close to such groups speaks as follows of them:

> Initially you have a small group of the "pure", gathered around one (or two) prophet(s)-founder(s); there is a very radical challenge to society and to the Church that approves it. Then the numbers increase, organization is needed, the first enthusiasm dies out, and people begin to complain that the days of the militants are gone and we now have nothing but "those who practice"....The "confessing group" has quietly become a "sociological group", and the process begins all over again with small groups breaking off to become "pure". So too, all the great orders have reformers as well as founders.

Such an analysis of groups so young ought not surprise us, since routinization takes place very rapidly, even if its full development at times takes many years and may in a sense never be complete. In the case of the pacifist anabaptists of sixteenth-century Switzerland and South Germany, the properly charismatic upheaval seems to have lasted less than two years.[20] What of the early Church? The study of Christian origins from this point of view has never been really undertaken, and it may be that the state of the documentation from that period would make such a study quite difficult. However, it would be of interest, at least beginning now, to study the informal groups in such a way as to allow answers to the questions we have been raising on the basis of Weber or even--why not?--of Engels.

The routinization of charism accompanies the formation of a new ecclesiastical body. Is the body in question a church or a sect? When people deal with informal groups they often answer this question before even asking it, and do so from a standpoint which has little sociological value. In using the terms church and sect here, we are referring to the ideal types constructed by Weber and his friend Ernst Troeltsch; the words convey neither compliment nor insult. To avoid all misunderstanding, we shall quote Troeltsch's own summary of his typology:[21]

> The Church is an institution which has been endowed with grace and salvation as the result of the work of Redemption;[22] it is able to receive the masses, and to adjust itself to the world, because, to a certain extent, it can afford to ignore the need for subjective holiness for the sake of the objective treasures of grace and of redemption.
> The sect is a voluntary society, composed of strict and definite Christian believers bound to each other by the fact that all have experienced "the new birth".[23] These "believers" live apart from the world, are limited to small

> groups, emphasize the law instead of grace, and
> in varying degrees within their own circle set
> up the Christian order, based on love; all this
> is done in preparation for and expectation of
> the coming Kingdom of God.
>
> Mysticism means that the world of ideas
> which had hardened into formal worship and
> doctrine is transformed into a purely personal
> and inward experience; this leads to the forma-
> tion of groups on a purely personal basis, with
> no permanent form, which also tend to weaken
> the significance of forms of worship, doctrine,
> and the historical element.[24]

We must remark straightway the significance of the mystical type, so little noticed and studied, for an analysis of present-day informal groups. To the extent that these groups recruit their members from the educated strata of society, they often become the beneficiaries of a theology which stresses the subjective elements in and explanations of the Gospel, rather than the objective elements, and plays down the normative value of ecclesiastical traditions.[25] Some "informal groups"--I know one--may in fact be examples of "the formation of groups on a purely personal basis". Generally, however, the attachment to "forms of worship" is kept, and we should speak of "groups with mystical characteristics" rather than groups of the mystical type.

The same distinction between substantival and adjectival attribution must be applied in dealing with the sect type. Informal groups seem generally to stress voluntary membership, the quality of the commitment rather than the numbers of the committed, effective obedience to the demands of Christian ethics, and the prophetic and eschatological aspects of the Christian message. On the other hand, the members refuse to think of themselves as having "experienced 'the new birth,'" and though they form a relatively closed group, they do not

therefore define themselves as "apart from the world". On the
contrary, they preach and practice "dialogue with the world".
Very often, they refuse to correlate the Church to the visible
space it occupies, and claim rather that it is coextensive with
mankind; in this respect they belong more to the church type
than most of the Churches do. But this universalist outlook
is not in harmony with the way in which they worship, for the
latter is so intense and so free from all sectarian forms as
to prevent "regular practicioners", to say nothing of non-
Christians, from sharing in it. Here, as with mysticism, it
is therefore better to speak of "groups with sectarian tendencies or traits" than of sects. Moreover, the sect always
emerges as not simply a protesting group but a dissenting group
as well. But, though the informal groups may be marginal in
relation to the Churches (toward which they may show either
attachment or detachment), most of them are not dissenting
groups, and this they assert quite explicitly. On the one
hand, their members continue to take advantage in many cases
of services offered by the parish from which they come; often
they play a role, sometimes an important one, in the parish's
activity. On the other hand, the general ideology of these
"communities" requires that Church reform, which is their
overt or covert aim, should be effected only from within.
Therefore they generally refuse to be thought of as dissenters.
The refusal is ratified and confirmed by the hierarchies of
the Church, since the latter want to absorb rather than eliminate these "informal" movements.

 The proportion of mystical and sectarian traits in these
groups must be determined in each individual case; the balance
of characteristics must be studied, as must the group's degree
of integration or detachment in relation to the mother Church.
No general or a priori answer can substitute for this kind of

prosaic research. In any event, it should be clear to everyone--
we repeat it at the risk of wearying the reader--that the label
"sect" is not an insult when used in its sociological sense. In
the same way, to say that a group is of the church type is not a
compliment. As the sociologist uses the terms, each refers to a
social group structured in a particular way. In reality, of
course, as our preceding remarks have shown, the types overlap
and blend. It is the specific balance of characteristics that
a group shows, that enables us to situate it in relation to the
ideal types of church, sect, or mysticism. Troeltsch makes the
point clearly: "From the beginning these three forms were foreshadowed, and all down the centuries to the present day, wherever
religion is dominant, they still appear alongside of one another,
while among themselves they are strangely and variously interwoven and interconnected."[26]

A religious order offers such a case of numerous interconnections and exchanges between the three types. Troeltsch
points this out in passing but his suggestion has not caught
the attention of scholars.[27] Yet it is undoubtedly only a study
of this kind that would enable us to situate the present-day
"informal groups".

The foregoing reflections based on Troeltsch do not contradict those focused on Weber's concepts. It may even be that
the two sets of reflections cannot be separated. Weber realized
this and introduced passages on the three types, inspired by
Troeltsch, into his posthumously published *Economy and Society*.
In fact, mysticism and sect correspond to Weber's prophetic-charismatic type, though the former lack some of the intensity
of the latter; the church corresponds to the priestly type,
while magic, or sorcery, of which Troeltsch does not speak,
corresponds to a permanent temptation that besets both church
and priesthood.[28]

The one thinker provides a justifying rationalization, the other an attempt to understand social phenomena as such, without expressing normative judgments. But one question remains unanswered: the relation between religious assertions and mass movements. If we adopt Weber's viewpoint and the passage from prophetic message with its radical challenge to institutions which bears witness to the message, we still do not know the precise connections between the overall change and the emergence of the charismatic. Weber did not claim that prophetism arises as a creation out of nothingness,[29] but he did not show in a sufficiently precise way what the relations are between the break in the old order of things and the sudden coming of the new. The ambiguity of the term "breakthrough" (*Durchbruch*) and the esthetic pleasure given by its use have perhaps something to do with the lack of preciseness. The opportunity offered by the current phenomenon of the informal groups should be grasped, we suggest, in order to come to closer grip with problems in an area in which Engels' views are not any more satisfactory than Weber's, because they are equally, though inversely, imprecise.

Generations, Social Belonging, and Socio-Religious Change

An American Protestant theologian has attempted to carry further the analyses of Weber and especially of Troeltsch. I am referring to H. Richard Niebuhr and his *The Social Sources of Denominationalism*.[30] In Niebuhr's view, a sect, in the sense given the term by Weber and Troeltsch, cannot last beyond a single generation. I shall quote Niebuhr, because though I disagree with his view, it is nonetheless not without interest for us:

> By its very nature the sectarian type of organization is valid only for one generation. The children born to the voluntary members of the first generation begin to make the sect a church long before they have arrived at the years of discretion. For with their coming the sect must take on the character of an educational and disciplinary institution, with the purpose of bringing the new generation into conformity with ideals and customs which have become traditional. Rarely does a second generation hold the convictions it has inherited with a fervor equal to that of its fathers, who fashioned these convictions in the heat of conflict and at the risk of martyrdom. As generation succeeds generation, the isolation of the community from the world becomes more difficult. Furthermore, wealth frequently increases when the sect subjects itself to the discipline of asceticism in work and expenditure; with the increase of wealth the possibilities for culture also become more numerous and involvement in the economic life of the nation as a whole can less easily be limited. Compromise begins and the ethics of the sect approach the churchly type of morals.[31]

Niebuhr uses the concept of "generation" without subjecting it to criticism, and this does not make the sociologist's task any easier. But, whatever be the meaning he gives the word, I think we must qualify what he says. Bryan Wilson has shown that in a sect there is always a first generation which continues to recruit itself.[32] Moreover, the American theologian's analysis seems applicable, if at all, only to the post-Pietism sects, but perhaps not to others. As a matter of fact, we sometimes see sects adopting more radically sectarian attitudes in the second or later generations than in the first. In any event, traits that are more or less sectarian and traits that belong more or less to the church type are generally intermingled in all generations, and it cannot be maintained that the sect type exists in its purity in any generation. In the real world we find only groups that more or less closely approach a given type; we do not find the type itself in its purity.[33] Having made this point, we must admit that Niebuhr has put his finger on a problem which all groups professing a religion come up against unless the group is made up exclusively of celibates: the problem of indoctrinating the children. If we may trust various reports,[34] present-day informal groups experience an almost insuperable difficulty as soon as the children in the group reach the age of reason; this is especially true if the group has adopted a strict community life. Here again it would be worth while to take the opportunity of testing the hermeneutic value of a sociological hypothesis that is as yet uncertain.

Niebuhr also took up the problem of schism, which he found to be typical of the second generation. In his view, schisms, which indeed are frequent in sects, reflect opposition between social classes. The very poor, in the second generation, refuse the changes in belief, ethics, and cultural practices, which the passage of time brings. Niebuhr sees class affiliations at work throughout the history of differentiation within Christianity: "In Protestant history the sect has ever been the child of an outcast minority, taking its rise in the religious revolts of the poor."[35] In addition, he sees the emergence of other movements, notably the Franciscans, as connected with the rebellion of the poor.[36] In his view, however, sects and religious orders are not "mass movements", as Engels uses the term. On the contrary, they are movements focused on individual prophets who gain a following among the poor, the latter being frustrated in their religious expectations, not in their social hopes as such.

But the poor and poverty have no monopoly of religious creativeness. Every social category creates for itself the churches that answer its needs. Thus there are churches of the

middle classes, others composed of immigrants, others still
which are based on language, ethnic origin, or skin color.
However, only the poor have enough inherent authenticity
periodically to attempt that return to the sources which
springs from a refusal to compromise with "the elements of
the world". In Niebuhr's view, then, sects receive an implicit
confirmation of their value by the fact that every church began
as a sect.

"Rebellion of the poor" sums up, then, for Niebuhr, the
thrust of primitive Christianity.

The judgment is that of the theologian and moralist.[37]
It can be challenged by pointing to the sects made up of intellectuals, or of people from the lower or upper middle class:
from the medieval Brethren of the Free Spirit to William Miller
and his adventists or the Darbyites of nineteenth-century
England.[38] The analytic key provided by Niebuhr surely does
not work. Contemporary sociology has made it clear that rich
and poor alike may feel frustrated. Indeed, at certain periods
it is perhaps only those who are socially secure who can rebel
against wealth and compromise.[39] A study of informal groups,
in which the economically underprivileged do not seem to play
a dominant role, could probably contribute to an understanding
of the role which social classes play in socio-religious change.

From the Dynamics of Change to the Analysis of Causes

In Niebuhr we see an uncritical blending of the problematics
of Weber and Troeltsch with that of Engels. We turn now to Ralf
Dahrendorf, a theoretician of social change, for what is undoubtedly the best key to understanding socio-ideological change in
the perspective which interests us here.[40]

A. The Problem of Authority

For Dahrendorf, class opposition, as the translation of inequalities in the distribution of property, does not provide a satisfactory explanation of social change. He sees change coming about chiefly because people want to acquire authority.[41] In society--every society--a dichotomy operates when it comes to the distribution of authority. In other words, certain persons and groups, who form a dominant minority, possess it, while the larger number of persons and groups, which are the dominated majority, are deprived of it. Social change effects a redistribution of authority, and it is in order to effect this change that interest groups engage in permanent struggle.[42] These various concepts can, I think, direct us toward a relevant and plausible explanation of the genesis of the present-day informal groups. It might even make possible a new and useful perspective in which to view the dynamic stages through which religious groups in general pass, as we have been explaining them here.

Let us look, from Dahrendorf's viewpoint, at what has been taking place in Catholicism since Vatican II.[43] The Catholic Church answers nicely to the model proposed. Authority, that is, the "probability that a command with a given specific content will be obeyed by a given group of persons", is evidently divided in the way Dahrendorf describes; at least the ideal and typical division follows the pattern he indicates. Until Vatican II authority resided in the Pope, with the bishops sharing in it only in a delegated and geographically restricted way. That can be said while neglecting for purposes of analysis the various kinds of subordinate authority and stressing the ideal and typical character of the description.

Even before Vatican II there were signs (some of them going back quite a few years) which showed that some of the faithful were dissatisfied with this state of affairs. But if authority was sometimes resisted, as in the priest-worker affair, it was never radically challenged. More specifically, ever since Vatican I, no one had tried to maintain against Rome an authority different from the latter's. The schism of Döllinger and the Old Catholics met with little success, nor did any of the subsequent crises give rise to any important differentiation that took people outside the Church. Within the Church, the most advanced thinkers condemned themselves as soon as Rome spoke.[44] So deeply had this dichotomized conception of authority been internalized that the protesters themselves did not realize they were challenging it.[45] Nonetheless a confrontation was building up, focused especially in Catholic Action movements, under the patronage of theologians, many of whom, down to the eve of Vatican II, could publish nothing without permission from Rome. In convoking the Council, John XXIII called for an updating, an *aggiornamento*. In so doing he was to anticipate the protesters, make what they wanted an integral part of the Church, and thus prevent a radical challenge from developing. Meanwhile the pontifical bureaucracy prepared for up-dating in its own way. Aware--whether in a fully conscious way or in a more subconscious fashion, no one will probably ever know--that if the bishops in council took their role seriously, they would question papal authority, the bureaucracy decided on the agenda and the conclusions to be reached. The most they would listen to was requests for changes in details. The fact was that this policy, coherent though it was with the traditional ethos, would fail. The intervention of Cardinal Liénart, right at the beginning of the first session of the Council, was to turn the meetings into unforeseen paths. The bishops meant to discuss

matters and make decisions. In view of Vatican I and the
definitions of papal primacy and infallibility, was such a
course possible? The question was raised, as we know, and
answered affirmatively. What were the sociological factors
that made possible such an interpretation which a few years
before would have astonished people, to put it mildly? We
haven't space here to engage in the analyses an answer would
require. In addition, a number of preliminary studies would be
required. We may note however that Vatican II would not have
been the Council it turned out to be, if the papacy, on the one
hand, and the episcopate, on the other, had not felt the need
of revising their "image". The bishops were unwilling any
longer to be simple errand-boys without responsibility of their
own; the papacy could no longer claim before the world to be
the sole authority within the Church. It was probably the
attitude of the papacy, affected as it was by the crisis of
credibility that had affected all institutions and values ever
since the Second World War, which made it possible for the
bishops to regard themselves as mature and responsible. Thus
the redefinition of roles of authority in the Church, as
Vatican II effected it, is related to the overall situation of
society as a whole.

B. <u>The Struggle to Redistribute Authority</u>: <u>The Bishops</u>

We may now put aside such very general analyses and concen-
trate on the struggle to seize authority. The bishops had to
look for allies who were in the same situation as they or shared
their aspirations. They found such allies in the theologians
who had been reflecting on the problems of authority and initiative in the Church: the very men, often, who had fallen under

suspicion in the preceding decade. The alliance would make it possible to put the problem of authority in the Church into a new perspective, by centering it on the two themes of episcopal collegiality and the priesthood of God's people.[46] The ambiguity of the texts which the Council produced in this area doesn't matter to us at this point. The important thing is that a theoretical redistribution of authority did emerge, one that favored the bishops and the faithful. The theologians and the priests of "second rank" (the ordinary priests) were forgotten, and the papacy was left in an ambiguous position.

This must be our starting-point, I suggest, if we are to understand what ensued and led to the present proliferation of informal groups.[47] Contrary to what might have been expected, the alliance between bishops, theologians, and laity did not last. In practice, the bishops had no intention of letting down the barriers for the other two groups. Ordinary priests were the first to realize this, it seems,[48] then the laity, as the crisis in the Action Catholique de la Jeunesse Française was to show. May 1968 did the rest, at least in France; but every country, it seems, has experienced its May 1968, even if at varying dates. Since then a new alliance has been formed between theologians, priests, and laity, and another, more implicit one perhaps between the pope and the bishops.[49] Of course, when you get down to the particulars of individual situations, things are not as clear as we are making them here, rightly or wrongly. But is it incorrect to think that the proliferation of informal groups presupposes the strategies just described and that in our present situation, in which the groups do exist, our analysis has a certain plausibility as an explanation? A Yes to the second part of the question and a No to the first are enough, I think, to justify us pursuing the present interpretation.

C. The Theologians

How is it that against all antecedent probability certain theologians, priests, and laity find themselves suddenly allies? The reasons are varied but they are connected with the ideology that came out of Vatican II. Because they played such an important role at the Council, the theologians thought that their critical role in the Church was now accepted. They were quickly disillusioned and found themselves at a distance from the bishops, who no longer needed them.[50] This is the origin of the conflicts which have caught public attention, along a path marked by congresses and warnings (from Rome, in some instances).

D. The Priests

The case of the priests would require lengthy study for adequate handling. Everyone is aware, however, that even in the highest echelons the priesthood is a problem for the modern world.[51] Not only has its authority broken down for reasons too well known to be mentioned here; in addition, the authority left it seems to priests to be taken away by the bishops. The latter, since the Council, in France at least, have introduced new pastoral structures. In the process, however, authority has passed to the deaneries and power to the various diocesan, regional, and national offices and commissions.[52] Yet at the same time pastors and assistants are bidden to preach "community" and "communion". The inconsistency is clear. When people used to criticize the parish, they were not suggesting a superparish would be better; when they attacked the episcopal staff, they were not looking for still more bureaucratic structures in its place. Forgotten men at Vatican II, the "second rank" priests are also the chief victims of the post-conciliar period. This felt frustration explains the protests raised by some groups against presbyterial councils appointed by the bishop and having a purely consultative role. This initial movement of dissatisfaction would be carried further by various organizations with a thrust toward a more radical challenging which focused on clerical celibacy and on the social and political isolation of the clergy.

The protesting priests very often joined informal groups in which laymen were in the majority. Such a move was to some extent surprising, seeing how the priests seemed concerned only with problems specific to the clergy. But to focus on this point is to miss the meaning of the move. At any rate, it is to fail to perceive how the move is related to the problem of gaining authority. The claims of the clergy, which we have mentioned, can in fact be interpreted as a rejection of episcopal authority, or, more accurately, a claiming of authority in the very area in which the bishops have traditionally exercised it in quite specific way, namely, in the ordination of "their" priests (as they used to put it). In demanding for themselves the right either to marry or to embrace celibacy temporarily or permanently, the right to adopt a profession and thereby achieve financial independence, the right (we must even say: "therefore the right") to intervene in the political sphere, the rebellious clergy were rejecting the idea that the minister of the sacrament of orders had a right to regulate clerical life. The locus of authority in its most specific exercise was thus being displaced (in desire, for the moment) from minister to recipient of the sacrament. The latter was being designated (in desire, again) as the ultimate regulator of episcopal action. The wish often expressed by the Fathers of Vatican II--that they might be and appear to be the servants of all--was being taken seriously. If the wishes of the rebelling priests were

to be heard, the priesthood of the "second rank" would regain
the authority it had long lacked, especially (in practice)
since the end of Vatican II, both in relation to the faithful
in the parishes and in relation to society at large. As a
matter of fact, and quite logically, the claim of independence
of the bishop is accompanied by the desire to restructure the
community of believers according to criteria suggested by the
requirements of evangelical action and not by geographical
considerations. This eliminates the likelihood of situations
arising in which the bishop must play the role, as with the
worker-priests, of the one who prevents the ordinary cleric
from keeping faith with those whom he has evangelized. On the
other hand, the present-day publics formed by the parishes hereby find themselves likewise emancipated from the bishops, and
the parish priest no longer need hide behind decisions from on
high when he wants to justify change but can accept, refuse,
or modify changes on his own authority. In the last analysis,
what we have here is a modern version of Richerism, even if the
individuals involved are not fully aware of it.[53]

E. The Laity

What have such clerical protests to do with those of the
laity? In point of fact, they do not win the attention of the
laity as a whole but only of one segment of the laity, the
segment for which the problem of authority in the Church is
the most pressing of all problems. We still have too few first-hand studies to provide an accurate description of the socio-professional affiliations within the informal groups. Nor do
we have any reliable knowledge of where the initiative in the
emergence of such groups lies: with the clergy or with the

laity. We do know, however, that the membership of these groups is drawn primarily, if perhaps not solely, from among the militants, or former militants, of the Catholic Action movements, that is, from that segment of the Catholic opinion which has been most sensitive to problems of authority, or else from among the committed faithful who have been most affected by May 1968. This "population", whose socio-professional affiliations are perhaps less important than their position in the Church (set over against the majority of the laity and confronting the clergy), also is one that is accustomed to exercise authority in secular society, and this by reason, frequently, of its religious involvements. For a long time these people have heard it repeated that "the laity are the Church". Vatican II, in the form of numerous speeches at the Council, confirmed that these people were indeed the Church. Admittedly, the final official documents do not state this without qualifications. Nonetheless it would be interesting and probably quite instructive, to study the texts of the speeches by the bishops on this theme during the Council. We would undoubtedly find there much more of a "wildcat" theology than was later officially adopted.

We would have to go a step further and see how information concerning the ongoing Council, especially as disseminated by the press, affected the laity. The very process of communication probably gave undue emphasis to certain elements of what was said at the Council. We may also ask, at least as a working hypothesis, whether such communications did not further certain policies of the bishops. This is not at all unlikely, to the extent that, in the hypothesis we suggested earlier, the bishops were at that time looking for allies over against the pope and the "second rank" priests. In the event, however, the authority offered to the laity, especially to the most committed among them, was not in fact given.[54] Their only recourse was to take it for themselves, for the contradictions laid bare in the system by the way the Council functioned enabled them to do so with a minimum of guilt feelings. The alliance with rebelling clerics made it possible for both the laity and the clergy in question to reduce still further the limits of the psychological insecurity either group might experience. The policy adopted by the hierarchy in regard to the groups that emerged from the alliance was a policy less of condemnation than of biding time and trying to absorb the groups, and it provided a large measure of justification for internal separatism (a reality even if a seeming contradiction) in the eyes of those involved, insofar, of course, as the latter still felt subject to any moral claims on the part of traditional authorities. The fact that these authorities can perhaps no longer take effective steps against the informal groups shows how much their ancient function has lost its plausibility in the eyes of contemporary society. Within the Church no less than outside it there is uncertainty about the locus, the subjects, and the agents of authority.

In their own way and with their own goals in view, the informal groups provide one solution to this problem. Each of them is in effect a locus of authority with its own laws and its own network of power; here is where decisions are made about the religious concerns of the members. The degree of autonomy varies, of course, according as the group claims more or less self-regulation and as the concrete circumstances of its existence allows. They supply a rather good example of what Georges Gurvitch called "pure social law".[55] Yet this relative autonomy and more or less extensive takeover of authority are somewhat ambiguous. On the one hand, the more radical informal groups claim equal rights for all members in the matter of authority and decision. On the other hand, the groups are probably rare in which the fact of a man's being a priest or a former priest does not give additional weight to his views, unless even greater heed is paid (with the blessing of any clergy members) to some "lay prophet" in the group. We would have to have case studies made in order to find out what exactly does go on. Is "declericalization" enough to turn any priest members of the group into purely functional ministers? But even if this were so, the danger of "reclericalization" is probable, if we may judge by what happens in sects whose original thrust was totally egalitarian. In any event, if Dahrendorf's hypotheses prove correct, authority must *in practice* be distributed in a dichotomized way in these micro-societies no less than in every other society. The clerics who are looking there for a new social authority in a non-traditional role must necessarily sooner or later oppose the laity whom they continue to insist are the Church. For if the Richerism of the priests shows up in rebellion against the traditional bishop-priest relationship, the congregationalism of the laity rebels against the traditional priest-faithful relationship.

F. The Sacraments

The parallelism of the two processes we have just been describing is seen to be complete if we reflect on two points: the problem of the sacraments and the problem of politics. Up to the present no investigator, be he journalist or bishop, seems to have found an informal group which rejects the traditional sacraments of the Catholic Church or which celebrates them without the mediation of a duly ordained minister.[56] In some groups indeed, all the participants say together the words of consecration at the Eucharist, but there is always a priest or former priest in the congregation, and this is enough to take a good deal of the steam out of the rebellion implicit in the practice. The same can be said of the "agapes" celebrated by some groups; even though the groups refuse to commit themselves on the precise theological meaning of these rites, the presence of priests or former priests renders the problem the same as the one just mentioned. Perhaps groups do exist which celebrate the Eucharist or agape without the presence or mediation of the clergy. If there are, they have escaped the attention of investigators and in any case are not representative of the informal group movement as a whole.

On the other hand, wherever a Mass (the name used is not important) is celebrated in an informal group, a protest is being made and its meaning is rather clear. People are here refusing a minister who would be imposed on them by the administrative system. The celebrant is a priest chosen by the members of the congregation, and he celebrates in the way and for the intentions which they decide. In this way, whatever be the form the rite takes, the regulation of the sacrament, which has traditionally been the clearly defined area where the ministerial priesthood declares its specific character, passes from the minister of it to its "beneficiaries". This amounts to saying that we no longer have a consumer laity, but a laity which provides services for itself and regulates the sacraments.[57]

Take the case of baptism, and we will see even more clearly that the challenge issued by the informal groups is aimed at the acquisition of authority. We know that the rejection of infant baptism is a characteristic trait of numerous groups, and the rejection is becoming more widespread. But what is the issue in this limited strike against Christian initiation? First of all, it is the authority of the ordinary minister to decide on the manner and time of administration and, in extreme cases, the necessity of the sacrament for salvation. Then, and most of all, there is the right of this same minister to decide on his own who

is or is not a Christian; that is, to determine the boundaries
of the Church. The rejection of infant baptism, therefore, like
the attitude of the informal groups to the Eucharist, has to do
with taking authority over the sacraments (*the* area of clerical
privilege) away from the minister and giving it to the recipient
of the sacrament; in other words, the non-clerical Christian is
seizing authority. If rebellious priests are claiming the right
to regulate the bishop's ministry and to subordinate it to their
purposes, the rebellious laity are looking--consciously or not--
to take for themselves the authority of the priest.

G. Politics

The same conclusions emerge if we analyze the place politics
has in the informal groups. These generally give it priority
among their concerns as being the sphere in which the Gospel is
realistically and effectively preached. In doing so, they are
pursuing the line adopted by Vatican II which defined the common
priesthood of all Christians by relation to the structures of
the "world". However, the positions taken by the informal groups
often veer more to the left than the hierarchy intended,[58] and
the authority of the episcopate and ultimately of the papacy are
being challenged.

The same kind of challenge, but in the opposite direction,
was issued in the years before World War II, in connection with
the Action Française. There would therefore be nothing very
original about the contemporary challenge, were it not for the
fact that the current attitude in the political area brings with
it a number of consequences for sacramental practice. In the
informal groups, even the celebration of the Eucharist takes on
political significance, not only at the level of the self-

interpretation provided by the groups themselves, but also at
the level of a sociological analysis of the rites.[59] I am
alluding to the way in which the groups organize the liturgy of
the word and the litanies of intercession. The readings chosen
for the first part of the Eucharist are often taken from the
Bible, but they are also taken at times from works--even theological writings--that are secular and politically oriented.
In any case, the commentary on these readings, in the form of
a dialogue which replaces the sermon is often the kind that
stirs political reflections or raises questions of political
commitment. The same slant shows in the prayer intentions
offered by members of the congregation. Consequently, the
Eucharist takes on a deliberately political meaning and in this
way once again shrugs off hierarchic regulation from outside
the group. It even evades regulation by any priests present,
including the celebrants, to the extent that the "material to
be eucharisticized" is provided by the sharing of news, reflections, intentions, and action by the members of the group.
Authority is once again transferred from minister to congregation, whatever be the conception in the minds of those present
of the theoretical relationship between minister and congregation or of the nature of the sacrament. In this way the
boundaries of the Church are also challenged, at least implicitly, since many of the informal groups consider political
involvement as a constitutive factor in the Christian profession.
Therefore only those who share the group's socio-religious
ideals can share its Eucharist. Each group, consciously or un-
consciously, is thus identifying the Church with itself and
claiming the right to determine the boundaries of the Church
and the norms for Christian life. Authority resides in the
congregation. Here we have, at least implicitly, an authentic
congregationalism, even though it stands in contradiction to the

tendency we stressed earlier to recognize no boundaries for the Church except those of the world itself.

Limitations of Challenge

We noted above the ambiguity of certain practices and attitudes in the informal groups. Their position in regard to ministerial priesthood strikes us as the most typical. At bottom, and despite a clear congregationalism, these microsocieties hesitate when faced with the choice between being a church and being a sect. As we said earlier, they cannot be regarded as sects in the sociological sense of the word. At the same time, they show strong sectarian traits. Why then do they not pass out of the one type and into the other? The reason is the high importance given to politics, that is, to a church-world relationship which is characteristic precisely of the church type. We often hear of representatives of the Churches finding fault with the informal groups for this attitude. The sociologist can only be astonished at the misunderstanding. Christianity of the church type, be it Catholic, Orthodox, or Protestant, has always justified and even sanctified the Christian's involvement in the political order. Only the modalities have varied, with the stress being put at times on the individual's passivity, at times on his activity; never has the individual been allowed simply to refuse the obligations laid on him by the state.[60]

Up to now, however, the hierarchy has controlled the choices open to the Christian in the political sphere, so that even worship acquired, in the sociologist's eyes, a supervised political meaning. In fact, as Werner Stark, the Catholic sociologist, has observed, medieval Christianity shows all the signs of being a religion that is identified with the social organism, although this is, strictly speaking, possible only for religions that are established.[61] Today the Catholic hierarchy acknowledges the relative autonomy of politics. In so doing, it is stripping itself of some of its authority and claiming to transfer it to the laity. But the latter receive their real competence in this sphere from quite a different source. Therefore they do affirm their independence by exercising freedom of choice, whatever be the decisions or preference expressed by the hierarchy, but they do so by reason of the logic of the social system to which they belong and which they do not challenge.[62]

In short, as I see it, the assumption of a sect-like position is motivated by the desire for a church-type accomodation to historical reality as men experience it today, a reality in which authority can no longer be thought of as connected with the place one occupies in a hierarchy, but is connected with the real qualifications of individuals. Such, at least, is one interpretation that can be placed on the informal group phenomenon as we now have it; the future, of course, may bring changes. Thus, in my view, the contradictions within the informal groups are those of the Church itself.

Conclusion

Our aim in this essay has been to suggest some lines for sociological interpretation of the dynamics of present-day small groups. To do this, we have had recourse to classical problematics. In a sense, therefore, we need draw no conclusions here. That we leave to those who will work to gather the facts of the case and to interpret them. It is clear, however, that if the classical problematics which we have proposed can shed light on the contemporary situation, reflection on the latter can also help refine the problematics themselves in various ways. This means that the study of the informal groups has a special interest for the sociologist. I hope that specialists in contemporary Christianity will realize this and not once again let the opportunity pass for investigating an exciting phenomenon.

CHAPTER 3

Sociological Prolegomena
on Informal Groups:
An Essay in Institutional Analysis

by

René Lourau

Base communities are not something new, nor are they typical of "modern" times, that is, of the era in which the capitalist system of production has prevailed. We find them in the age of the pre-capitalist system of production (Middle Ages) and in places where the Asiatic system was practiced (pre-Christian and post-Christian Palestine). We are dealing, then, with a massive historical fact, one kind of response to the action of institutions.

At the present time, moreover, base communities are not simply an ecclesiastical phenomenon but affect every sector of social life. Insofar as the informal group is a historical response to oppression or repression by the state or any other institution (such as the Church) that exercises hegemony, it does not differ notably from the political party or the industrial organization. As a matter of fact, the term "informal group" originated in a psycho-sociological discovery concerning American industry in 1925. In that year Elton Mayo uncovered the existence of non-official communications networks, that were not provided for in the organizational charts and thus conflicted with the communications lines set up by the authorities. During the same period Moreno was showing that behind the organizational organigram a hidden sociogram was at work, that is, a structure of informal relationships. In the twenties, too, Trotsky was pointing out the impossibility of separating "party" from "faction" or sub-group; thus the informal was making its entrance into political thought as well.[1]

In the forties, experimental psychology and, later, clinical social psychology went more deeply into the theory of groups and the methods for analyzing and leading such groups (methods summed up in the general term "group dynamics"). Group dynamics, in the strict sense of the term, is a theory and method invented by Kurt Lewin, an experimental psychologist.[2] Lewin rejected the view widely held in the older collective psychology and in a certain type of sociology, and showed that a group is not a loose sum of individuals which acts after the fashion of a non-conscious being or an animal, but a structured whole with a history, which undergoes or chooses various developments in function of very important variables that exercise an influence in the social field in which the group moves as well as in the field of the individual and in the field constituted by the group as such. The type of leadership exercised, for example, is highly determinative for the structure and development of the group. The well-known experiment with the "three climates", on the eve of the Second World War, shows that a group's aggressivity varies according as the leader is autocratic or democratic or simply lets things take their own course.

Other experimentalists, such as R. F. Bales, were later to bring to light the fact that two leaders may exist side by side in a group. One is the traditional type of leader: the man given the responsibility of guiding the group because he is regarded as the most capable and dedicated and because he "likes that sort of thing" (that is, giving orders). The other is more of an underground leader who reflects what the group does not say rather than what it officially says, and brings to a focus the affective responses of all the members or of some important sub-group; he performs these functions in a passive way, like a mirror reflecting the unconscious levels of the group's life.[3]

The Englishman Bion discovered the same two leaders in his practice of group clinical psychoanalysis.[4] The first type of leader he calls the work-group leader; the second, the basic-assumption group leader. Bion sets up a system of "valencies" for groups, in the light of his observation of religious groups. In every group, he maintains, two valencies are at work, though not necessarily in a permanent way; they can succeed one another, be in conflict with one another, or exclude one another. There is the valency proper to the basic-assumption group and the valency proper to the work-group. A work-group does not spend its whole time working. Even when it is working or thinks it is working, it is the locus for phenomena which have to do with the structure, leadership, orientation, etc., of the group. Conversely, relations of production exist in base groups which regard themselves as having no productive function.

We may say, then, that the phenomenon of informal groups, now experienced by the Church, is a very ancient historical phenomenon and a widespread social fact in the contemporary world. We ought to be put on our guard, by this fact, against the moralizing and aprioristic approaches that in the guise of "science" simply give voice to a conservative ideology and to a class outlook which does not dare sail under its own colors.

Our brief recall of how the group has been an object of study may suggest, moreover, that group psycho-sociology and religious ideology may have something in common as they confront the small informal group. That is the point we will take up in the first part of this essay: that the potential collaboration of religious knowledge and science is extensive and highly important for explaining the "base communities" phenomenon in the Church.

I. Psycho-Sociology as an Ideology of Salvation

Sociology began to be of interest to Church authorities when the crisis of the parish as the basic geographical unit of organization became evident for all to see. This crisis was connected with the more general problems of the urban explosion, the shift in relations between city and countryside, and the industrial revolution; consequently it is a social crisis and has other aspects besides the purely religious (cf. below).

Religious sociology has traditionally been developed almost entirely by means of monographs dealing with parishes and dioceses; the monographs, in turn, have been based on the annual statistics drawn up by the dioceses. The aim of these statistical inquiries is to get a picture of the extent to which Christians practice their religion, and information is sought chiefly about the basic acts of religious conformism: baptism, marriage, burial, communion, and support of the clergy, as well as about the age at which baptism is conferred and the periods of the year at which most communions are distributed.

In France, as in other countries, this initial sociographic approach has, with increasing frequency, been supplemented by inquiries concerning the idea of religious affiliation or belonging. The theory concerning the groups to which people belong and refer themselves, when added to sociology and social psychology, helps to flesh out the rather uninformative concept of participation in acts of worship. In addition, historical research sees a vast and almost completely unexplored area for study opening up before it.

Religious sociology is the branch of the humane sciences that is best calculated to provide an answer to the social problem felt by Church authorities and by all those professionally involved in pastoral activity, be they clergy or laity (with responsibility either for directing organizations or for providing guidance and inspiration). But in their daily activity with the masses, all these various "preachers" of the good news feel the need of further information and further questions and answers and of obtaining these by methods that are less purely objective in nature and more closely related to the kind of "psychological action" in which these people are daily involved. At this point they turn to the psychoanalytic and psychological study of groups.

The Psychoanalysis and Psychology of Groups

In point of fact, psychoanalysis is also of interest to the theologian, and indeed to the theologian more than others. We have seen numerous efforts to render to Freud what belongs to Freud and to God what belongs to God. Of course, the borrowings from psychoanalysis differ in character according as the God the theologian worships is the God of Ivan Illich or the God of the archbishop of Burgos, and according as the psychoanalysis in question is that of the "strong ego" or the much more severe psychoanalysis of Lacan. In any case, the theologican likes endless conferences and association with the most integrist kinds of psychoanalysts, especially when the discussion concerns the sacrament of penance and the work of the spiritual adviser. The theory of the unconscious is also put to work exploring the symbolism of the other sacraments. But here, as in his dealing with the positive sciences which preceded psychoanalysis (astronomy, biology, paleontology, sociology), the theologian is well able to preserve what Breton, speaking of the unconscious, called "the unsmashable nucleus of night" that dwells in man.

The question of the sacraments involves the competence of the theologian, on the one hand, and that of the pastoral worker, on the other. The priest engaged in the pastoral ministry is not primarily concerned, for the most part, with points of dogma or canon law. The questions he raises about baptism, confession, communion, confirmation, and marriage spring from daily life and specific social contexts. In addition, unless he is in a parish or religious organization whose membership is highly educated, he rarely has occasion to discuss with his flock such questions as the morality of castration. On the other hand, he must at any cost maintain, day after day, a certain level, quality, and diversity of adherence to the Church. His professional task, somewhat like that of the teacher but in a more open way, consists in constantly patching the rents that develop in the social bonds uniting the masses to the institution; participation, reference, fidelity, obedience, submissiveness, belonging, commission, and acceptance are some of the categories with which he works. To do so, he needs tools and arms which he is less likely to look for in the total-explanation visions of sociology or psychoanalysis than in techniques for action. It is clear, then, that the psycho-sociology of groups will provide him with these instruments and arms, almost tailored to his needs.

The popularity of group methods with some sectors of the clergy would not have become as widespread as it now is except for the mediation of laymen who were put in charge of pastoral activities, in such roles as moderators of youth movements, guides of meetings, and leaders of cells of students and teachers within the national organizations of which we shall be speaking further on (*Paroisse Etudiant* [Student Parish, i.e. parishes made up of student populations], *Paroisse Universitaire* [university parish]). It was in and through organizations that were religious in purpose, that these methods found entrance into ecclesiastical institutions as such. But for some years now, both priests (regular and secular) and laity have been faithfully involving themselves in group reunions, psychodrama, group dynamics, etc., and also learning how to conduct these; the reunions, etc., have been organized by the associations of psycho-sociologists that have been springing up in France. Pedagogical experiments were already being carried on in religious houses or in religious organizations of laity before the *Education Nationale* stopped making grimaces of distaste at the splendid instrument of "participation" which they have in group dynamics. At the present time in France there are at least two organizations (A.M.A.R. and C.E.R.E.P.), made up either of ecclesiastics only or of ecclesiastics and laity together, which are devoted to the training of formation leaders in the area of psycho-sociology. Their clientele is chiefly religious and ranges from superiors of congregations of women to parish priests and includes the whole gamut of Christians involved in formation and animation of various kinds. Such a clericalization of certain sectors of scientific study and its application was foreshadowed among the specialists in religious sociology who were religious or at least believers (Boulard, Chélini, le Bras) and among the psychologists and psychoanalysts who belonged to the Church (Beirnaert, Oraison). We may recall, apropos of psychoanalysis, that the monastery of Cuernavaca, Mexico, where the superior, Dom Mercier, had in recent years been pushing an experiment in group psychoanalysis, has now been closed as a result of the experiment.

The abundant psycho-sociological literature that is Christian in orientation or commitment has been insisting on certain basic points with regard to the crisis now being felt in institutional Christianity (by this phrase I mean religious institutions and, above them, ecclesiastical institutions). There is, first of all, the matter of the relations between the priest and the groups. The priest, like the teacher, has been prepared by his training to focus almost solely on his own and other believers' connection with institutions, the latter being regarded bureaucratically as decision-making bodies. The group as such represents a vast theoretical and practical problem, which can be expressed in a second question: that of the specific social relations that exist within small natural groups. A third question has to do with the relations these groups have or ought to have with institutions through the mediation of the hierarchy of clergy or laity who are in charge. Finally, in addition to knowledge of the various kinds of relationships involving the group, the priest wants to know about new forms of pastoral action that are inspired by group techniques.

The connection between the language of pastoral activity (a language in which theology, canon law, moral theology, liturgics, and mysticism are all used) and the language of experimental and clinical science is established by *mediations* that are essentially *philosophical*, beginning with *personalism*. For, Emmanuel Mounier is still very influential in progressive Catholic circles.

Personalism

Personalism developed initially among the young Christian intellectuals who, in the years between the two World Wars, had to confront what the Spanish philosopher, Miguel de Unamuno, called "the agony of Christianity" as well as the growing strength of Communism. To this extent, personalism was a new version of social Christianity, attempting to turn its back on the right-wing "social" teachings that had held the field in the nineteenth-century Church. It was not enough from now on

to "rally" to the republican regime with its pomps and its works
that were economically and socially suspect. There was need of
involvement, but on the side of the disinherited classes, in
order to help them in their struggle against the dominant class.
Not that the class-struggle will be taken by these Christians
of the left as the basic theme of all history (only a few
"inspired" people and some "Christian communists" would go that
far, and Mounier would denounce them). Temporal involvement
was regarded both as necessary and as insufficient: commitment
in the realm of the spiritual continued to be the "cover" or
justification for political undertakings.

This political side of personalism already gives us a
glimpse of the other, philosophico-religious side of the doctrine. If there is involvement at the side of the workers, the
peasants, the exploited, this is the expression of a new "rallying" rather than of any questioning of Christian ideology. The
modern philosophical bases of personalism are to be found, on
the one hand, in the mystical socialism of Péguy and, on the
other, and above all, in the "Christian" variety of existentialism.

What I am here calling mystical socialism had for its main
content the attempt (now seemingly condemned by history) of
certain Catholics to assign politics its own "proper" domain;
in a well-known antithesis Péguy called politics in this
narrower sense "the mystical" and contrasted it with "the
political" as meaning a fall into compromise, materialism, and
violence. In this new Christian conception of the political
order, the cult of Joan of Arc fits in harmoniously with support
given to the working classes and to the underdeveloped countries.
In other words, nationalism and patriotism stand guard behind
this mystique. The now well-known path followed by Péguy himself is exemplary in this respect.

We must recognize, however, that this part of personalist doctrine is the one least able to hold its own and that present-day disciples of Mounier, even if they continue to make the pilgrimage to Chartres which Péguy and Mounier praised so much, draw their inspiration much more from the philosophy of Kierkegaard, Husserl, Jaspers, Heidegger, Unamuno, or Gabriel Marcel, than from the couplets of Péguy with their early version of fascism. The *duality of commitment*, temporal and spiritual, leads to a tragic vision of existence.[5] In his *Existentialist Philosophies*, Mounier lists as major themes "personal conversion", "attachment", and "the revealed type of life".[6] In *Personalism* he enumerates "the structures of the personal universe": embodied existence, communication, intimate conversion, confrontation, freedom under conditions, highest dignity, and engagement.[7]

In face of the solicitations and ultimatums issued by the political revolution, Mounier's existentialism has come, although by different paths, to share the ambiguities which mark Sartre's existentialism. The critique of rigid institutions, for example, becomes in Sartre a theory of institutionalization as the *inescapable calamity* which awaits revolutionary groups and movements, and is accompanied by a serious distrust of Marxist organizations as far as their functioning and strategy are concerned. Now it is not an accident that after 1968 we should find not only Sartre but also the leaders of the *Echanges et Dialogue* group among those backing an organization for helping imprisoned leftist militants.

The Heideggerian themes of nothingness as source of the negative, of primordial anxiety in the face of death, and of knowledge that does not seek to know anything (and is therefore condemned to know only this Nothing) pick up the rightist Hegelian (Kierkegaardian) theme of the "knight of faith" who is entangled in the dark forest of the negative. The category of negation is here stripped of the natural and historical reality which enabled it to be the springboard for the materialist dialectic, and is used to rehabilitate the idea of transcendence. Personalist humanism salvages God by distinguishing between good and bad revolutions, good and bad politics, and by harping ceaselessly about the satanic dialectic of ends and means. At this level, Mounier turns out, in the last analysis, to be quite close to Catholic thinkers who come from the right, for example to Bernanos, who wrote:

> I repeat: the revolution of 1789 was the revolution of Man and was inspired by a religous faith in man, whereas the German, Marxist-style revolution is a revolution of the masses, and its inspiration is a faith, not in man but in the rigid determinism of the economic laws which regulate an activity that is itself inspired by self-interest.[8]

From Personalism to Groupism

It remains for us, at this point, to show how personalism, at a certain moment in its development, allowed itself to be invaded by group methods and gave pre-eminence to the group over against the institution.

The tragedy of communication between individuals and between the believer and God is not simply a philosophical "theme" (to use Mounier's term). That theme, like any ideology, has an objective basis, and it is the function of the theme both to hide the basis and to express it in a distorted way so that it becomes acceptable to believers or disciples. We need not look very far to find the basis in this case. Mounier and his personalism themselves point it out when they analyze the dissolution of certain forms of religion, the inadequacy of ecclesiastical or religious institutions for meeting the needs of the modern world, etc. Christendom is dead!: such is Mounier's own diagnosis.[9]

The judgment is a very severe one, as Mounier speaks of "the agony of Christianity" (a theme taken over from Unamuno), the threat of a "spiritual Sedan", and a "silent apostasy".

> The contemporary world no longer comes in contact with genuine Christianity, and the word of God has become a dead letter for it.... Christianity's words are no longer accepted, its gestures have no more meaning; the world has lost the key to the Church's languages, and the Church in turn has lost the key to the language men speak. The Christian lives like a madman in the world: he speaks but is not understood, and he thinks everyone else is mad.

The "strong stink of apostasy" which Bernanos denounces Mounier perceives even in our most orthodox behavior: in "the oppressive Masses", and "the dreadfully empty sermons" as well as "in the scatterbrained writings of our young Christian communists". In the final analysis, it is not the death of Christianity that is written on the wall but the death of western, feudal, bourgeois Christendom. A new Christendom will be born tomorrow or the day after tomorrow from new strata of society and from new graftings of non-European origin. But "we must not quench this new Christendom with stench from the corpse of the old".

Here we have a thoroughly sociological outlook on the religious crisis. "Exegesis is sociology," writes Roger Mehl, "because revelation is anchored in history." In fact, Mounier is more radical than the non-Christian sociologists who have long been accused of objectivizing faith and destroying religion. Durkheim was defending himself against the charge that he was making sociology "a weapon against religion", when he proposed his erroneous, conservative view of human institutions: "It is an essential postulate of sociology that a human institution cannot rest upon an error and a lie, without which it could not exist."[10] To this incredible statement, here disguised as a "postulate", Gabriel Tarde, an opponent of Durkheim whom modern sociology has unjustly forgotten, had already given an answer:

> Think of a hypothetical State in which everyone without exception--the priest in his pulpit, the newspaperman in his office, the deputy or minister on the speaker's platform, the candidate for office during his campaign, the father and the husband in his home--were to say, write, and publish exactly what he thinks and as he thinks it. Would a single one of the institutions on which society is built--family, religion, government--last even a day, given the present state of morals and minds?[11]

"It is Fréjus All Over Again"

Christian institutions are not as *credible* today as they used to be. As Tarde was implicitly suggesting, this loss is simply a concomitant or consequence of the slow breakdown of the consensus on which all institutions (economic, political, educational, orthopedic, etc.) seem to be based; in fact, however, the very crisis they are experiencing proves that in the last analysis their objective basis also consists of material strength. "Christendom is dead", as Mounier was already perceiving in a vague way. What is progressively disappearing is, in fact, a certain ideology concerning institutions, an ideology which "positive" sociology has always made it its business to justify, right down to our own time. A "spiritual

Sedan" (and not only a spiritual one) threatens numerous institutional organizations that had long been regarded as self-evident and perfectly reasonable; the French crisis of May-June 1968 was an illustration of this new state of affairs. On the eve of his departure in 1969 General de Gaulle was reported to have spoken in the following metaphorical terms of the sudden collapse of his power: "It is Fréjus all over again. The Pope too will have his Fréjus barrier." Personalism has come along at a given moment to announce that the unforeseen likelihood of a sudden breach in the "barrier" which institutional Catholicism throws up against its opponents has now become a reality. The breach has steadily widened and become more visible; *a groupist ideology is attempting to close it.*

Here are two examples, one practical and the other theoretical, one Protestant and the other Catholic, of this attempt to renew the social fabric with the help of techniques super-added to reality.

In the first case we are dealing with one of those Protestant centers of which I shall be speaking further on in discussing the counter-parish. More specifically, the center is an urban one in a large French city. It is characterized by the presence of a permanent officer, the pastor who is in charge of the center for "study and encounter", and by a rather wide diversity among the people who frequent it. Whereas most of the other Protestant centers go in for cultural activities that have more or less clear political overtones, this center has chosen to specialize rather in guidance that relies on group techniques. Small-group meetings are analyzed in terms of "motivations", "attitudes", "dependency", "blockage", "affective level", "meaningful discourse", "non-directiveness", "non-assertion of the group", etc., etc.; the whole vocabulary is that of clinical psychology as applied to limited groups. The center functions, at least in part, like one of those

centers for psycho-sociological training that act as substitutes
for the University and are connected with the ongoing training
and orientation of the large Parisian organizations which
specialize in the "sale" of human relations.

The second example is taken at random from the Catholic
literature of groupist inspiration that is now being published
in such abundance in France, Belgium, and Quebec, after having
taken the Anglo-Saxon countries by storm. The example is a little
book on "small groups and the future of the Church".[12] In an
unusually candid way the author links scientific or parascientific
ideas of "becoming aware" and "culpability" with the Christian
idea of repentance. The penitential rite, he says, must take into account the crisis caused within the group by tensions due to
leadership, etc. "The group should be able to rediscover" the
penitential rite "at the end of its own proceedings, this rite
being the 'forgotten' dimension of these proceedings." Here the
rite of confession is identified with the regulation, drawn from
psychoanalysis for the treatment of groups, that everything must
be brought out into the open. "Such a confession [of guilt] is
the surest criterion for the proper functioning of the primary
group, inasmuch as the family and the small group are, beyond
all others, the place in which interpersonal relations should
make such a confession possible and support the person making it."

Such perfect convergence between religious ideology and the
scientific ideology behind psychoanalysis and the treatment of
groups does not cause us much surprise. The subjectivism proper
to these two ideologies contains in germ a common conception of
institutions and a common conception of change (change is individual, which amounts to a conception of revolution as interior conversion). Another point of similarity between the two is the
homology between family and small group, a homology postulated
in the name of the old sociological theory of the primary group.
Such a structural correspondence makes it possible not only to

legitimize the small group on the grounds that it is an affective structure, but also to give the family a new legitimation on the grounds that it is a small group and a matrix of affectivity. Thus we see family therapy being developed in the United States; here two or three generations of the same family meet with the psycho-therapist, as a group, to seek care. The most important point of connection between the two ideologies, however, lies in the running together of the psycho-sociology of groups and the sacrament of penance. Unlike a number of heretical sects, the Cathars among them, who straightforwardly substituted public confession (the *apareillement* of the Cathars) for the traditional sacrament and its secrecy, the groupist Christians, having appropriated group dynamics for spiritual purposes, add it to the sacramental ritual; this last continues to be the true reference point.

These remarks will give us some idea of how groupist ideology functions when it limits itself to being a critique that is integrated into the system, and thus reinforces the system it is regarded as attacking. Groupist ideology thus provides an example of *anti-institutional* action that does not become *counter-institutional* and is therefore, immediately or in a short time, reabsorbed into forms of *institutional* action. The italicized terms require some brief discussion before we take up the question of the passage from base group to action group.

II. <u>Typology of Groups and of Forms of Action</u>

With a view to going beyond the distinctions mentioned earlier, we propose the following scheme for discussion: work group, base group, and action group.

The first two names refer to the groups discerned by experimental social psychology (Bales) and clinical social psychology (Bion). I have added the third myself. Like the other two it expresses a kind of "valency" or potentiality, or reference point, rather than a type of group that can be observed and studied objectively at will. In fact, as I have elsewhere attempted to show on the basis of experiments in an educational context, the three kinds of group are both present and absent at every moment, and they become real successively or simultaneously depending on the strategy adopted by the group, that is, depending on the group's orientation toward what is outside it, this orientation being dependent in turn on an analysis by the group of the action of external forces on it.[13] Here we have an illustration of the theory that there is an interaction between the action of the group on the milieu and the action of the milieu on the group. Awareness of and reflection on this interaction produces the "group subject" which becomes aware both of the forces that shape it from outside and of the action it is capable of undertaking with regard to the outside. On the other hand, if the group believes itself to be totally determined from without or totally free in its choices, the result is that one moment in the dialectic becomes autonomous, and social determinisms or freedom (as the case may be) are transformed into ideology.

The work group can be defined as resulting from assigning autonomy to the action of the milieu; the rules according to which the group operates are imposed from outside. By this very fact the group denies that it has any valency as a base group; that is, it denies it has the kind of uniqueness as a group that make it possible for it to act on what is outside. The work group is a place for conformism.

The base group, on the contrary--and I remind the reader that we are dealing here with aspects rather than real objects--

stresses its own free action (its ideology is that of creativity and free expression) and plays down or denies the action of outside forces on it. The base group is the place for groupism.

The action group tries to bridge the contradiction between the first two kinds of group by articulating (in the sense of speaking about and analyzing) the two kinds of influence to which the other groups assign an autonomous position. This articulation or analysis deals with the way in which institutions weigh upon the group and the way in which groups may possibly act upon institutions.

The reader may already suspect that a link can be established between this typology of groups and a typology of the forms of action as established with reference to institutions. The aim of institutional analysis is to establish that link.[14]

Levels of Action

Institutional action, an idea already in use in Catholic Action movements after the Second World War, is defined as action in and by institutions and in dependence on institutions. It is not accidental, then, that such action should have given birth to an ideology and practice of group work that focuses on some task (intellectual, cultural, social, political) but is always implicitly tied in with the established order and existing institutions. These last serve as a model even for those attempts to create other institutions which were part of the purpose of Catholic Action.

Anti-institutional action, as we have noted in regard to psycho-sociology as an ideology of salvation, aims at a critique of institutions. But the critique, carried out by groupism which claims to be an alternative to rigid, dogmatic, bureaucratic, etc., institutionalism, really does not bring forth a genuine alternative. The reason is that it is carried on within the existing institutional system, even when it seems to be rejecting it. This does not mean, however, that such anti-institutional action is not effective. We can see that it is when we note the important role played by non-directive methods or their like within the schools. A letter has been issued by the Ministry of Education (January, 1971) to the effect that the experiments may not be continued without institutional authorization and control, because they tend to give rise to radical criticism, often without the knowledge of those conducting the experiments. In industry, too, the application of "human relations" theory (so much criticized and, indeed, open to criticism) has a boomerang effect, and the bosses who use it in order to maintain their own power and the capitalist regime sometimes see the weapon turned against themselves. As for the Churches, in the power relationships between hierarchy and base or between clergy and laity or even between one part of the bureaucracy and another part that is more modernized, groupist ideology may act like a strong cleanser in the system.

Counter-institutional action effects a critique, but not an unqualified negation, of the other two types of action. If it negates the simple negation introduced by groupism, it does so because such a simple negation does not act as a sufficient practical challenge to institutional action.

There is thus a renewal of institutional action but also a going beyond it when counter-institutional action attempts to provide an alternative to existing institutions, that is, when it tries to institutionalize new forms. Institutional action institutionalizes in the line of existing institutions, under the egis of the law which legitimizes these institutions and of the prevailing ideology which grounds them.

Anti-institutional action rejects institutionalization; it sees in the latter the death of spontaneity, creativity, and

the authenticity of interpersonal relations. The establishment
of counter-institutions or the choice of radical forms of action
are the two ways which make possible the third moment in the
institutional dialectic, a third moment which the other types
of action would either tamper with or reject.

Levels of Analysis

We must here state more exactly the way in which this
system of institutional reference points to a new level of
sociological analysis--new, that is, in relation to the kinds
of analysis already practiced in sociology as well as in social
psychology or political theory.

Social psychology, generally speaking, attempts to evaluate and even to measure the form and content of social relations,
using as its points of reference the attitudes, intentions, and
motivations of individuals, as well as the action of individuals
upon each other. This kind of investigation finds quite congenial the opinion poll which accepts, or pretends to accept,
the word of those questioned as really expressing their behavior
and action. Of course, a comparison of expressed motivations
with actual behavior enables the researcher to check the results
of questionnaires or interviews and to show differences or even
contradiction between word and action. But even this kind of
comparison deals in elements already ideologized: concretely
(to take only simple examples), the notions of "motivation" and
"behavior" which have been turned into autonomous abstractions.
The often unconscious theoretical basis for such a method is the
postulate that human subjectivities as such can be observed and
an analysis of their interactions carried out. Motivations are
referred to a matrix that is both subjective and intersubjective;

behavior is related to norms that are at times objective (as in the case of marriage), at times subjective (as in the case of the profession of Christianity). Such a procedure leads to results and interpretations that are dualist, being referred to both the psychological and the sociological levels. The individual's transcendental subjectivity is postulated at the start by the psychological or psychoanalytic conceptual tools being used, but in the end the individual is reduced to a set of double entry tabulations or analyses of contents. All that is left is either a statistical average or a statistical aberration. The concrete content of the individual's life and social practice are dissolved into a mixture of radical subjectivism and normative objectivism. The hidden dimension of his "motivations" no less than of his "behaviors", namely, the institutional dimension, is missing.

The same can be said, from a different point of view, of attempts by sociologists to eliminate subjectivity. Here the irrationalism that threatens social psychology is replaced by a rationalism based on the "functions" or "decisions" of the individual, regarded as a social "agent". The sociology of action postulates an autonomous sphere of action which can be objectivized by a comparison between the agent's *purposes* and *what he does* (or, as the psychologist would say, his self-actuations). Here no attention is paid to the role played by the imagination, to which the psycho-sociologist attaches such importance. Above all, however, the contradictions which form the Marxist point of view are the moving force in social praxis (and its theoretization) are reduced to divergences in behavior and strategy and to a simple pluralism of social undertakings. It is as though there were no central thrust to social life under the capitalist system of production. This central thrust, which plays a determining or overdetermining role in relation to all other drives, is the class struggle or struggle between the dominating and the exploited elements of society. The sociology of action thus necessarily involves the rejection or a modernizing adaptation of the theory of social classes and class struggle.[15] The point of reference used in actionalism is the "social system", the resultant of the forces at work in society. By taking effect for cause and by giving a privileged place to social *structure* and its specific functioning as compared with the historical dynamic of contradictions, this sociology leads to positions hardly different from those of social psychology. *Adaptation to change* becomes the magical formula. But, to what change, if not the one caused by the dynamism of capitalism and the strategy being followed by the dominant class? The value judgments implicitly contained in this sociology for managers are not to be rejected automatically (for, can any sociology really avoid all value judgments?), but for the reason that they conceal their true frame of reference and thus make understanding of social praxis impossible.

Institutional analysis *takes as its real point of reference historical movements and their contradictions*. It is thereby led to evaluate social action in terms of the relations which individuals and social categories, strata, and classes have to institutions. This type of analysis is therefore not to be confused with the "political analysis" of the theoreticians of revolution. In the view of these last the criterion of action is always internal to the party, organization, or political group. This explains why a militant of the French Communist Party considers it a political action to sell *Humanité-Dimanche* on Sunday morning, while for a militant member of some little Trotskyite group or, better, some little leftist group or movement the true political action will not be some form of propagandist ritual but an "exemplary action" that is public, aggressive, even violent, and of high symbolic intensity. For its part, the anarchist branch of socialism, often quite close in its practice to community-oriented Christianity, sees the building of counter-institutions as the criterion of revolutionary action. It is, therefore, to this particular historical current (one that, as we mentioned at the beginning of this essay, antedates both Christianity and the capitalist system of production) that institutional analysis chooses to relate itself; it is in that current, at least, that it looks for its criteria of sociological evaluation.

As a matter of fact, both of the directions taken by action groups raise problems. On the one hand, the action group in the strict sense of the term is defined by the activism that consists of exemplary actions, but it does not necessarily envisage a counter-institution or community form of life. On the other hand, the base community or base group (this second name occurs in the vocabulary both of revolutionism and of psycho-sociology--which heightens its ambiguity) may either turn in upon itself and away from political action in all its forms, yet still be a group-witness to a political alternative, or may be the locus of the common life of militants who engage in the activism of which we have been speaking. We shall try to come to closer grips with this delicate point by comparing the activist groups and the rise of counter-parishes.

III. Action Group and Counter-Parish

The scheme proposed above (under "Levels of Action") should really contain not three but four divisions.[16] For the moment the scheme may be reformulated as follows:

      institutional action -- work group
      anti-institutional action -- base group
      non-institutional action -- action group I
      counter-institutional action -- action group II

In this scheme we use the term "anti-institutional action" to mean that while the action is critical of the institution it nonetheless develops within the institution (in a partly imaginary opposition between the group and the institution) and for the purpose of transforming the institution. The term "base group" is taken in the psycho-sociological sense of the words and includes the extensions allowed in this use of them.

Non-institutional action, on the contrary, is a doubly negative strategy. First, this action refuses the established norms for change that hold within the institution, and becomes instead a deviation that is not acceptable to the institution. Second, the intent of such action is not to transform the institution, even "radically", but simply to destroy it or at least hasten its demise.

"Action group" is here synonymous with base group in the political sense of this last term (a group arising from the base) and not in the psycho-sociological sense it also has (a small informal group that stands in parallel to the official network of power). But, to avoid all ambiguity, I prefer to speak of action group I rather than base group II. For, as we shall see from the description of a little revolutionary group in the Church, the fact of being a base group and even the fact that it is a group rising out of the base are much less important to the action group we have in mind than is the fact that it looks to immediate action.

The term "counter-institutional action" has here a somewhat more precise meaning than when we used it earlier. It refers to a struggle against the institution (and thus is quite close strategically to non-institutional action) but a struggle that uses other means than unregulated challenge or exemplary action. The kind of action meant here looks to the construction of counter-institutions; the purpose of the latter is, in part, to unify the little "base groups" (action groups I) and make them more effective, and, in part, to foster social experimentation and a style of life that will anticipate the development of productive forces and the resolution of contradictions at the level of relations of production. Such action, therefore, has a utopian dimension that is more or less marked according as the strategy of struggle is to a greater or lesser extent uninhibited or, on the contrary, is masked by an ideology of non-violence and by what Marx, speaking ironically, called a belief in "peaceful transformations".[17] Within the Churches action group II can also be assimilated to the base group (base community), but only in a sense different from the two senses already given to the term "base group". Since counter-institutional action requires some kind of decisive "self-actuation" in the sphere of daily life, the group which thus actuates itself can be called an "action group", even if the action is not political action in the sense of militancy or activism. We shall see this in the case of the counter-parish.

1) An Action Group I: C.A.R.E.

C.A.R.E., or Action Committee for Revolution in the Church (not *of* the Church) arose spontaneously in May-June, 1968. I was able to observe its birth and many of its actions until it disappeared at the end of 1969. I had known several persons in this group (among them my future wife) as "clients" during a sociological activity in September 1967. This fact largely explains my being able thus to observe the group, even though, given the nature of the group, such observation would normally require, if not active participation, at least presence at the scenes of action and some ideological and political involvement.

a) <u>Formation of the group</u>. During May-June, 1968, in France and especially in the Latin Quarter of Paris, an onlooker could readily have found verification for Sartre's theory about groups.[18] Groups "in process of fusing" were legion. The multiplicity, diversity, and extreme speed and ease of contacts, encounters, and social relations generally, whether on the street, in ongoing general gatherings, or in institutional locales set up for the purpose, could have been noted by all observers or observer-participants. The wave of socialization that swept over France in those few weeks was a sociological phenomenon that left a permanent impression not only on the sociologists who came in contact with it but also on the whole of the revolutionary movement, including the fringe reform groups whose presence in the movement was short-lived.

A very few days saw all the phases which Sartre finds a revolutionary group passing through in its formation. Acceleration and its corollary, the transitoriness and speedy obsolescence of social forms, was one of the most striking aspects of the May movement. This acceleration was considered a negative characteristic only by those who are ignorant of or deliberately reject the sociology of crisis and, more generally, the sociology of the institutionalizing and deinstitutionalizing process as this takes place in our times (obsolescence is increasingly affecting even industrial and commercial organizations, whose forms are seemingly more stable or more rational). The "fusion" of the group, the "oath" which binds the members, the "brotherhood of terror" which unites them against the outside world, all these very quickly led the "series" of several dozen people who were meeting regularly at the Saint-Yves Center (rue Gay-Lussac) to organize themselves into a small group of about fifteen active members. To the extent that activism gained the upper hand, the selection of members took care of itself. Other dimensions of the group--work, function as base--were either eliminated or pushed aside. Reality was too urgent.

Reality set the pace: C.A.R.E. was formed in accordance with the hegemonic model of the moment. Even its strategy was not its own: the aim of the movement was to overturn the existing order, and such a purpose was accompanied by utopian wooliness but also by a great deal of institutionalizing energy. Tactics too were derived from the movement: occupation and exemplary action. Every day brought news from the factories, universities, and very diverse organizations, that showed the power of these tactics.

The moment of definitive foundation (that is, of organization for the purpose of coherent action) was unusual in that it corresponded not to a bureaucratic movement but to an action, namely, the first action taken. This was the disruption of Sunday Mass at Saint Severinus Church in the Latin Quarter, not far from the Saint Yves Center.

Why Saint Severinus? Partly because it was close by, but mainly because this parish was known for its up-to-date liturgy and pastoral practice (the parish had a center where the young people of the Quarter gathered for cultural activities and where help was given to young workers). In the choice of Saint Severinus we can see what is specific in the rebellion of May, 1968. The influence of situationist theory is evident: the attack is to be made not on the strongholds of conservatism or reaction but on the advanced representatives of the kind of reformism and criticism that is still integrated into the system. This is why during the 1960's the Internationale Situationniste did not attack traditional sociology or Stalinism but the modernist, anti-Stalinian sociology of the *Arguments* team. In the department of sociology at Nanterre, those who would later be the guiding spirits of the March 22 Movement set their sights on Michel Crozier, a representative of the most up-to-date sociology, as much and more than they did on François Bourricaud, who represented traditional Durkheimian sociology.

In ensuing disruptions the aim was almost always to tear the mask from attempts at modernization in the Church: ecumenical conferences, meetings of liberal laymen, etc.

b) *The disruptions*. Here is an incomplete list of disruptions caused by C.A.R.E. between May, 1968, and the end of 1969. Mass at Saint Severinus; meeting of the Paris University Parish (a meeting of Catholic teachers in secondary and higher education); gathering of the bishops to deal with the crisis of the clergy; Mass in the Sorbonne chapel at the opening of the 1968 academic year; ecumenical service at the Orthodox Church in the Rue Daru, where the highest authorities of the Catholic, Protestant, and Orthodox Churches of France were gathered; an ecumenical vigil in the church of Saint-Germain-des-Prés, inspired by Protestants from Taizé monastery; the episcopal consecration of Father Daniélou, recently appointed a cardinal, in the chapel of the Catholic Institute.

On a different level, that of anti-institutional action, we may recall the participation of the non-lay members of C.A.R.E. in an "intercommunion" organized by Catholics and Protestants and held at the home of one of them.

The technique for such disruptions can be described as comprising several steps: preparation for the disruption and composition of a broadsheet; brief "wildcat" occupation of the place of disruption; seizure of the podium and distribution of broadsheets, along with some symbolic actions; if occasion offered, discussion with those present, after the disruption of the meeting or service; communique to the press or publication of another broadsheet describing the reaction of those "challenged".

The themes to be found in the broadsheets and in the speeches during the disruption dealt with the political involvement of the Churches. Great stress was laid on the class struggle and on repression, especially with regard to Latin America. Local current events, such as the prohibition laid on Father Cardonnel, could also be used for purposes of attacking ecclesiastical collusion with the politicians in power.

The manner of the disruptions was highly non-institutional. The chief element was the seizure of the podium, which meant a symbolic shift in relation to the service in question or to the bureaucratic conventions of the meeting being disrupted (set agenda, right to speak given only to members of the organization or invited officials, etc.). In terms of institutional analysis the actions of the disrupters introduced a "wildcat" factor, but there was no physical brutality, at least on the side of the disrupters. This fact is to be explained, in part, by the composition of the disrupting group which was made up of Christians or people strongly influenced by their religious training; in part, by the fact that the number of women in the group was almost equal to the number of men.

Broadly speaking, in the division of work the women's task was to distribute the broadsheets or to handle the small group discussion, while the men were to seize the podium and to perform any other actions which would require a certain amount of strength: gaining entrance to the meeting or service when this was difficult, putting the organist out of action, escaping from laymen or clergy who might react violently.

The reactions of those "challenged" were strong and sometimes brutal. There were the summoning of the police or cooperation with the police when the latter came on the scene quickly. During the disruption of the ecumenical service at the Orthodox Church, at which the archbishop of Paris and various Orthodox and Protestant authorities were present (and

M. Couve de Murville, Minister of Foreign Affairs and future
Prime Minister, was booked to come), those present passed from
exclamations of outrage to insults and from insults to action,
and violently ejected the young people who had spoken a few
words and tossed out some broadsheets in the midst of the
service. Those present who did not help in "cleansing" the
church expressed deep emotion and spoke along fascist lines.
Frequently, when the disruption occurred in a place of worship,
the organ was used to drown out the voices of the disrupters
(therefore the need of putting the organist out of action).
At the service in Saint-Germain-des-Prés the Protestant monks
were relatively "understanding" in regard to the disrupters
who demanded the right to speak. But laymen tried to take the
microphone from the unannounced speaker, while a crowd of
Catholic religious women shouted themselves hoarse with Kyries
and Our Fathers, which, of course, created all the noise needed
to defeat the speaker.

One aspect of the disruptions must be noted, for it highlights one characteristic of C.A.R.E., that is, the youthfulness of its members. I am referring to the symbolic gestures, which at times closely resembled those used in the classical school protest. For example, during the disruption of a Protestant service (this disruption was intended as a follow-up to the Saint Severinus affair), the words "You are the camphor of the earth" were accompanied by the throwing of camphor balls and the seizure of the bible which was laid on the side-walk, that is, "in the street". On other occasions, less conventional gestures were used. You will not expect me to speak of them in detail.

c) <u>Structure and dynamics of the group</u>. Catholics were in the majority, and the members were mainly students and young teachers. Many had gotten to know each other within the framework of the PU (University Parish) during sessions organized by this institution during school vacations.

Among the Catholics, most were lay people. The non-laymen were some leaders of *Echanges et Dialogue*, a movement of radical priests which was then being formed. On the Protestant side the members were chiefly young Protestant pastors and their wives. There were also a few foreigners, chiefly Belgians.

It is difficult to assign a very precise number to the membership. As we have already indicated, not all by any means of the many people who met at the Saint Yves Center entered C.A.R.E. At the beginning, there were about fifteen, perhaps twenty; then when the letdown from May set in, there remained a nucleus of about ten, later five or six, *active* people, plus the few priests already mentioned who did not take an open part in the disruptions.

The priests were present and active, however, in the preparation for these disruptions. The priests supplied the needed workrooms and other means for the laymen who met to discuss or mimeograph the texts. But the priests were much less visible when it came to public action. The usual ruler-subject relationship was not entirely eliminated between clergy and laity. In fact, we may speak of two sub-groups within C.A.R.E. The priests engaged in clerical strategy and action in their opposition to the powers that be, while the laity did not necessarily derive their strategy and type of activity from the ideology represented by the radical priests. The priests wanted to change the Church from inside, not because they professed a reformist outlook, but because they had learned from several decades of experiences and knew that by leaving the Church and marrying a priest lost all power over the Church. Deviation due to ideology or passion almost always created a crisis that was a dead end.

The laymen, for their part, did not hide their wish to dismantle the Church not simply as an institution (a bureaucracy) but as a grouping of people, a "christendom". This emerges clearly from a collection of interviews conducted while passions were hot and published by a priest of the group.[19]

The same outlook became visible in the course of the group's evolution and final dispersal. In this sequence the group followed the same path as most of the groups that had been formed in May, 1968, under the pressure of events. The numerical outflow was irreversible, beginning with the opening of the 1968-1969 school year. The government's assertion of control of the situation made its effects felt in all institutions. There was, then, a reduction of the group's size, and by the end of the 1968-1969 school year the nucleus consisted chiefly of people who had known each other before in the P.U., before C.A.R.E. was started. Furthermore, the tendency to organize and institutionalize the deviant group coincided with the loss of the group's original institutionalizing energy. A bulletin, *Lien*, attempted to bring about the federation of various groups in Paris and the provinces, but C.A.R.E. saw this organizational phase as a weakening of its original thrust and purpose. The very way in which the group's activity was carried on already represented a decadence as compared with the first days: in the early period everybody had a share in all decisions, but *Lien*'s attempt to create an (admittedly very flexible) federation came from decisions "at the top". Such regulation at the national level was but a reflection of regulation by the public authorities, by events, and by the restraints put upon the May movement.

In this final phase C.A.R.E. could have chosen to turn into a work group or into a base group in the sense of a group of friends who had no intentions of engaging in action. Some members of the group did eventually chose this second way, continuing to see each other after the activist phase had passed. Contacts were also kept with some priests of *Echanges et Dialogue*. Two members of the group who had known each other since the P.U. session at Hendaye in September, 1967, asked a leader of the radical priests' group to marry them in an unconventional way in the parish church of the Charonne sector of Paris, a sector known for its revolutionary traditions. In this instance, there was a deviation from the course which led from lay movements, via the enthusiasm of May, 1968, to a position in the Church that represented both integration and marginality. For others, the return to normality after the upheaval of 1968 meant a definitive departure from the Church and the faith. A young Belgian Franciscan left the priesthood and married. A young teacher--my wife--married, broke definitively with the Church and temporarily with her family. A young pastor became a leftist militant. One leader left for Algeria and training. There was a diaspora. Once defunct, C.A.R.E. would not come to life again as a group working on problems of faith or politics, or as a band of groupist comrades, or as a base community taking the counter-institutional path.

2) Counter-Institutional Action and Counter-Parish
(Action Group II)

The parish as a basic territorial institution of Christianity is dead. The Catholic Church is still profiting by its hegemony over the masses and the kinetic energy communicated to these masses by centuries of history. But lay movements are ceaselessly being destroyed by their own contradictions, while the dialectic of temporal and spiritual finds its practical form in a conflict between ecclesial institutions (the bureaucracy) and religious institutions (the movements). Faced with the choice between norm and movement, the Christian institution has finally chosen the norm. The small-group remnants left by the movements are coming into open conflict with the bureaucracy or becoming marginal.

Like the Roman Church, the Reformed Churches have been deeply shaken by the urban revolution. A second Reformation is under way, due not to a Luther or a Calvin but to the pressure of urban life.

Relations between city and countryside, the understanding of which is essential if we would comprehend the development of the capitalist system of production, have changed far more radically in a few decades than they did when heavy industry was first introduced. In fact, it is not simply the relations that have changed; the two terms in the relation, city and countryside, have themselves changed their very nature. Between them a third element has taken its place: the suburb, which is the only place of continuous growth. The central sections of the city are being emptied or their population is being expelled and replaced by new strata which can pay higher rents. The countryside is becoming a place for the tourist-consumer, despite some attempts to decentralize industry. The suburbanite, who must spend so much of his time in endless daily travel, lives neither in the city nor in the country; he lives among the increasingly abstract symbols of city and country life. Amid the urban phenomenon he is as it were the synthesis, never quite complete, of the impossible city and the impossible countryside. His little garden, his summer-house, the nearness of woods or polluted river, the "fresh air for the children" symbolize--to his imagination--his return to nature. The segregated living, the price of property now that the speculators control it, the nearby superhighway, the heavy traffic at rush hours, the supermarket, the billboards, the small-scale reproductions of the city-dweller's pleasures (concerts, recreational clubs, nightclubs, discotheques), all these supply a pale image of the city.

The city means all of this: all these signs of natural and civilized abundance, and all the deficiencies that hide behind such signs. To begin with, there is the lack of socialization and the collapse of neighborhood units, and no amount of publicity about rebuilding "villages" and cottages of cut stone with pitched roofs can make people forget these things.

Amid this transformation of the traditional environment and social scene the parish tosses about like a straw in the water. It tries to follow the growth of the suburbs, the centripetal and centrifugal migrations, the abandonment of some sections, and the desertion of rural areas. Church walls rise up, concrete or prefab. But the movements so congenial to the new urban populations are too rapid, even if one does not build in concrete. In the North, churches are up for sale, right in the middle of heavily populated areas. At Sarcelles there are too many parishes for the population.

Christianity has suggested a number of responses to this situation which recalls the period when Christianity was first implanted in pagan lands. Here we will discuss only two of these responses. One is the Protestant changing of the map which attempts to replace the old parishes with new "undertakings". The other is the counter-parish movement, which comes from below but is at times encouraged or controlled by the bureaucracy.

a) "New Undertakings" in the Reformed Church of France

These are of two kinds: the centers set up in rural areas and the centers set up in the cities or suburbs.

These centers are, in varying degrees, counter-parishes. But all the centers have some traits in common with the counter-parish.

The counter-parish is a form of parallel but not necessarily "underground" or oppositional Church, as is the counter-parish of Isolotto at Florence which is in opposition to the official parish and the bishop. The traditional parish generally continues to exist alongside, or not far from, the counter-parish, and has a clientele which tends to become more and more clearly distinct from the heterogeneous clientele of the counter-parish.

The counter-parish is the responsibility of a pastor who may or may not have been officially detached from his strictly pastoral duties (saying the office, training children, etc.). He is paid by the National Federation (Reformed Church of France), but this does not prevent regional authorities from controlling and criticizing the action of this missionary who has parachuted down through the local hierarchy.

The counter-parish sets aside, partially or completely, the usual preaching activity and assigns itself a different mission: to bring together individuals or groups with varying objectives, without applying any strict criteria of religious affiliation. Some people look to the rural or urban center for a meeting-place they otherwise lack; others see in it a place for reflection, intellectual work, information, and culture, where they can make up for their own defective formation and for the deficiencies of the educational institutions; still others look to the center as a place for withdrawal or rendez-vous with a view to militant action. In other words, some intention of temporal involvement may always be present, but it by no means implies a unity of outlook and action among all who frequent the center (although this may be true of a very small number of centers).

The counter-parish is not a territorial institution. Its boundaries are fluid, and it would be better to speak of a sphere of influence. Moreover, the opposition between "with walls" and "without walls", which partially expresses the distinction between rural center and urban center, has consequences that are both material and symbolic. At the material level, the absences of walls (of set locale) means that those in charge of the counter-parish come to live among the people "like a fish in the water". At the symbolic level, the existence of walls implies the idea of a refuge for groups of young people who have nowhere to gather, and thus the idea of temporal administration and, consequently, of a conscious or unconscious control or pressure by the hierarchy.

These various characteristics of the counter-parish can, speaking roughly, be reduced to one: the counter-parish is a criticism-in-action of traditional Christian institutions (that is why I have chosen the term "*counter*-parish"). Its existence and development represent a tacit or open opposition to the territorial institutions which surround it and possibly to other counter-parishes as well. In contrast, the conflict with the hierarchy is less inevitable, to the extent that the hierarchy is disposed to shut its eyes to these *sociological experiments on living people* and content itself with financing them and regulating them only in a very flexible way.[20]

The problem raised by the counter-parishes which have gone farthest along the path of radical criticism is this: If a counter-institutional movement is accepted and even encouraged by the hierarchy, what chance does it have of resolving contradictions which it seems inclined rather to "live with"?

b) The Base Community Movement

This subject is being handled in other papers of this colloquium, and my intention here is simply to situate the question in the sociological context developed in my own paper. Inquiries such as those conducted by Danièle Léger (see next

chapter) or Henri Gougaud as well as various other works provide
us with only the beginnings of a knowledge of this sociological
phenomenon which affects far more than just the Churches.[21]

This is how I would formulate the problem which these
communities raise: How do these communities (whether or not
they be Christian in origin and obedience) stand in relation to
the various types of action which I have proposed in a somewhat
simplistic scheme and tried to illustrate by current or recent
examples?

The element of institutional action is present in these
communities to the extent that some of them are connected to
the bureaucracy either through some of their members or through
respect for the sacraments or through obedience to hierarchy
or Pope. This is true, for example of the various "New Life"
communities. Moreover, the political involvement connected
with such institutional action is revealing as to both the
ideological basis and the practice of this new kind of Christian
community. The P.S.U., with its modernizing and leftist ambiguities and its integration into traditional political life,
corresponds fairly well to this kind of base community.

The anti-institutional element comes to the fore inasmuch
as the base group (in the psycho-sociological sense of the
term) constitutes as it were the chief temptation for such
Christians as are desirous of reestablishing the transparent
kind of social relationships that characterize the small group.
These small groups are not communities in the sense of being
stable units characterized by some collective ownership of
goods. They may exist as centers for periodic encounters, as
places for renewal, for ongoing training, for the raising of
questions outside the narrow perspectives of immediate practice.
Many people involved in teaching or formation, cleric or lay,
come to advance their own formation in places and under guides
who show them what kind of person the good leader is and how

a group functions well. As we saw earlier, in these circumstances psycho-sociology becomes an ideology of salvation; political conflicts are left behind in an outside world, in some separate temporal sphere.

Using the example of C.A.R.E. we have identified non-institutional action with the qualified activism of the "leftist"; this kind of action is a militant version of counter-institutional action, and may inspire permanent or semi-permanent base communities. In such instances we are dealing with groups of militants who want to engage in collective political involvement and a collective life-style: raising children together, pooling incomes and possessions, gradually discovering how to live with others and themselves in the absence of such social relations as involve domination. That is what these people are looking for, not as an end in itself but as the condition for coherent revolutionary action. The separation between private life and (militant) public life is regarded as something to be eliminated.

Finally, counter-institutional action in the limited sense (action group II) reveals the ambiguity we have already noted in connection with the two current movements: the official or semi-official counter-parish movement, and the more spontaneous base community movement. The counter-parish shows potential for action that is in turn institutional (by its links, at least financial, with the hierarchy), anti-institutional (by its tendency to groupism and to "revolution through education"), and non-institutional (in the case of the more "leftist" Protestant centers which are open to the non-Christian strata of the population and are actively involved in revolutionary political action). Its counter-institutional potentiality, however, can be gauged only by the gradual or sudden demise of the traditional parish. As long as the counter-parish remains simply a parallel institution and continues to celebrate its cultural or ideological counter-Mass for intellectuals, it will not accomplish the essential mission of every counter-institution: to unify a coherent social base around clear revolutionary goals.

The choice between the reformist and the revolutionary strategies is being ever more clearly forced on us. For that reason, the debate between institutional Christianity and group Christianity will prove to be offering false alternatives.

CHAPTER 4

The Politico-Religious Ideology of Informal Student Groups
An Essay in Interpretation

by

Danièle Léger

At the present time, especially in confessional circles, a truly amazing amount of attention is being given to the subject of small-group formation. By that I mean the development of small groups which remain on the periphery of "officially approved" ecclesial institutions and are known by various names: base communities, brotherhoods, critical groups, informal groups, study groups, etc. The abundant literature on the subject is proof enough of the interest being taken in it.

Yet at the very time when essays in pastoral interpretation are multiplying and pastoral strategists are trying to absorb the groups (we even hear of "getting spontaneous groups started"!), there is often something problematic about the identification of the groups and the judgments being passed on their extent and formal variety. The uncertainty is due in part to the easily observable shifts in attitude on the part of Church authorities, who vacillate between enthusiasm and distrust of the groups. The uncertainty in turn begets contradictory evaluations of the whole phenomenon.

In the view of some, the flowering of spontaneous groups is something radically new; from it they expect a genuine renewal of ecclesial institutions, a death warrant for classical-style groupings (parishes and traditional movements), and a real hope for "the future of the Church". To others, on the contrary, the very existence of the informal groups is not certain: "Everyone talks about these base communities. Where are they?" In this view, attention being paid by religious organizations to a phenomenon that is so diffuse and marginal is simply an indirect way of questioning their own ability to adapt to a cultural and social situation in which their traditional influence has waned. Finally, between overesteem and minimalization there is a third tendency which is even more calculated to increase the confusion, and that is the tendency uncritically to assimilate the small groups to categories which, in principle at least, are better marked out and more easily manipulated (the category of sect, for example).

The first requirement, then, of any attempt at interpretation (such as I am being asked to give under the heading of "the politico-religious ideology of informal student groups") is to make it clear what one is talking about when one speaks of "informal groups". Current opinion, as I have indicated, says either too much or too little. In point of fact, however, any attempt at a sociological perspective on the growth of the base communities runs into the difficulty of coming to grips with the extreme diversity of the groups that remain marginal to official institutions but call themselves "base communities" and thus solicit the attention of the observer. This is true even if one restricts oneself to a particular population such as students. Thus a first examination of the makeup of student groups does not bring to light any constant factor that could be the basis for a working hypothesis concerning the conditions under which such groups come into existence. It seems, in particular, that the genesis of the base communities is not connected with a specific age group. By this I mean that, although differences of style between groups do depend on age, the young students who are just beginning their studies are neither more nor less likely than their more advanced elders to form "spontaneous groups". Nor does intellectual specialization seem to dispose some categories of students rather than others to establish informal groups or base communities.

If we limit ourselves to a straightforward description of the empirical reality, the first thing we observe is that both in circumstances of origin and in concrete ways of functioning the groups are extremely varied. Varying points of departure intermingle, different combinations being at work from group to group: students who are in direct reaction against the way in which the Catholic Student Center attached to their faculty operates; groups of friends who decide they want to formalize their relationships by regular meetings; students interested in the same political goals or desirous of investigating the problems posed by the practice of a particular scientific discipline; groups looking for ways of communal religious expression which will allow a greater degree of participation than is provided by the traditional practices of ecclesial institutions; etc. A great diversity also comes to light when we consider the declarations of the members concerning their own "project", the objectives and future they envisage for their group. Finally, the way in which the groups function does not provide a uniform basis for judgment. We may be dealing with a team or working group that meets once a week; we may be dealing with a brotherhood or community that is experimenting with a more or less full-time common life. All sorts of combinations are possible, even if all the groups in question may call themselves "base groups" or "informal groups" or "base communities".

There is a strong temptation, therefore, simply to produce monographs without end on each individual case or series of cases. And admittedly any attempt at a more comprehensive approach does seem notably to reduce the rich complexity of the reality being observed. To this difficulty we may add another:

the secretiveness of most experimental groups which see their
freedom dependent on preserving a certain clandestinity and
are reluctant to discuss their doings with a third party.
Finally, if we take into account the frequently ephemeral
character of these groups (especially when they set out to be
completely absorbing "communities" that will assure the members
as integral a common life as possible), we will understand the
difficulty observers have in grasping the informal group phenomenon as a whole and, much more, in reducing it to any quantitative terms. We will also understand the great weakness of any
and all generalizations.

In view of these various considerations, my intention here
can only be to offer a dossier, and one that is provisional and
continually being improved. For practical purposes, my exposi-
tion rests on observation of about thirty groups, made up exclusively of students from Paris and the provinces. I have
used written documents produced by some of the groups; statements solicited or simply recorded at meetings of the membership; and, for some groups, direct participation in some of
their meetings or liturgies.

With the help of these various sources of information, and
bearing in mind the inevitable limitations of any general pre-
sentation of such a diversified phenomenon, we can attempt a
"profile" of the base communities among students. That will
be my object in the first part of my essay. The profile will
then serve as a point of reference in an attempt to understand
the "logic" of these groups and to relate their "project" (insofar as the initial description has enabled us to grasp it) to
their concrete situation in regard to ecclesial institutions
with their regulatory systems. Finally, in the third part of
the essay, we shall understand the ideology of these groups
to mean the complex structure of collective representations
which express both the concrete situation of the groups and the

imperatives they derive from that situation. We can then ask, for these specific groups which are determined by their twofold character as student group and confessional group, what mutual relationships exist between the representations, regarded by the groups as "political" or "religious", of their relations, be they "spontaneous (or lived)" or "imaginary", to their surrounding world.[1]

I. Profile of the Student Base Communities

At the risk of excessive schematization, we can claim three traits to be characteristic of the groups we have observed. The traits are very widely found and can serve as the basis for an attempt to interpret the politico-religious ideology of the groups.

1) The first noteworthy point is the importance which the groups attribute to the events of May, 1968.

It was during the academic year 1968-1969, that is, immediately following on the May Movement, that spontaneous groups or "base communities" began to spring up outside the classical groups of the Student Mission Movement, the University Catholic Centers, and the University Catholic Action. It is probable, however, that if we take into account not only the groups we have observed but all the groups which now call themselves base groups, we will find a good number that were established well before May, 1968.

The process of small group formation did, however, intensify in the months following the ebbing of the May Movement. In addition, whether by stimulating the formation of new base communities or by radically affecting the outlook and functioning of those already in existence, May 1968 was a "decisive moment", a "breakthrough", the "privileged occasion for a new awareness" and a "renewal of outlook" both on the future of society and on the role of the Church in society.[2] May 1968 brought new thoughts, to which those involved attribute, often explicitly, the growth of new group forms.

The reference to the events of May, 1968, so widespread in 1968-1969, has lost its force by now, especially among the younger students. But the importance still attributed by the base groups to politics, to the theme of "human liberation", and to that of the emancipation of human expression, are witness to a perspective that may not have first come into existence in May, 1968, but certainly became widespread among Catholic students as a result of these events.

2) The second trait that is generally characteristic of the groups we have observed is the concern that a common religious commitment should not be the only criterion of group membership, but that "the community should be a place for mutual exchange at all levels: personal problems, political problems, social commitments, etc." This concern is widespread and effectively operative.

Observation of the way the groups really function as well as of the formal statements of the members shows that in every case the common sharing in the same political task and in the life of the local university legitimitizes and makes possible, in the eyes of the members, the properly religious life of the group. A "political consensus" and the same "political practice" are often said to be the reason the groups came into existence, and it is in function of this "established fact" that the participants will define the content of a "quest" which they call religious. The very use of this terminology points to a reversal of the kind of functioning with which the classical groups and especially the Catholic Action teams are familiar. The content of the faith is no longer the stable and unquestioned reference point when it comes to "action in the world". Now the content of faith is the problematic thing, while the ways of sharing in the life of society are defined in an apriori fashion, without any reference (at least explicit) to religion.

We may state this point a little more broadly by saying that in most of these base groups the possibility of a shared religious expression depends on the existence among the members of a "political consensus" (if not of commitment to the same political organization); the lack of such a consensus would render empty any religious agreement, such as might be formalized, for example, in shared worship. More than this, the possibility of a shared religious expression depends on the existence of an "authentic group life".

A student at Limoges said: "We become members of a base community in order to satisfy the more or less open need of avoiding isolation and joining others so as to escape anonymity and live in a properly human way." Others speak of "sharing life in all its dimensions"; "achieving effective solidarity with one another"; "sharing experience".

Here we have the key-words in the life of the student "base communities" and the objectives most often formulated by the members, whatever be the manner in which their particular group may function.

We must bear in mind, however, that the groups which really try the experiment of an all-embracing common life are a minority of all those which call themselves base communities. Of the thirty or so groups observed, only one became, for six months, a thorough-going commune with a complete sharing of possessions. Most of the time, the groups require of their members only a weekly meeting for work and discussion; the meeting often includes a shared meal and a liturgy or shared prayer. Sometimes, three or four members of a group live together, but the community as such has a larger membership which meets at regular intervals. In any case, a lasting sharing of all possessions is rare; more often, the group sets up a fund to which each member contributes.

Nonetheless the desire for a fuller, if not total, common life is widespread. It is worth noting that, in most of the groups with which I have been able to establish some direct contact the group meeting is generally viewed as a limited realization of that more intense common life which the members would like to enjoy. If we are to gain a rounded appreciation of the group phenomenon as a whole and a correct interpretation of its real thrust, it is essential that we take into account the aspiration toward community, even if the intensity of the desire and the importance given it are out of all proportion to the present functioning of the base groups.

The will (seen most clearly when we look at the collection of groups as a whole) to achieve this kind of multi-dimensional sharing is undoubtedly effective only in a limited way and to the accompaniment of numerous difficulties. Yet, ephemeral and precarious though the groups be, and however illusory the communal goal which they set for themselves may be in some cases, this goal does constitute a specific characteristic of the base communities.

The possibility, then, of shared religious expression, is connected in all the groups observed, whatever be the manner of their functioning, with the existence of effective solidarities between the members of the "community" or "team". These solidarities are found in all the areas of life which they do not categorize as religious, and especially in the area of political choices and action.

The basis for a shared life in these groups is no longer the religious commitment as such, with the group then determining what the consequences of that commitment are to be for the

social activity of the members. On the contrary, it is the
common social life that legitimizes the specifically religious
expression of the group. Membership in a base community cannot be acquired simply on the basis of a previous religious
commitment whose existence is determined solely by the officially sanctioned religious actions of the person seeking admittance. Rather all must "seek to reach mutual understanding
of the meaning of their experience"; the important thing is that
"each person express himself truly, freely". We hear these
formulas in the groups we have encountered; they express in
various ways the twofold aim that is characteristic of the
student base communities:

To liberate the religious life of individual and group
from isolation by articulating a shared religious language
based upon those effective, "socio-political" solidarities
which have largely ceased to play any part in traditional
groups in which the members are not really dependent on one
another in any way.

To reject, consequently, any externally imposed program of
investigation and expression; especially any program arising
out of an apriori definition of religious faith which would be
established by an ecclesial body with power to determine the
norms for individual and group religious experience.

3) This twofold aim corresponds to a typical reinterpretation of the usual maxim to be found in ecclesial institutions
and among their militants: "the whole of religion in the whole
of life". Now, on the contrary, it is the group's "being together" or the totality of relationships prevailing in the
group that provides the basis for the group's religious life,
and not vice versa. This viewpoint must be related to a comprehensive radical challenge leveled against official ecclesial
institutions, be they parishes, Catholic Action movements, or

student centers. It represents the third characteristic mark of the base groups which we have observed.

The various criticisms of the ecclesial institution as a whole may be grouped, somewhat schematically, around three main points: the Church is repressive; the Church is compromised; the Church is alien.

1) The Church is repressive by reason of its hierarchic structure. The concentration of power exclusively in the hands of a few men, the lack of communication within the ecclesial body, and the weight of the bureaucracy: these elements have all been challenged by the students we have questioned, in the name of "Christian freedom".

But the criticism is mainly directed against those intra-ecclesial "ideologists", the theologians, to whom those in power assign the function of justifying the overall functioning of the body. In support of this interpretation of the theologians' role and of the control exercised over their work by the hierarchy, the students point to the "repression" of those who stray from orthodoxy. Thus, the "Schillebeeckx affair" or the "Cardonnel affair" in their time drew a strong student reaction. The students were almost totally indifferent to the objective content of the theological debates involved in these incidents, but they were very sensitive to the procedures adopted by the Church in dealing with the men in question.

2) If the Church can in this way be reproached for being a "repressive structure", the reason frequently assigned is that it makes use in its own sphere of the methods of domination and intellectual repression to be found in society at large, while trying to justify them in religious terms. Correlatively, the Church finds itself being blamed for accepting the prevailing ideology which such methods foster. As a result, all those whose political commitments lead them to challenge the existing social and political organization of

society find themselves automatically "marginalized" in the ecclesial institution whose social functioning they question. Many of the base communities we have observed are far from developing in equal measure a systematic analysis of the political order, but the themes we have mentioned are widespread among them.

3) Under cover of language that claims to embrace all mankind, the Church thus shows that it is in fact bound up with a social order and a morality that is individualist and liberalist in spirit. Consequently it is alien to all who reject the socio-political order on which the Church depends. The political explanation of the foundation of this criticism will be more or less incomplete, depending on the group in question. It is very largely true, however, that the classical dichotomy between a "Church" that is by definition, holy, universal, and set apart from the conflicts and struggles to which society is subject, and the "world" in which these conflicts and struggles are played out, is less and less acceptable to a growing number of students. These students are applying to the specialized functioning of the group we call "church" a more or less systematic analysis of society as such.

In the name of its own postulated "holiness" and the revelation on which it is based, the Church stands off from other social groups; it claims to be "set apart" within society at large. The degrees of opposition may vary, but here we have the essential point that is rejected in the criticisms leveled against ecclesial institutions by the base communities we have studied. The students in this critical movement apply to the Church an analysis of social reality which contains no explicit religious reference and is usually described as "political". They are attempting a demystification of any claim to be an "exception", whatever be the theological justification offered by the religious group in question. The rejection of any "apartness" for the religious group takes positive form in the quest for total integration into the life of society. As a base group in Montpellier put it: "We want to be full-fledged sharers in the world's life." From this point of view, there is a radical difference between the groups and sects. The groups then are no longer appealing to a theological vision of the Church's mission within society at large in order to justify a full and total participation of Christians in the life of society in the name of apostolic effectiveness or the requirements of the gospel. On the contrary, they are rejecting in advance any claim of the Church to limit or direct such a sharing in society.

In the eyes of many groups, the Church is subject to internal conflicts that are incompatible with the "holiness" she claims. More than that, they do not allow her preaching a specially privileged role. Theological discourse is simply one of numerous competing ideological discourses to be found in the marketplace at a given moment; it has no special status and therefore cannot claim exemption from the criticism that may be leveled against every socio-cultural discourse of a particular time and place.

The Church is often blamed for having "claimed a monopoly on the means of salvation" and thus giving its members the privilege of standing apart from history and "judging" it. Moreover, the groups do not allow the Church any right--certainly not one based on the revelation she claims to embody--to declare the meaning of history and to determine the eschatological goal toward which mankind is moving. That kind of reference is, in any case, useless and ineffective when it comes to the historical process of man's emancipation.

Such a stance is, obviously, that of the more "radical" base groups we have observed in the student world; the members of these groups were all politically on the far left. But traces of the same outlook are to be found in groups less vigorously opposed to the prevailing social order and the ecclesiastical organization. We will note further on how, in some instances at least, religious representations of mankind's future have been wholly or partially incorporated into a vision of the end of history which those concerned call "political". It is a vision which deliberately disassociates itself from any theology of history.

It seems, for the moment, that most of the base communities are elaborating a critique of ecclesiastical functioning which consciously avoids any religious reference. The point, then, is not to set up a new ecclesiology against the prevailing ecclesiology. It is to subject the Church to the demystifying effects of a political analysis that is valid for society as a whole.

We must note, however, that this "secularization" (to use a word that has been rendered valueless by the variety of its applications) of the critique made against the ecclesial institution can be and most frequently is accompanied by a challenge to the Church's functioning and teaching in the name of evangelical purity. The latter is regarded as betrayed by the organization; it is often seen as incarnated in the first Christian community portrayed in the Acts of the Apostles.

A "political" critique of society as a whole, including the Church, and a "religious" critique of an ecclesial instituion that is corrupted by its compromises with an unjust society, when it ought to be denouncing and fighting the injustice of the world: the two critiques are correlative; they lead to and reinforce each other; sometimes they blend into one. According to the group in question, according as circumstances seem to offer greater opportunities for exercising a transformative action on society as a whole or, on the contrary, bid the group turn in on itself, the amount of each kind of criticism will vary.

The components, however, are constant, and we can say, generally speaking, that the base communities issue a double challenge.

It is a challenge to the increasing fragmentation of social life; to the dispersal of human activity into carefully isolated spheres; to the resultant anonymity, of which these groups are all the more sensible, living as they do in universities afflicted with gigantism and in which the degeneration of university life forces the individual back into the isolation of his private work. This challenge, initially a partial one caused by a special set of circumstances, develops into a global challenge to the whole functioning of societal relations and can take the form, or tend to do so, of attempts at revolution.

It is also a challenge to the Church's isolation from the life of society; to the foreignness of the traditional language the Church uses; to anonymity within ecclesial institutions, where only a formalistic liturgical life guarantees an increasingly unstable cohesion within the group.

II. Logic of the Base Communities

A. "To Change the Way of Life"

It is clear enough from what we have seen that the terms "base community" or "informal group" are not being applied to a homogenous reality. A simple group of friends in a private little world, a study group meeting at regular intervals, a brotherhood which carries its experiment with community living to the point of a complete sharing of possessions: in short, a very great variety of groups likes to call itself "base groups". The only requirement is that the members, uncontrolled by any official ecclesial institution, should define their own purpose and mode of operation.

This last statement makes it possible to maintain that the group phenomenon within the student world does not totally elude definition. For, in point of fact, the whole range of experiments can be ordered around a single proposition. A student in the Faculty of Science at Orsay, and a member of a brotherhood, put it this way: "In the last analysis what we want is to change the way of life."

1. A Counter-Society

Observation of the base groups shows that, in various ways, and with more or less innovative energy, all are trying to effect among their members a new style of relationships, very unlike that which usually prevails in society and particularly in the University.

The aim is to replace anonymity, the struggle to survive, and individualism, with the "acknowledgment" of each person in the group. The person is to be part of the group, not by reason of a juridical acceptance or by a function he exercises in it, but by sharing co-responsibility. The complete sharing of tasks, the absence (at least in principle) of anyone who is "responsible" for the group, and the desire that general objectives and methods of operation be the result of collective decision, even if this means difficulties in practical functioning--these are among the most constant traits we have observed in the student base communities.

Degrees of "totalization" may vary, but the constant intention of these groups is to avoid the fragmentation of social relations and the widespread and increasing dissociation of work, leisure, political militancy, friendship, etc., that now prevails in society, and to create instead a small-scale but unified structure that will be a microcosm of a radically different kind of societal life, in which the various dimensions of the members' lives can "be lived in unity" (I am quoting again the student from Orsay).

Personalization of relations, co-responsibility, and unification of social life: these are the three aims which the student base communities set for themselves, even if they less often bring them to fulfillment. The aims represent, of course, an opposition to the real situation of the University students with its isolation, lack of responsibility, and marginalization in relation to society. They also sum up the counter-society which May, 1968, may have foreshadowed, especially to those who took part in the Movement. The student base communities came into being, for the most part, in the immediate aftermath of the events of May and as the impulse behind those events ebbed. They often seem to be micro-forms of the counter-society which was glimpsed during those exciting days and straightway shunted aside into the realm of imaginary possibility; they are the derided witnesses who refuse to let the utopian ideal die out.

2. A Counter-Church

The kind of relationship to the ecclesial institution which the base communities want to have is a specific expression of the all-embracing determination to renew all social relations.

What is specifically new about the groups when it comes to the Church is their endeavor to apply here the characteristic thrust of the groups as such: freedom of the group to create; rejection of any externally imposed program of activity; definition by the group of its own objectives and practical forms; redefinition, if there be place for it, of the status of any clerical member, who is to be chosen by the group in most cases and admitted on the proviso that he renounces any privileged status and consents to be simply one of the members; rejection of any programatization of religious expression; a taste for "intimate liturgies" in which all the participants are actors, and not passive spectators; etc. All these elements, found in most of the groups we observed, can be regarded as significant manifestations of the attitude of self-sufficiency which marks relations between the base communities and Church authorities.

B. Church or Sects?

The points just made in the preceding paragraph are those which the observer is tempted to rely on if he wishes to assimilate the development of base groups in the Church (or at least of the radical fringe of these groups) to a development along sectarian lines.

If we refer to the characteristic traits of a sect as Ernst Troeltsch summed them up in a now classic definition, there is no doubt that the base groups do show sectarian traits in varying degrees. On analysis most of the informal groups prove to be small in membership; made up of voluntary, strongly motivated people; based on the intense personal experience of each member and the collective experience of the group; strongly opposed to the priority given to "numbers" in ecclesial institutions which seek out the masses, and to the claim of the Churches to a "holiness" which is belied by the real conflicts within these bodies.

At the same time, however, we must recognize that the rejection of the Church systems is often more verbal than real. In fact, the observer of these groups finds the discrepancy between words and facts highly interesting. The discrepancy is most evident in matters of liturgy, for here, better than anywhere else, we can see how individual and collective mentalities are influenced by those very religious prohibitions whose passing is so vociferously proclaimed. In this sphere which has traditionally been reserved to the priest (we are speaking chiefly of the Eucharistic liturgy), we find a real paralysis of the imagination. To excuse themselves and to compensate for the paralysis, the membership often claim with great intensity that their real purpose is to create "open spaces" in which no externally imposed orthodoxy will hinder the free expression of the participants and no ministerial specialization, which in any case is without theological justification or practical value, will be permitted. In fact, however, and without the members even realizing it, catechetical stereotypes are undoubtedly operative, far more surely than any system of control and sanction by Church authorities, to set limits to the exploration into "new types of expression".

Moreover it is striking how, after calling for the revamping of religious language and of the operation of ecclesiastical institutions, the groups tend to settle, for the short or longer run, for the forms they had initially rejected or, despite their original violently worded claims, accept accomodations that are specified and granted by Church authorities.

A further fact to be considered is that the groups maintain their "commitment to the task of changing society". In this the base communities reject the "unworldliness" of the sects. This alone would be enough to establish the distinctions between informal groups and sects. (We leave aside the fact that the "commitment" often does not take the concrete form of participation in a specific political organization, but remains either a verbal adherence to a revolutionary cause or an episodic participation in particular actions.)

The groups we are discussing are composed for the most part of Christian students with a past history of militancy in Catholic organizations on the school and university scene. They are examples of protest which remains almost entirely within the Church; they are part of the "protest within" that

Joachim Wach described. What they are interested in is not
breaking off from the Church but exercising their rights by
changing the Church or stimulating it to change itself. The
groups that call themselves base communities, critical groups,
or informal groups, seem indeed to threaten the ecclesial body
with a possible schism, for they give a dramatic form, in words,
to their marginal situation in religious society. In point of
fact, however, the kinds of internal organization and operation
they adopt show that they are really asking for a new distribution of power in the Church.

We also find in these groups a particular form of a tendency
that is characteristic of radical challenge from within: the
tendency to mark off within the Church an extra-territorial
space, as it were, which then provides a base for action.[3] This
tendency, along with the discrepancy between words and action
which we have been noting, allows us to conclude that what the
groups really want is the reform of the overall religious
society. For the time being, we cannot anticipate the direction
the whole movement will take, and whether "resistance" will win
out over "submission" or vice versa. It is more likely, in
fact, that there will be as many developments as there are
groups. Generally speaking, however, it is clear that the consultation--mandate pattern which until recently governed the
relations between lay militants and hierarchic authorities is
now passing. It is true enough that the practical steps taken
by the groups seem unsure and quite limited in scope when compared with the claims frequently issued by the same groups. But
the quest for emancipation from all external tutelage (thought
of as paralyzing imagination and action) is certainly the
driving force in "the movement of small-group formation in the
interests of radical challenge", and the development of the
"informal groups" is certainly, at least in part, an example of
that movement. (The only norm the protesting groups are willing

to accept is the Gospel, which the Churches have supposedly obscured, betrayed, distorted, or simply watered down.) What the small-group movement represents is a call for a new kind of social intervention on the part of the Church and a radically different kind of organization of society.

III. **Essay in Interpretation of the Politico-Religious Ideology of the Student Base Communities**

From the ideological viewpoint the novelty of the informal group phenomenon among students seems minimal. In the history of the Church, examples are constantly cropping up (think of the conditions in which many religious orders were founded) of the kind of protest that developed within "little groups" of a marginal kind which attacked ecclesial institutions for compromising with secular society. The protest was religious and directed against the Church organization for failing in its true mission, but along with the religious protest there was always a more or less camouflaged political protest. The latter was part of the very claim that the Church's betrayal was due to its peaceful co-existence or even collusion with the social status quo.

In the case of the base communities we find that the two aspects, political and religious, of the challenge issued received a special explicitation. Moreover, a socio-political critique of society at large (including a critique of the religious society and of Church-society relations) seems to replace, or, more often, be added to, the kind of critique of the religious society which implies a radical critique of the socio-political order.

To be more specific, we find that two tensions are at work:

Church	Society
ecclesial counter-model	social counter-model

Now, the identification by the protesting small groups of ecclesial and social counter-models used to work most of the time in favor of the ecclesial counter-model, but today it seems to be working in favor of the social counter-model. The latter takes the form of a utopia, with the base groups as attempts to bring the utopia into existence on a small scale.

How has such a shift taken place in groups which, for all their variety of forms, share at least one positive goal: to be the locus for an "experience of community" (even if only imperfect) that would be wholly unlike the kind of life imposed by the university situation and the kind of participation in the Church that is usually provided by traditional institutions? That is the question we would like to face, even if for the time being we can only suggest factors that would contribute to an answer.

The critique of the institutional Church often arises out of the dream of a new society, a utopia that owes much to the inspiration of May, 1968. The critique is expressed in political terms by most of the base communities I have observed among the students. This is to say that the rejection of the bureaucracy, the criticism of the way authority is exercised in the Church, and the challenge to the ideology expressed in the Church's teaching, language, and concrete action, are all part of a more comprehensive socio-political critique of institutions generally. The Church is accused of having obscured precisely the subversive character of the Gospel message. This is why the base communities, intending as they do to play a role in the ecclesial institution, speak for the most part of a radical renewal of society as a whole and therefore of both religious society and political society. In political terms, the Church is blamed for having established an unwarranted dualism between political society and religious society and thereby concealed the revolutionary thrust of the gospel ideal. The groups expect that such a socio-political critique of ecclesiastical institutions will enable the Church to carry out in the proper way its prophetic mission and fulfill its real task which is to "preach the kingdom".

The twofold phenomenon of a secularization of religious Messianism and a sacralization of political ideas is quite clear in all those groups--and there are many--which align themselves both with the classless society of communism and the early Christian communities of Acts when they try to justify their wish to do away with the water-tight bulkheads between social, political, economic, intellectual, and religious life, or simply between "profane" life and "religious" life.

This intertwining of religious and political themes can partially be explained by the kind of preaching which formed many militants in the youth movements who today are often to be found in the student base communities. That preaching was focused on the obligation for the people of God, the Church, and each Christian in particular to make visible the Messianic work already accomplished by Christ and now operative in history. Based as it was on the idea of "the Christian's mission" in a world that must be changed, the preaching automatically tended to give every socio-political commitment of a Christian a properly prophetic character; it turned every such commitment into a vicariously Messianic action, both individual and collective in nature. The goal was to "take over" the world of school and university, to "be present there", and to "give a Christian interpretation" to its varied situations, in order thus to share in the *building of the kingdom*.

In this context, correlations were established between the religious themes connected with the expectation of the kingdom and the political themes of radical challenge to society such as was implicit in a Christian's commitment:

eschatology / common good of society
kingdom / perfect society
redemption / liberation from oppression and alienation
Church / classless society
Messianic banquet / free access for all to the good things of earth

Thus, political protest had as its starting point and constant reference-point a properly religious choice, that of active expectation of the kingdom. The logic inherent in political action and, specifically, the contact with other militants who did not need any religious reference to motivate and energize their choices and political commitment undoubtedly led to a growing separation of the "political" and the "religious". Among the student members of the base communities none of those we know referred the political activity or experiments of their group to the requirements of building the kingdom. On the contrary, in groups with strong political preoccupations, there was much talk of the autonomy of political options, and of the inner coherence proper to political analysis, both of which, it was maintained, were not admitted by official institutions.

Despite all this, an initial Messianic vision continues to lend the political project a breadth and radicality; nor does the fact that the themes of Messianic expectation have been secularized into themes of radical challenge make any difference. The goal is to remake society as a whole, to reshape social relations, almost to re-create man himself. An integral humanism, based on an original religious reference, continues to inspire political choices and behavior.

Consequently, apart from such moments as May, 1968, when the emergence of a new world becomes credible, it is rare that the utopian vision underlying political commitment can stand up to a confrontation with the technical demands, austerity, and strategic concessions of a real political "program". In fact, for a number of reasons--the hazards of political action, the practical impossibility of effecting the goals of the initial project through concrete political militancy, and the distance between utopian vision and actual results, of which students are cruelly aware in the vacuum created after May, 1968, and in the present breakdown of the university--a new *expectation*, religious in character, is coming into existence. The failure of the political project is renewing the credibility of the Messianic project.

Students no longer expect the religious society to play a "prophetic role" in relation to society at large. They no longer ask the Church, as they did earlier, to offer secular society a religiously based model of a counter-society. At the very moment when the waning of the Church's influence is everywhere evident and bears witness to the failure of the Church's efforts to acculturate the world to itself (by Christianizing society) or to acculturate itself to the world (by giving a religious dimension to "values"), the increasing social marginality of religious groups invites them to turn inward and engage in that questioning of "Christian identity" which provides so much food for reflection in the student base groups, rather than to look outward in an "apostolic" effort to master the situation in which the groups find themselves.

At the same time, however, the Church is being asked to make its own mankind's aspirations for a new world. It is being asked, not to lead men to God, but to bring God back among men through a comprehensive sacralization of daily life.

We have, then, on the one hand, the evident lessening of the Church's influence in every area of society and the absence of any Christian social project that could mobilize the men of our contemporary technologico-industrial society, and, on the other, the weakening of any expectation of changing, by political means, a dominant system that seems able to swallow up every radical challenge as it arises.

Such is the complex backdrop against which the multiplication of base communities is taking place (a process unleashed among students by an unprecedented breakdown of the university). It also explains the politico-religious ambivalence of the whole development. Even if their protest remains at times largely verbal, these informal groups are seeking a way out of this twofold process of social marginalization, this twofold prison.

In its extreme form the movement may take the form of small cells of protesters, who attempt in an artificial religious environment to create a totally new society; they cannot envisage a large-scale upheaval of the dominant system, whether in the Church or in society at large. Their doubly repressed protest takes shape in small-scale social forms which confront a disqualified religious establishment and disqualified political hopes for society at large with an experimental countermodel of Church-society relations. In their eyes, this countermodel alone can make credible the possibility of a radical renewal of both Church and society, something that at the present time seems wholly improbable.

This kind of protest must at the present time develop within a closed box, within small groups of people, and in deliberate or forced isolation from the life of society. The protest is, as it were, in a state of hibernation. No one therefore can, at the present time, pass accurate judgment on the subversive power such protest may have latent within it or the kind of radical change it might cause in, for example, the socio-economic conditions of contemporary society.

CHAPTER 5

Group and Person:
A Philosophical Reflection

by

Maurice Nédoncelle

If the philosopher is indeed, in Plato's words, a "synoptic man",[1] no one listening to this conference will blame me for taking a broader view of the "group" than is taken by such specialized sciences as psychology and sociology. This broader view implies no contempt for such sciences; on the contrary, I shall frequently be referring to their conclusions and shall move along my own path with a sharp awareness of the lurking dangers. A philosophical reflection must, however, envisage all sides of a subject, starting with elementary observations concerning it and rising if possible to the more difficult problems that yield only to the reflective mind.

Starting with the elements means, in this instance, examining the animal basis of groups. Reaching the heights means scrutinizing the nature of the transindividual subject and asking if that can replace the transcendental and even the transcendent subject. In between these two extremes it is desirable that we consider the specific character and functions of human groups, bearing especially in mind, of course, the informal groups which are the proper subject of our colloquium.

I. *The* *Basis* *in* *Animality*

Living species are not usually concentrated in one territory or composed of perfectly identical members. Each species breaks down into groups and sub-groups which contain differentiated individuals among whom dominant or recessive characteristics are distributed by heredity. Competition develops between individuals but also between groups. For a group is, as it were, a group of chromosomic genes that is different from other pools. Some biologists conclude that the inequality of groups, which depends on the inequality of the individuals, is an instrument, wielded by the species itself, of natural selection at the species level. Such selection is not to be confused with the selection that depends on external factors and has preoccupied the attention of the Darwinian school. For example, a troop of baboons is attacked; some of its members defend the group vigorously, even at the risk of their own lives, and they do it better than the baboons of other troops. Isn't this pehnomenon one key to the evolutionary process?

> Those populations in which the innate compulsion to give warning ran the strongest most obviously possessed the superior capacity to survive. A quality perhaps once the property of but a few populations spread, through group competition, to become today the property of the species.
> Society is the gene pool's testing ground. With fine disregard for individual fate, natural selection must look on the competition of groups for phenotypic evidence as to how genetic possibilities are working. And while you and I amy shudder, at first thought, concerning gods so harsh, on second thought we may look a bit closer and glimpse immortality in our mirror.[2]

These lines are from a book that enjoyed great success in the English-speaking countries. Its author, Robert Ardrey, is an immensely erudite zoologist. He is a clear-minded thinker, given to the sardonic and to occasional black humor. He is, finally, a very able popularizer and perhaps one who generalizes somewhat rashly. One thing is certain that the concepts he uses are not always precise, beginning with the concept of "group" which sometimes designates a highly localized and hierarchically organized assemblage and sometimes a rather scattered and amorphous assemblage such as the group of individuals whom a city-dweller knows and meets about the town.

I am interested in the zoologist's observations here because they suggest the basis in animality for human societies. I shall therefore cite a further passage which concerns our species. The passage will show how Ardrey, like the non-conformist colleagues on whom he draws, can throw off numerous suggestive remarks.

> In the human species, language as a rule forms the sharpest barrier between populations, and that is why the line of language forms usually the national boundary, and why, with rare exceptions, political boundaries enclosing varying language groups tend to enclose trouble as well. But even within an interbreeding population of common language, still religion, geography, allegiances of custom or occupation, economic class, even degree of education all tend to reduce to smaller groups any high probability of meeting and mating. And so the smallest unit of truly equivalent chance is known as a deme, or isolate, and Dobzhansky has suggested that among people even today isolates number hundreds, rarely thousands. A study of marriage records in France has revealed the paradox that in the mountains such isolates average about 1,100 while in Paris, where one would expect broad mixture, they are only about 900.[3]

We would probably turn up similar figures for the seal colonies of Alaska or the elephant herds of Tanzania.

The stimulating and accurate idea behind the hypotheses concerning detail or the bold statistics seems to be the following. The human species retains its roots in animality, and these are always ready to make their presence felt and to affect our higher activities. We too find ourselves divided into competing groups for reproduction or combat. We too are capable of descriptive communication with our likes, yet incapable of communication in other respects, incapable of authentic communion; moreover we have a further source of division the animals do not have, namely our language groups, so that like the animals but more readily than they we can build up hatred for the stranger. Such attractions and repulsions, often connected with possession of a territory, condition our collective survival. If a maddened crowd is stirred to action by a descriptive signal, it even dispenses with human language; it becomes a brainless monster; it crushes any individual who holds onto his reason and wants to apply it. The human group which abdicates its humanity becomes worse than a tribe of rampaging apes; it withdraws into a world in which society exists, not consequent upon individuals, but prior to them, and sacrifices individuals to its own ends.

Human societies are the discoverers of what Ardrey calls the individual and what I would prefer to call the person. Or rather: the person, hatching laboriously out of the chromosomic pool of some hominoid group, produces civilizations.[4] Human order is different, therefore, from an order among mere animals. Its balance is due to compromise: on the one hand, society must recognize that the individual is the only source of civilization, whether scientific, artistic, or political; on the other, the person, while rejecting any kind of crowd-existence, must recognize that men are created unequal and cannot wholly escape from their territories, hierarchies, competitions, and fear of strangers.

In the depths of each of us, there is a reptilian being. That is clear enough to be a commonplace. But Ardrey adds another disquieting idea which is less of a commonplace. He is struck by the survival in human groups of biological traits which may be seen in other higher vertebrates: on the one hand, the association of males, and, on the other, the instinctive grouping of individuals of the same age, and especially of the young. We surmise that for Ardrey the monogamous family which brings into harmonious unity individuals of varying sexes and ages is a late and fragile creation of the primate phylum to which we belong. He asks whether in the present time of crisis the existence of sub-groups of young males is the prelude to a radical restructuring of the social order, the consequences of which would be incalculable as far as our morals and institutions are concerned. He thinks that the three basic desires of the human being are for consciousness of one's own importance, a stimulating life, and security, but also thinks that it is not easy for society to satisfy all three desires simultaneously. He has but limited confidence in the future of our species and distrusts egalitarian utopias and feminist mystiques on the ground that they hide our true condition from us and increase the dangers of imbalance, violence, and degeneracy.

Let me say once again that Ardrey's involved book does not offer decisive proofs but only working hypotheses concerning group selection, hypotheses based on the genetics of populations. It would be only too easy to criticize some of the ways in which he tries to tie together his rich harvest of facts. It cannot, however, be denied that he has given us fascinating insights into the reality of the animal foundations of man's life.

II. The Human Superstructure

The life of the pre-personal group is a spontaneous one; the group forms an affective "community" (*Gemeinschaft*), with bonds that are superficial or deep as the case may be, but lacking any element of contrivance and with a membership that is largely determined by spatio-temporal proximity; there are individual differences between the members but the overriding factor is shared impulses and tastes. We cannot find what is original to human groups in the zoological series in this primitive, concrete form of the pre-personal group.

At the other extreme, a group can be defined in a purely abstract way as a logical class which the mind applies to things or people. The task then is to apply a uniform criterion and assemble various phenomena which have some characteristic in common. Thus, round pebbles on a beach, octave volumes in a library, and bald vicars-general form distinct groups. It seems clear that even though the human mind in its work is constantly defining classes of this type, nonetheless the simple aptitude to be put into such a class is not what is original about a human group.

What is it, then, that forms the superstructure which man adds to the animal substructure and to purely logical classifications? It must be something involving consciousness and intentionality: a willed association of persons, and an association which, initially at least, is created by these persons. On the other hand, we cannot reduce the group to the bond that links two consciousnesses, as in a pair of lovers or a pair of friends. For the purpose, the means, and the kind of sharing are different in the dyad and in the social group properly so called. A group exists only if over and above the intersubjective dyad there is a collective whole, and over and above the dyadic relation a more complex kind of relation. The social "we" presupposes not only the "I" and "Thou" but a plurality of "thous" or a "you [plural]"; it also presupposes that the field of consciousness includes not only the "he" (or "she") that makes its appearance at moments when the "I-thou" awareness weakens, but also the "they" who can co-exist with the "I-you", no matter how strong our sense of this latter relationship may be.

In other words, there is a human group when consciousness knows and wills its connection with a collection of consciousnesses, among which it can perceive particular "thous", and when it perceives itself as a whole that is situated among other consciousnesses which are analogous and complementary to itself. Thus, having first an egocentric representation of the whole collection, each member of the group then moves outward in a decentralizing way in favor of the other and of the collection as such. The capacity to do this is not simply imaginative and pragmatic as it doubtless is in other vertebrates which are sufficiently high on the scale. The capacity in man is also a rational one, for it is straightway linked to a concern for truth and a conception of justice. Human language is a condition for the possibility of the group as thus understood, and language manifests the rationality we possess. Each member of the group shows that he has a viewpoint on other viewpoints, by the fact that the linguistic tense a speaker uses to relate everything to himself and his present existence is matched by the chronological time proper to events, and by the fact that the linear and objective sequence of events is accepted by the whole group of speakers without any misunderstanding in principle.[5]

The total consciousness or, if we prefer, the "we" of the group is not identical (as we indicated above) with the "we" of dyadic communion. The reason is that in the former case distance, both spatial and temporal, necessarily enters the picture. The distance can be as minimal as you like, but it does enter into the very context of the social relation, and this for several reasons.

First, the group includes persons whose presence cannot be simultaneously active in relation to the others nor simultaneously perceived. This, if for no other reason than the complexity of the respective developmental processes peculiar to those persons. However compact a cultural, professional, or even familial group may be, it involves spatial absence, a delay in communication of information, and suspensions of interaction.

A second reason is that the group not only includes but is also included. The consciousness each member has of it is not a consciousness of comprehensive societies or of mankind as a whole. We always situate the group within a larger whole of which it is only a small part. Here again distance or rupture makes its appearance, inasmuch as the boundaries of the group are also the boundaries of our attention and information; the territory that lies beyond us is both indispensable and unknown, htat is, foreign to us.

Finally, a third kind of distance shows up in the group. This distance lies in the very heart of the "we", that is, of the relation between person and community. For, since this "we" is not the "we" of authentic interpersonal communion but only of functional communication, a long-range project that is partly independent of each individual lays a duty on the members of the group. In regard to the members this project is as it were an object, a goal, and a method; it motivates their action to a greater or lesser degree. We might compare it to a tapestry on which many hands are engaged. It has a pre-determined woof and warp: these are the essential or conventional norms accepted by the group. It also has a design which is being made visible by threads of various colors: these threads are are the individual contributions which make up the history of the group. When intellectuality becomes a far more important factor than the animal basis, "society" (*Gesellschaft*) puts a damper on "community" (*Gemeinschaft*), and we witness the victory of ideology. (Our vocabulary reflects the difference, for we speak no longer of a "group" but only of a "grouping".)

This analysis shows that the human superstructure of a group tends to make a lasting choice possible and therefore to make the liberty of persons become possible with the permanence of their association. But the analysis also shows that this tendency is limited on all sides. It is limited quantitatively, since a group always represents, as it were, an area carved out of a larger whole and since the greater the novelty of the group, the more limited its membership will be. As a result we see the formation of sub-groups within the group in order to keep the members from being lost in the shuffle and their common spirit from being crushed out. From the viewpoint of numbers, it is normal that the word "group" should be connected with the idea of smallness.[6] If the group becomes over-large, it ceases to be itself, and turns into a crowd, an assemblage, a movement, a party, a Church, a people, a State, etc., and now has all the nuances these terms carry with them. As a consequence of its smallness, a group can exist for only a limited time, for if it grows old but does not disappear, then it is no longer a group and has become an institution. In the light of what has been said, it is clear that "group" is not a substantive which allows no plural; there cannot be one group unless there is more than one; perhaps there cannot be a group which does not contain virtually within itself one or more anti-groups.

In addition to limitations created by numbers there are also qualitative limits: the prestige and possible dominance of the founder or the leader who succeeds him, the prestige

and dominance of other influential individuals who create an
overriding spirit that crushes opposition, even if the spirit
be more or less reformable. Out of this situation comes the
dominance of certain images or ideas, then that of regulations
which insure the free play of these images or ideas. It may
happen that to a certain point there is a creative fidelity
to these original ideas, revivals of them, creative transformations of them. But it can also happen that the enthusi-
astic collaboration which marked the group's beginnings ends
in a depressing uniformity, while the members become nothing
more than an echo chamber for a single singer or a wornout
record. A group is not limited simply from outside; it is of
its nature contingent and even mortal.

III. The Fulfillment of the Person and the Mediation of Groups

When we ask whether or not the group fulfills the person,
we are trying to determine the functions of the group in relation to the person. As soon as we ask the question, we realize
that these functions are many. Here is a list, far from complete, which can serve as a springboard for reflection.

1) The group can be a kind of mirror for the members.
Each one projects on to it something of his real self and something of his ideal self; the result is to some degree a mingling
of horizons, to the extent that belonging to a group implies
the representation of the other members insofar as all form an
affective or functional "we". Dwelling in contemplation of
the individual or collective self is a stage in the formation
of persons, but it can also quite easily be a stage in their
deformation. To look at oneself in the mirror is useful when

one is combing one's hair or cutting one's beard. It is still more useful to look at the rear mirror of an automobile or the radar screen of an aeroplane when you are trying to see the relation between the path of your own vehicle and that of other vehicles. But how disastrous when a person stays in this posture too long and turns into a Narcissus! Esprit de corps is a form of looking into the mirror. Depending on how much scope the person or group gives it will be a source of strength or weakness for those who have absorbed it.

2) The same ambivalent kind of mediation is to be seen in another function of the group, that of disassociating and sorting out personal images; what might be called the prismatic function. The group then acts as analyst and selector; it creates nothing, yet it transforms the members by the very fact of registering the variety of their contributions. The prismatic function changes us without our noticing it, just as the elements in the air act on those who breathe it in. But, whereas the air accepts and fuses together all the effluvia, the group filters out all but certain contributions, either by determining what activities each member is to exercise towards the outside world, or by giving greater prestige to certain persons and ideas, or, finally, by simply allowing those laws to operate which control the messages coming from the various members.

Special mention must be made of professional activity, for this is one way in which the individual builds a personality by entering into mutual relationships with others. A doctor, for example, sees other people as patients. The group formed by his colleagues and the group formed by sick people force him to select the images he forms of himself and others, and to do so by way of a certain kind of work performed on nature. The impress of personage on person is immense; it means the building of the self through specialization of experience.

But the impress does not begin as an addition from within or without consciousness; it begins as a subtraction of certain virtualities from consciousness and a choice of the relations consciousness is to have with other consciousnesses.

3) If we compare the group to a melting-pot, can we ascribe to it a more directly creative role? It does not seem so. The new metaphor indeed supposes that something more than a selective process goes on; it says that there is a combining of the personal contributions of each and a synthesis that then works back upon the individual. But the creative power of ideas and initiatives does not reside in the melting-pot; it resides in the ingredients which are put into the pot and which come from persons. The melting-pot is only a meeting-place for elements which are in harmony or conflict with each other. Everything latent in the good or bad influence of the group on the members and their cause comes in the last analysis from the members themselves. What can indeed be creative is the influence of one person on another. But in the group this influence passes through a phase of anonymity. We must realize that an anonymous influence is not an impersonal influence, for it is but the outward form of thoughts and actions that have their origin in individual consciousnesses. The trajectory of these ideas and actions is pre-given, their encounter pre-determined. The only thing specific to the group as such is the laws governing encounter; they alone make up its irreducible being.

4) The fact that the group acts as a vehicle in so many ways also means that it acts, as it were, to tighten or relax tensions. It distributes pressures. In principle, the fact that persons participate in a group lessens the internal shocks between them and creates solidarity among them. But the union which gives strength will at the same time harden the attitude of each person toward what is outside the group. If the group

is a closed group, it will surround itself with a buffer zone
and develop a cenobitic indifference to the environment; if it
is an open group, it will doubtless welcome new members and
ideas and integrate these with old, but it will perhaps be
only all the more hostile to other groups, which it will look
upon as anti-groups. Opposition can develop among the members
themselves and give rise to stubborn sub-groups. In any case,
a group is always a pressure group, and will distribute the
pressures it exerts, within or without, by means of sympathy,
indifference, and antipathy. Once again, we note that there
is nothing strictly speaking creative about the group as such.
We can add, however, that it is not only a vehicle with its
own specific laws, but also an amplifier of interpersonal
influences, and that the amplification is increased in an odd
way by its passage through the anonymous accumulation of individual contributions.

Mirror, prism, melting-pot, tightener and relaxer of
tensions: all these comparisons indicate ways in which the
group mediates. The generalization suggested by the comparisons
is clear: the groups, as specifically human, do not create
anything personal or superpersonal, but transmit something
personal to persons whose condition it is to be living at a
spatio-temporal distance from one another. The function of
the groups is to overcome the distance, while not departing
from the axiological neutrality proper to them as such. The
value of what they transmit does not derive from the fact of
transmission. Like a radio set, the groups rather detect and
amplify utterances whose scientific, esthetic, or moral quality
is independent of the radio sets themselves. Their mediation
is not inventive, but communicative. And they can eventually
wear out. In this generalization the reader may glimpse a
distant but valid application of the neo-Platonic doctrine of
emanation.

Putting a label on functions is indeed not enough to make their nature evident. Mediation is a word, and the reality can be conceived in various ways. Basically, it tends to have two meanings and to shift readily from the one to the other. Sometimes mediation is the act of an intermediary who links two extremes without reducing them one to another and without himself ceasing to subsist *between* them. At other times, mediation is the movement in which the intermediary unites the two extremes and becomes part of their new configuration or binds them together in his own unity. A tool is a mediator of the first kind; a living organ is one of the second kind. The mediation of a group, like the mediation of language, includes both forms. We may illustrate the distinction by a very simple example. In a football game, each team is a sub-group and constitutes a "we together" which ideally binds the members together like a living organ for the purpose of winning the game. On the other hand, the group made up of the two opposing teams forms a "we" that is much more external to the players, since it is internally divided; it exercises a mediatorial role like that of a tool. The tool has its weaknesses; that is why a referee is needed in order to bring the two teams together, or to reconcile them, and thus avoid the total rupture of the functional "we" which the teams must form if there is to be a match.

The example also instructs us that the mediation of the group is exercised not only among consciousnesses but also between consciousnesses and values. In the example, the rules of the game and the ideal of the sportsman come from elsewhere and become part of the match to be played; mediation takes place in this regard by reason of the consent of those who engage to play the game.

In brief, group, players, and values all become mediators each for the others; they form a unity without losing their

identity. Yet it is quite clear that the focus of the various
mediations exercised by the group remains the action of the
persons involved. Consciousness of the "we" procedes from
that center at different levels. We cannot determine in advance the developing content in which the mediation of the
group will be exercised, for that content is by definition
unpredictable and unstable.

IV. The Informal Groups

    The instability just mentioned is a striking trait of the
informal groups. The very expression "informal group" may be
a redundancy. For a group represents a beginning. In time,
either it consolidates and becomes institutionalized, or it
breaks up and dissolves. In either hypothesis, it disappears.
In the life-history of societies, the group seems to be a
manifestation of a youthful period, and the adjective "informal" says as much. An informal group arises out of the
desire for brotherhood; it wants to do without the division of
labor and without hierarchy, but how often it proves abortive!
The graveyard of such associations is well filled. When they
do continue to exist and seem to prosper, they quickly turn in
upon themselves; how often brotherhoods become clans!
    In our own day, the success of the so-called informal
groups would be inexplicable, if there were not, behind the
awkward name, a reality that we can explore. An informal group
is rarely an invention without forebearers and with a goal
never before known to men or a face not turned aggressively to
anyone else. Ordinarily it carves out a place for itself within an older society, and stands over against an institutional
framework which it judges cold, useless, or even intolerable,
and which serves to set off the new reality of the group. The

group is therefore almost always bent upon secession and radical challenge. But the group is not therefore synonymous with a simple "gang" that rejects all obligation toward institutions. The informal group is the expression of a need for reform; it bursts through the ice-pack but does not leave the ocean. It claims rather to restore fluidity to the ocean and to make it navigable once again. It sails along, sails filled with the euphoria of a rediscovered springtime; it does not know what it is to be sated.

Yet, if the group is not quickly swallowed up by the waves, it will meet the fate that growth brings, for the increasing number of members will automatically destroy the equality which the original promoters intended.[7] As ideals become more explicit, the structure becomes complicated, and exchanges are paralyzed. In such conditions, how can applications for new memberships not fall off? The group must either change into an institution or else mutilate the consciousnesses of its members by refusing them any food besides fanaticism and any future except anarchy. It would be foolish to run a large store the way you run a stall on the street. The law of social biology is pitiless: the more rapid the growth of an informal group, the more ephemeral its existence as an informal group. Yet to limit the number of members and ideas would simply be another way to destruction, for then the group would become a secret society, and a secret society is not informal but hyperformal.

Does the informal group have no role, then? Of course, it has. It has a very important, but also a very uncertain role. The informal group acts as a mediator. But is it to mediate life or death for the institutions it aims to reform and the values it aims to promote? The attitude of rejection of the established order, with which the group begins, almost always contains the risk of malicious joy at another's misfortune (*Schadenfreude*). Will the group cause a new sap to rise in the old trees? Will it invent new programs, take the citadel by assault, and do better than the old personnel did? Or will it hasten the disintegration of the society without being able to offer anything but false charisms? A philosophical reflection must be courageous enough to utter a moral caution. We have just pointed out the danger of negation. But negation is not the worst thing, provided it be felt as a source of suffering and accepted as a means. The worst thing is the theoreticians' cheap claim to genius and their tyrannical certainties. The existence of the informal groups is in itself a source of hope. But when at a given moment such groups begin to proliferate everywhere and in every area of life, the moralist is disturbed, for he sees in this the sign that modesty is passing through a crisis. The historian and the sociologist, too, are disturbed, for they see in this proliferation one symptom that the paths of society are blocked off, or even the proof that decadence is well advanced.

The person can find in the informal groups a fuller scope for his own individuality, for the ideas at work there are fresh, and collaboration between the members fervent. The person can there find shelter from the abuse of power or the pressure of the mass media. But he can also fall victim to a mirage that will destroy him in a very agreeable way and with a deadly subtlety beyond that which any other collective mediation can exercise.

V. From Transindividual Subject to Logos

As I begin the last section of this essay, I would like to express both homage and remorse. The homage is for Lucien Goldmann, recently deceased, who reflected a great deal on the transindividual subject and the transcendental subject. The remorse is for the fact that, due to circumstances, I did not accept an invitation he gave me to discuss the subject with him. If I depart here from some of his conclusions, it is with gratitude for the stimulus those conclusions afforded me.

Some months before his death Goldmann presented a paper to the *Société Française de Philosophie*, and here is how he summarized his ideas:

> The central concept in positive dialectical thought is that of the transindividual or collective subject.
> From the viewpoint of positive science, this concept has the advantage that, in the genetic structuralist study of social life and historical processes, it can account for a large number of empirical data. In the privileged case of cultural products, especially literary products in which the text presents us with all the immediate data, this concept allows the establishment of relatively simple models which make it possible to understand the text almost in its entirety or at least to an incomparably greater extent than does any other interpretative or explanatory method.
> From the viewpoint of philosophy, the concept renders superfluous the concept of the transcendental subject and enables us to avoid a series of false alternatives: subject--object, judgments of fact--judgments of value, continuity--discontinuity, explanation--interpretation, process--structure, mechanicism--idealism, theory--action, science--philosophy.[8]

Let us take the main points in this summary. In Goldmann's view, the person may be explained in two ways. On the one hand, there are his organic particularities, or what he calls the individual and libidinal sector. On the other, there is what this person accomplishes with other persons; this sector is bound up with work and history. Now, from this second point of view, each of us belongs to many groups: familial, professional, cultural, etc. Here we have collective subjects which link consciousnesses without being reduced to them (taken in isolation); these collective subjects are therefore transindividual subjects. It is they who, by their intermingling in each person, give the latter his originality. It is they who have created civilizations and even the mental categories with which we understand social relations. To explain Pascal or Racine, for example, we would indeed have to know what was idiosyncratic about these authors, because this element is not unrelated to the groups they chose to enter. But the range of explanation we can give their work is extremely limited if we do not look beyond the individual subjects to Jansenism, the Nobility of the Robe, etc., for without reference to these their writings remain almost unintelligible to us. Among all the transindividual subjects, one occupies a privileged place: social class. The reason is that this is the only group which in its praxis looks to society as a whole. The weakness of philosophers who deal with the individual subject is that they neglect the structure of historical phenomena. The weakness of the structuralists is that they neglect functionality. The dialectic of the transindividual subject overcomes the duality in these systems and makes it possible to account, without any important remainder, for social facts and especially for cultural facts.

Despite our differences of terminology and orientation, I am in agreement with a number of these statements. It is clear enough that the person is not a monad without windows and doors and that it exists only within a network of persons, so much so that in this sense it is radically social. The relation to other persons is part of the person. But I fear that Goldmann's analysis unduly diminishes the role of the self in favor of the non-dyadic group, in which communion (difficult enough and only intermittent even in the dyad) degenerates into communication, even when the group is itself a magnificent structure built on our animal foundations.

There has always been discussion about whether great men explain society or society great men. The debate is often circular and barren. It is certainly true, however, that the great man, whatever he owes to the groups that shaped him or serve him as sounding-boards, alone has the spark of creative genius which transcends its sources and opens up new vistas for mankind. Had Mozart lived in the neolithic age he would certainly not have written a concerto for flute, harp, and orchestra, but he would have extended the range of the art of sound. With all the more reason, Homer or Racine would not have been reduced to dumbness by being translated to earlier centuries, for a poet has no need of complicated material in order to pour out his soul. Goldmann, like the Durkheimian sociologists, is forced to concede the existence of this unknown but which is the talent of the individual, and to grant that it rises above the available technical resources and the influence of predecessors (although he does call this talent "a virtuality elaborated by the collective subject": p. 102). I would prefer to say, then, that we reveal ourselves to ourselves through the mediation of society and that in so doing we also renew the intersubjective bonds. There is a transindividual subjectivity, but there is no transindividual subject.

Another reservation concerns the privilege allowed to social class among the supposed transindividual subjects. It is arguable whether social class is indeed a more direct way than others to the dialectic at work in society as a whole. The difficulties experienced by the Nobility of the Robe in the seventeenth century contribute very little to the explanation of Jansenism, since there were aristocrats of this type everywhere else, among the Jesuits, the libertines, and so forth. Moreover, if Pascal shows a strong preference for the Passion of Christ, we must say that what is fundamental in his faith belongs to an entirely different sphere than that of the social categories of his day and is hardly intelligible at all in terms of these categories. What is at issue here is a transcendent world. There are many "we's", and that formed by man and his God has different dimensions than the "we" formed by a man and his caste.

With this we come to the thesis of Goldmann which causes me most difficulty: Goldmann thinks that by asserting the transindividual subject he can do away with the transcendental subject. He blames Brunschvicg for avoiding dualism by positing an impersonal *cogito* ("I think") that is not empirically verifiable. This is not the place for discussing Descartes or Husserl, or for giving the reasons why I prefer a transcendent subject to a transcendental subject. But I would at least like to claim for philosophy the right not to think its task done when it reaches the transindividual subject of the sociologists. How, we may ask, can the scattered multitude of empirical groups form a coherent "we" or even a whole that can be co-ordinated? How can the categories of thought, the verification of truth and error, the criteria of progress and degeneration win absolute status when empirical reality supplies us only with a series of brute happenings? If all these things do not depend on an absolute which transcends temporal episodes, then history is simply a blind thrust operating through enslaved consciousnesses.

But consciousness is not enslaved. It rises above and passes judgment on the very conditionings to which it is subject. Consciousness is a perspective on the whole of reality. The primacy of its personal vocation releases the "we" from its possible alienation in groups and lays the foundation for a hypersocial "we". The simple fact that at this very moment each of us is questioning himself about himself and the world is enough to put us in contact with a Logos which stimulates persons to such questioning and links them together in that questioning. The metaphysics of the Logos is easier to forget than to refute, for those who pass it over in silence still live by it, even if unwittingly. Above and beyond the groups which pave the way for the person and which the person creates, the person discovers in itself a community which is no longer of this world, a transcending of its own being into being, an act which illuminates its action, and a gift which bestows its freedom upon it.

CHAPTER 6

Church Structures and the Informal Groups

by

Georges Casalis

Preliminaries

I have been asking myself what it means that I should be speaking precisely at this point in the conference, in between two groups of lecturers, the sociologists and the historians, to neither of which I belong professionally. I am a "practical", or what the Catholics call a "pastoral" theologian; this means that I am called upon to reflect critically on the concrete implications of theology and on the theological presuppositions of ecclesial practice in all areas of the latter. I can see, of course, that it is important for me, as I come to speak, to have listened carefully to the panoramic descriptions of the sociologists; and indeed I have honestly tried to give them my close attention. On the other hand, I suspect that the historians will soon be telling me that what is supposedly new today is really quite old and in no wise original. That will doubtless be a salutary lesson to those (and I am probably among them) who think at times that we must re-invent the Church and theology. As for those of my colleagues who will speak as systematic theologians, or ecclesiologists, they must forgive me if I trample a bit on their flower-beds, for I am sure that they will not be following the tracks I have left!

We have heard a lot already about "observation". My viewpoint is a different one, for, although I have not been a regular member of any informal group, I have been directly involved in the existence of a good number of them and am a co-editor of the publication *Bulletin de liaison des communautés de base*.[1] Although it is three years behind on what is being done, for example, in Italy, the purpose of this magazine is not to direct or be a central office for the life of the informal groups (they neither want nor perhaps need such an organ), but simply a place where those who want to use it may meet and share. Thus I had to smile yesterday as I listened to Mr. Lourau, for in the three analyses he gave I found several elements of my own biography; what he calls "the institutional", "the anti-institutional" and "the counter-institutional" all clash in me, but now I recognize them for what they are, and I find myself interiorly in a situation that is both uncomfortable and salutary.

I will add one further preliminary remark: my attitude in this lecture, as it is in my life generally, is to listen and to sympathize. There are two reasons for this attitude. The first is that in my view the basic attitude of any theologian must definitely be one of openness to all the questions and challenges that fill the world, among them the challenge of Jesus of Nazareth. To close oneself to men's questions is to condemn oneself not to hear the call of the Gospel. I shall be trying therefore to reflect back to you a whole series of questions and challenges as I hear them. This does not mean, however, that I agree with all the answers or attempted solutions which are offered. However--and this is my second reason for being a listener--I recently found by experience that in this area in which passions are roused on both sides, even the slightest taking of a critical position is utilized ("exploited" would be better) against those whom one is attempting to interpret. A recent article that was adopting a very inflexible position against the informal groups made its own a question I had felt forced to raise in an essay that was in fact 95% positive in its evaluation of the groups![2] I shall therefore reserve for the discussion period some critiques which I do not think it useful to formulate in my lecture itself. Moreover, it is for those who will be engaging in the "Theological Reflection" part of our colloquium to attempt answers and solutions.

Pluralism of Structures

What do we mean by "structures"? We certainly mean the visible organization, the historical form, the habitual ways of acting which the Churches have. But the word "structures" also, and inevitably, refers to the mental structures of the Churches, to their ideologies and theologies, their explicit spiritualities and their collective subconsciousnesses. In speaking of structures I cannot stop at what is purely external, that is, the juridico-architectural aspect of institutions, because the latter implies or expresses an overall attitude, a view of the world or understanding of reality which cannot be separated from the outward forms. We acknowledge, do we not, that form and content are inextricably connected? It is evident, then, that structures, like words and language, are not "innocent" but in their objective reality imply choices, compromises, and psychological and spiritual orientations. Barth reminded us some years back that the structures of the Church could either express or betray the community's obedience to the word of God; that they could be the sign and vehicle either of impiety and heresy or of fidelity to men and Christ, of domination or service.³

That the existence of the informal groups raises questions there is no doubt. We need only look at the vast literature it has provoked, the occasional lengthy bibliography with entries from many languages, or the huge pile of documents in Father M.-D. Chenu's study as he prepares for a book which he admits may never get written. In a bygone period--and the very fact tells us how much things have changed!--we would have had condemnations or excommunications, strict admonitions and warnings to get back in line. These would have been the only answers to questions which are, in fact, challenges to or even inquisitions against the traditional structures of the Church.

Today, however, we find in all the Churches and at all levels a basic uncertainty about the institution. The hierarchies, universal and local, stagger under the repeated blows of the attacks and criticism, the challenges and crises they must face: crises of personnel, vocations, Christian identity, and theology. In all these crises the very existence of the Church and its future presence in the world have become uncertain: "When the Son of Man comes, will he find any faith on the earth?" (Luke 18:8). Whether or not they are aware of the eschatologico-apocalyptic nature of the current *krisis*, the ecclesiastical authorities, whatever their stamp, no longer have either the strength or the desire to launch the condemnations of a former day. Almost everywhere, the tactic is to be flexible and to cultivate the secret hope (a cowardly and shameful one indeed) that perhaps the informal groups will assure the future, if not of Christianity, at least of the essential thing: Christ's presence among men. Perhaps, like the cenobitic communities during the barbarian invasions, these little pockets of Christians will sow the spiritual harvests of a future day. A few years ago, Paul Ricoeur was already saying: "The non-parish will save the parish." Is the Church's best hope, then, to be found in the very element which now issues her the most radical of challenges? Like a father who cannot forget that the survival of his name depends on an unworthy or hostile son, ecclesiastical institutions are always torn between fear and hope as they confront the informal groups!

This suggests a first and basic point: evidently, there are lateral channels or parallel ways of communicating the Gospel to our contemporaries. Whether we like it or not, perhaps the only real evangelists today are those who reject all confessional labels and adopt a "wildcat" fashion of expressing Christ to our fellow-men. Consequently, whatever be their personal theology, people have taken a practical attitude to the groups and have, willingly or unwillingly, accepted the fact not only of plurality but of pluralism when it comes to ways (even within the same institution) of voicing the Gospel in the contemporary world. Henceforth the institution will be living in a difficult, painful, and contradictory confrontation and companionship with the "counter-institution" or even the "anti-institution". Yet we can hardly complain of such a situation if it proves to be the definitive barrier against the deadly trio which Cardinal Suenens attacked at Vatican II: clericalism, juridicism, and triumphalism!

It is clear that the basic question all Church institutions must face is that of the diversity of ways in which the Gospel can be manifested and communicated in our world. All ecclesiological patterns are radically relativized, as the hierarchic structures (collegial and conciliar or presbytero-synodal) of the various institutions (Catholic, Orthodox, and Protestant) are confronted with the creation and development of mobile, flexible, and provisional groups which are adapted to their immediate situation, original and inventive, and responsive to events. This does not simplify the overall situation, of course, but it is undeniably taking place. Speaking at the Montreal meeting of the World Council of Churches in 1963, Ernst Käsemann maintained that nowhere in the New Testament can we find a universal ecclesiology being applied. What we find, rather, in the great variety of forms and life-styles is a kind of "ancient ecumenical confederation", which showed as much internal variety as we see today between the various institutions and the informal groups taking shape within or alongside them.[4] In Käsemann's view, the facts he adduces are evidence that we never have the Gospel *in itself* but only *in a particular set of circumstances*, that is, in numerous refractions of the original message in numerous socio-cultural contexts which are irreducible one to another. The only bond of cohesion for the confederation is the common reference to Christ who is acknowledged and confessed as always present, transforming worldly reality, and bringing to light the essential unity between the most widely varying communities. The unity can only be eschatological, but it must already find expression in respect for the most varied forms and languages.

If Käsemann is right, does it mean that we must return to the early Church? No: you cannot simply bypass two thousand years of history. However, we are experiencing today a salutary sloughing off of a lot of rules and formulas, ecclesiological patterns, and ecclesiastical habits, as they are radically questioned and challenged from within the Church itself. The novelty which makes our present situation like the early Christian situation described by Käsemann is precisely that the "counter-institution" is to be found not just outside the institution but within it. The very people who stand apart from the Church and challenge or reject it are sometimes the very ones who also most seriously call it to account from within. Moreover, the same thing is happening everywhere, to such an extent that it is quite useless to change over to another Church to escape it. For this reason, too, most of the Catholics who challenge their Church do not dream of becoming Protestants. Why should they when they will only find the same reasons for opposing structures that are inflexible and falling ever further behind the advance of history?

What we are seeing today, then, is both a reduction and a radicalization of fragmentation, for it is within ourselves that we are being broken up.

Analysis of Some Definitions

At this point some remarks about language are necessary. There is widespread perplexity when it comes to naming the informal groups. Each name, in fact, is an implicit reference to an ecclesiology and is especially significant if those who apply the name are not themselves members of an informal group, for in using the name they are revealing and defining themselves.

I have collected the various names I have come across, and I shall offer you a few samples, along with their ecclesiological implications. For example, when we speak of *base communities* we mean that they have come into existence without any initiative from the hierarchy. Consequently, the name necessarily includes a reference to a summit or apex, which is that of the pyramidal structure of the Church in question. This is why the theologians of the informal groups have large reservations about this particular name.

What of *wildcat communities* [*communautés sauvages*]? Are we saying that these groups are not yet civilized or domesticated?

Or that they are in open rebellion against communities which are wisely and prudently integrated into their socio-cultural context?

Informal communities: Is the point that form--authentic form--is to be found in other communities, namely, the ones from which the new groups are splitting off?

Marginal communities: Are we saying that these communities are on the periphery of society, the institution, the faith, and Christ himself (each of these being regarded as centers of reference)? But, if so, will we admit that the traditional institution is itself just as marginal when it comes to the Gospel?

Floating communities: Does this mean that the other communities are not solidly anchored, or does it mean that they are in danger of going under?

Call them *underground, spontaneous, small,* or *new*; call them the *third Church*. Each name raises questions which require serious reflection and ecclesiological self-scrutiny. Language, like structures, is neither neutral nor innocent, and we would do well not to be naive about it.

The basic issue, as we have pointed out, is therefore the undeniable practical challenge to every institution, no matter what it be, and the appearance on the scene of a variety of forms of Christian existence within a plurality that involves radical confrontations. I do not hesitate to maintain that these confrontations seem infinitely more positive than such manifestations of identity crisis or indifference as betray only a deep existential despair within the Church. The multiplication of informal groups may be disturbing on several counts, but at least it is a heartening sign of life and creative inventiveness.

Against this background, I shall discuss four large questions which the informal groups put to the structures of the Church.

Four Questions Among Others

The four are (1) communion as the center of ecclesial life; (2) relation of the Church to the secular powers; (3) the new way of theology; and (4) evangelical inventiveness.

Without trying at all to be exhaustive, I shall review these four points, noting at the very beginning that each question is asked in most of the informal groups but is assigned varying degrees of importance depending on the group.

1. Whatever be their particular purpose (spiritual renewal, search for better liturgy, knowledge of the Bible, charitable activities, ecumenical action...), *all* the new communities in the Church depend for their origin on the members adopting a critical attitude to the traditional forms of Christianity. The parish, as being an impersonal mob, is rejected as a legitimate and valid grouping of the Christian people, and the critics try to organize a defense against the increasing anonymity of the large cities and the industrial rhythm that is imposed on religious expression. "I have eight thousand parishioners; I meet their needs": I heard that one day from a city pastor, and he didn't smile when he said it; a very active patriarchal type, quite jealous of his authority. We cannot help but understand the protest against the kind of supermarket pastoral care which such a ministerial style brings with it. We cannot help but sympathize with the need of personal knowledge and sharing which is felt in places where people have, perhaps for generations, been deprived of it. People will no longer accept a religious world that is unrelated to reality, a Church made up of consumers who are fed with standardized rations and of casuals who stop in while passing through, with sacraments and services being the only occasions for an individual (not a personal) contact with the

pastor. Birth, puberty, marriage, and death have become occasions and pretexts for ambiguous rites that bless, i.e. guarantee, life, at the cost of leveling down the Gospel so that it becomes an adornment of the status quo rather than a criticism of it and a pledge of hope through the proclamation of the Cross and Resurrection. As R. Bohren says, the casuals cause the Church to transform Jesus Christ into Baal, the god of fruitfulness, and to preach this life as the supreme good instead of teaching men to turn it upside down by bringing into it a liberating love.[5] In short, as numerous Catholic writers have pointed out, the casual churchgoers are a permanent source of de-Christianization, one that is fostered by the Church itself.[6]

The informal groups refuse to accept that the Church should be confined to the "suburban captivities"[7] of personal and collective life. This is why the search for true communion and true sharing is accompanied by reflection, which they deem highly important, on the professional or civic commitments of the members. Sometimes, to concretize and to test the seriousness of the whole undertaking, a common-life group is set up, with all the dangers that involves in present-day society.

What the groups express is a very determined will to be adult Christians. The members are bent on being responsible for themselves in all matters, even the sharing of the word. If we adopt Maurice Nédoncelle's statement that human groups must offer their members a three-fold satisfaction, in the areas of identity, security, and stimulation, I would say that the traditional parish deals with identity and security, while the informal groups look rather to identity and stimulation. The opposition between the two is clear: what is predominant in the one case is religion's role as source of security (I remind you that for Luther security is the contrary of faith!); what is essential in the other is apostolic action and risk.

This attitude of the informal groups implies that the members reject the monologist, the man sent by providence, be he ordained or not, the "virtuosos of religion", as Schleiermacher called them. On the other hand, we find a vigorous demand for theology, an intense desire for knowledge of the Scriptures, and, frequently, the effort at a socio-political competence that is correlated with the certainties of the Gospel. If we ask what "clerics" can deal with and help Christians of this kind (supposing that these Christians are still looking for, or can stand, any cleric!), the answer is clear: Only clerics who are themselves this kind of people can have anything to say to these individuals. It is in this context that we must understand (regarding it as a profound need emerging from faith itself) the demand which is being formulated these days and widely put in practice in the priestly lives of a number of the clergy: the demand for freedom in the three areas of love (therefore a rejection of the *obligation* of celibacy), work, and active involvement in the political sphere.

We must ask ourselves at this point, however, whether a Christianity thus defined is not in danger of becoming elitist and remaining alien to the great mass of "sociological" Christians, that 80 to 90 percent in France who, motivated more by religious superstition than by faith, continue to have their children baptized.[8]

2. The second question concerns the relation of the Churches to the secular powers. Whether as a deliberate policy or not, this question is connected, in most of the groups with which I am acquainted, with a political critique of the structures and ideologies of the Churches. (I must admit, of course, that my personal convictions have made me selective in the kinds of groups I approach!)

In this very large area, which alone would provide material for contrary exposés, I shall mention only the following points.

a) The first attack by the groups is on the claim, and requirement, of apoliticism that is made by most of the Churches. For it is clearly a meaningless question to ask whether or not one should "be politically involved"; whether one should praise or blame a "politicized" sermon; whether or not the ideal pastor is a man who never "gets involved in politics". It is meaningless because one is involved whether one likes it or not: involved from the very moment of the birth that makes us part of a complicated web of economic, social, cultural, religious, and political solidarities and makes us from our first days one of the privileged or one of the victims. This is so true that I can only repeat here the entirely serious witticism I have used elsewhere: Man is a political animal and his first political act is to be born. The real question, therefore, is not whether, but *how* you are politically involved: whether you shamefully submit to (for I do not really believe that there is an honest ignorance in this matter) or lucidly take upon yourself this involvement which is at the very heart of every human life. Thus Dorothee Sölle recently answered a questioner who blamed her after a lecture for not having said enough about sin: "You're right. I forgot that I eat bananas."

b) One conclusion from what I have just said is that neither the silence nor the words of the Churches can be politically neutral. You may recall Martin Niemöller's words in 1945: "We have too often spoken when we should have been silent; we have too often been silent when we should have spoken." In the preface to a recent book I tried to show that all speech, and especially any that claims to be apolitical, has a positive or negative political impact.[9] It is clear that centuries of submission to the secular powers have politicized not only the language but even the most elementary reflexes of the Church. It has even falsified the most accurate translations

of the Bible. For example, the versions continue to tell us
that Barabbas was a "robber", whereas the Greek word *lēstēs*
in the time of Jesus and in the language of the New Testament
writers means a revolutionary or guerrilla.[10] And when Harvey
Cox, following Barth, analyzes the nature of sin he is rightly
amazed that it should be described in general terms as "a rebellion", thus making every rebel and revolutionary a sinner,
while other elements of sinfulness are neglected, such as the
lack of solidarity, failure to shoulder one's historical responsibility, laziness, and cowardice. Such an emphasis and
corresponding neglect are not accidental, he concludes, because
the established has every reason for not giving Christians too
much encouragement to stop being passive![11]

c) It is clear enough that the structures of the various
Churches correspond to well-defined types of political regime:
Catholicism to divine-right monarchy; Protestantism to liberal
bourgeois democracy. For this reason they are habitually unable to challenge the order of which they are often only a
cultural image, even if that order did not give birth to them.
On the other hand, the Churches are powerful agents of socio-
political integration,[12] even when they are faced with a system
which has become hostile to them yet continues nonetheless to
be closely related to them (a good example is the Orthodox
Church and the Soviet regime).

The informal groups remind us that the central question
for any political analysis is the reality of the class struggle,
for it is the key factor in social confrontations and a dividing
line that passes through every collectivity and every community,
including the Churches. It is impossible to believe any discourse (including also, and even most of all, the discourse of
reconciliation) and any gesture that would claim the right to
ignore that struggle. Here I include the action of the World
Council of Churches in supporting anti-racist movements, even

if that action represents an extraordinary progress by comparison with the paternalism that held sway a few decades back, and still does, in large sectors of Christian thought and action. For, what the poor and oppressed want is not that we be generous but that we be *with* them in order to set them free. Here once again the real question is not whether we acknowledge or deny the class struggle, but what side we take and what solidarities or complicities we make our own.

A few months ago at Amsterdam, a Paraguayan priest put into unforgettable words the point I have been trying to make:

> In the eyes of us priests who are involved with the peasants the society we live in offends not the poor alone but Christ himself. "What you do to the least of my brothers, you do to me." If men prevent the poor from seeing, they prevent Christ from walking the roads of the world. We priests have no intention of being atheists but we refuse to use God's name to bless an unjust society or to require of those on the fringes of society a patience or conformity that only degrade them.
> We priests will not preach violence, but neither will we connive at the institutionalized violence which exploits the great majority of men for the profit of a few. We will not connive at the violence of those in power, nor become their accomplices through a shameful silence.
> We priests will not turn communist, but neither will a stupid fear of communism keep us prisoners of a society that is neither Christian nor human. We are committed to the way of change and will support the thrust toward humanizing change, whatever may come--even if the well-to-do desert us and call us communists.
> In the name of the peasants who are committed to collective and personal liberation, I ask you: "ON WHAT SIDE ARE YOU?"[13]

I have quoted this long passage, even though its author is
a Latin-American priest, because in its general orientation
and especially in its tone it reflects the commitment and
positions of many informal groups here at home.

Everywhere certain questions are asked: Is the Gospel
also a message of political liberation? Can the Churches be
forces for political liberation? Does being a Christian mean
being a revolutionary? An affirmative answer to these three
questions is at the basis of these groups, and wherever the
answer is taken seriously, men are beginning once again to
believe. As a worker put it to me recently after a conversation on the Gospel and the class struggle: "You have just
wiped away two thousand years of Christian history."

The taking seriously involves two steps: a critical reading of the ecclesial reality (for example, under the three
rubrics of ecclesiastical possessions, power, and knowledge in
a given society), but in the context both of a comprehensive
political analysis and of a concrete commitment to action
(solidarity with migrant workers, sharing the struggle of the
working-class, refusal of military service, etc.). An important place is assigned to this rediscovered unity of theory
and practice, a unity that is characteristic of Christianity
but constantly frustrated in the "clerical alliance".

Such a search for unity represents a violent attack on
traditional habits and conformist faith; undoubtedly it sometimes leads men close to atheism. (I am speaking of something
much more essential and tragic than Ernst Bloch is when he
speaks of atheism within faith.[14]) For the choice is clear
and a formidable challenge to traditional Christianity: The
primary goal at the human level (all the informal groups with
a predominantly political orientation say as much) is the
liberation of man as he lies crushed by oppression and

exploitation; it is to overturn alienating social structures and therefore to join forces with all (even non-Christians, Marxists, etc.) who struggle here and now against these structures. There is inevitably the danger of confronting other Christians, but if we refuse to face this danger, we will be admitting implicitly that our "primordial" solidarities are not essential solidarities after all! Once again, we must come to understand what it means to say that the class struggle takes place within the Churches themselves. To recognize the fact is not to make it something absolute that relativizes the Gospel; it is simply to recognize that no faith can serve as an excuse for not getting involved in the great historical task of freeing the slaves of whatever time and place.

Isn't it simply fraudulent, then, to say that what unites us as Christians is stronger than what separates us at the political level--since that would mean that political choices, fellowship in the same struggles, and revolutionary commitments are all unimportant, secondary, optional, and not to be taken seriously? One of my colleagues, a dear friend, said to me once, here in this very University: All revolutions are laughable in the light of the Gospel of reconciliation. That is true enough if one means only to stress the definitiveness of the cosmic reconciliation which Christ effected, and the provisional nature of every political revolution. But the statement is radically false if one concludes from it that the Gospel of reconciliation can serve as an excuse for avoiding revolutionary action, or even that this truth can be credible to those, individuals or peoples, whom one leaves in their state of enslavement.

For many informal groups there is an evident contradiction between the Gospel of liberation and the Church of submission to the economic and political powers. The basic question the groups raise may be put this way (I quote a recent statement): "Must we stop the struggle in order to believe? If so, we prefer to renounce belief and go on struggling. If we cannot belong to the Church while sharing in the struggle, we will leave the Church."

Here we have a real, desperate alternative that is being faced by men today. Does it reflect an unacceptable politicization of the faith? Or a prophetic protest against the culpable connivence of the Church with the powers that be? Morvan Lebesque once said: "What separates me from the Christians is not God, but their astonishing capacity for accomodation."

3. The third question concerns the nature of theology. If it be accurate to say, with the informal groups, that theology is an authoritarian form of knowledge, the expression of the Church's ideological alignment, and a justification of the established powers, then it is indispensable that such an authoritarian discourse be eliminated and, after it is gone, a different kind of theology be born. The new way being opened to us is that of an evangelical hermeneutic of reality as it is experienced in the fight for liberation. A necessary counterpart of this would be a political hermeneutic of the Gospel texts in light of the experiences and requirements of that same struggle. "Everything depends," says Paul Ricoeur, "on a close collaboration between understanding of the Bible and understanding of our own times."[15]

If we understand "hermeneutic" to mean "critical interpretation", then there can be no question simply of a new alignment such as the notorious "clericalism of the left". The latter is often held up as a threat but it is in reality mostly a myth, since clericalism, which aims chiefly at maintaining the Church's privileges, is basically counter-revolutionary! No, what we mean by our "hermeneutic" is a process of hard mutual questioning,

that is, an ongoing dialogue between our analyzed experience
and our faith which seeks self-understanding in the light of
that experience.

Such a process cannot but lead to some startling reversals,
especially the rediscovery of the decisive importance of history
and the collectivity. These are completely ignored by the
Bultmannian hermeneutic, because it refuses to enter into the
dialogue and mutual critique of exegesis and politics. A result of this rediscovery will be a new definition of man; man
will be seen as an historical, social being who becomes a
person only within these two basic dimensions of the human.
Consequently there can be no valid anthropological statement
whatsoever except by a mind that is actively involved in both
dimensions of life. Any study of the human reality which would
attempt to ignore these dimensions would be condemned to meaninglessness from the very outset.

It seems then that we are living through a period when the
formulation of the faith, and, consequently, the rediscovery of
Christian identity, can take only one form. That form is an
account of the historical experiences of the communities which
today are taking over the apostolic ministry and following,
wonder-struck, the footsteps of Christ as he advances through
a world that is moving toward its consummation. On more than
one score, the informal groups are pioneering explorers. They
cannot, therefore, but be at odds with those in the Christian
family who continue to recite the creeds of the second, fourth,
and sixth centuries and to believe and live as if, since those
days, the world had only gone backwards.

4. Our fourth point is evangelical inventiveness. In the
perspectives we have been indicating, the community gathering
will play a decisive role in the critical reading of reality
and the faith, in exposing ecclesiastical treacheries and

ideological myths, in detecting the traces of Christ in the world, and in bringing to light the Gospel hope for reality in all its aspects. The Office, the liturgy, and the sharing of the word will, in these circumstances, be a celebration of life as understood in the light of the Gospel, and a discovery of the good news about Christ who liberates all men and the whole man.

For the informal groups, this celebration, at once political, critical, and lyrical,[16] is almost everywhere the occasion for a surprising outburst of creativity. All cultural resources--music, poetry, gesture, audio-visual techniques, publicity, information--contribute to bear witness to the cosmic extent of the miracle worked by the Gospel and to the spiritual meaning which all reality has. In this bold, joyous inventiveness should we not see a sign of the authentic Christian roots of these informal groups?

The Christian character of the groups is also to be seen in their solid indifference to the whole juridico-institutional structure at both the confessional and ecumenical levels. Here, invitation, imagination, and happening replace rules and discipline and participation in the communion of the universal Church. The celebrations of these groups transcend even that communion, for the groups give prophetic witness to the reconciliation and recapitulation of the entire cosmos when they celebrate the Eucharist which is the eloquent sign of the down-to-earth reality of salvation, of solidarity with the hungry, toiling masses, and of the boundless joy of former enemies when they are finally united in the bonds of peace.

What we find in these groups is an atmosphere of prophetic boldness and clearsightedness, a flowering of charisms, a spiritual dynamism, that remind us of certain manifestations of Christianity among Black Americans, Soviet Baptist, or Brazilian

Pentecostalists. What we see is a new outpouring of the Spirit who is at work in the informal groups.

Do the Churches understand all this?

Concluding Remarks

1. Let me say once again that I have hardly, if at all, expressed the criticism or reservations I have about the groups. But others will not be slow to take on this task.

2. I would like, however, to stress one point: the informal groups are raising for all the Churches (and especially those which are ready to take their challenge seriously) the question of episcopacy, that is, the question of a ministry of unity which, in an attitude of listening and openmindedness, will watch to see that the charismatic explosion does not trail off into sectarian fragmentation. I cannot dwell on this point, but it is a major problem.

3. I do not think we are entering an areligious age. Neither do I think we are on the threshold of the adulthood of mankind; it seems to me that men like Kant, Bonhoeffer and even Bultmann have been victims of an illusion in this respect. On the contrary, everything seems to indicate that we shall see a strengthening of the structures and influence of the great pagan religions, including a domesticated Christianity. Moreover, as I see it, there will soon be a gradual break between the Churches which are prisoners, and instruments, of religious alienations, and the people of faith who, in imitation of Christ, live out in their lives the exodus and detachment of men at the service of the world.

The informal groups confront the Christian masses and Christian institutions that have largely become the servants

of Baal, mammon, and Caesar. Are these groups not the proof
that the Spirit is present, enabling men to live in joyful
boldness and inventive hope the existence of a minority who
await the kingdom of Man while fighting even at the cost of
their own lives for the life of all men?

PART II

History

CHAPTER 7

The Johannine Group and Apostolic Christianity

by

Joseph Schmitt

Our contribution to the colloquium deals with the New Testament, that is, the apostolic Church. Its aim is to provide material by way of counterpoint to the problem which occupies our thoughts today.

Early Christianity, in point of fact, took shape without needing first to seek out ways of accomplishing a liberating reform. It fixed the message to be preached, came to a decision with regard to eschatology, and defined its ministries, institutions, and structures. This work, not yet completed at the end of the apostolic age, was done by the various Churches and by a very few groups which transcended the boundaries of the local communities and are still remembered in the New Testament. Early Christianity was pluralist, at least if we mean by the word the very complex doctrinal and institutional heritage it had received from its varied origins. But none of the apostolic communities--not James and the "brothers of the Lord", nor even the Hellenists around Stephen and Barnabas--corresponds to the so-called informal groups of modern and contemporary Christianity. In fact, apart from circles which went over into heresy, the Judeo-Christian and pagan-Christian groups started with a basic unity in faith, worship, and spiritual experience, and developed toward a mingling of thought in which the contribution of each group already shows clearly the extent to which the original pluralism had lessened.

The Johannine group provides an example of what we are saying. This group was made up of intimates of him whom the fourth gospel calls "another disciple" (John 18:15, etc.) and is at the source of the development which Johannine traditions underwent down to the end of the first century. What we have to say here is not an analysis nor, much less, a synthesis of that development. We shall simply be recalling some of the conclusions reached by recent literary and doctrinal criticism of the Johannine writings.

One prior observation is necessary, however. It concerns the immediate sources of our observations and, more particularly, the informational value they have in what concerns us here.

The ongoing debate concerning the literary problems of the fourth gospel and first letter of John brings out the fact that the texts are rooted in the Johannine tradition. The disciple's testimony proves to be active at the origin of the gospel and at various points in its as yet incomplete formation. The transmission of that testimony was long and extremely complex. The received datum was seen ever anew in the light of a developing thought, of a changing pastoral and spiritual situation, and probably of new cultural and religious situations. Consequently, there were in M. E. Boismard's phrase fragmentary and progressive "re-readings" which affected both the narratives and the discourses.[1] The gospel shows traces of these various adaptations and, in accordance with redactional techniques used by the ancients, even juxtaposes them sometimes to parallel passages of which they are the revision or for which they provide motivation. We cannot here give detailed evidence for this aspect of the fourth gospel, though in our view it is to be seen from the Prologue on. We may simply note that all the re-readings arise in the oral transmission of the Johannine testimony, as Rudolf Schnackenburg has reminded us;[2] they are prior, therefore, to the redactional glosses, even where these latter underline a development which the former had already initiated. Most important, the re-readings cannot be the work of a single author, as M. E. Boismard rightly insists in his discussion with F.-M. Braun on this point.[3] Spread out as they are over a period of growth and along different lines of development, and being anonymous by reason of their identical literary traits, the re-readings are clearly the work of a group. In all likelihood they are the work of more than one generation of Judeo-Christians who were disciples of John. In saying this we state both the unusualness and the critical interest attaching to the re-readings.

Analysis of the gospel allows a first conclusion which throws exceptional light on the theological pluralism of early Christianity. The conclusion is that the Johannine tradition, with its very special character at the point of origin, does not evolve simply in the direction of a regressive particularism. Rather, as it develops and breaks its original Judaic connections, it adapts to other, more widespread, currents of thought and even to the synoptic tradition.

As evidence we offer a few of the best-known texts.

1) The pre-Christian hymn which makes up verses 1-5 of the prologue (1:1-18) is one of the chief vestiges of Jewish dualism. It deals with the Word (1) and his various roles in creation (3a), the fall (3b), and the eschatological event (5), and climaxes in the assertion of the victory of light over darkness which did not "overtake" it or--in the adversative interpretation of the aorist *katelaben*--did not "overpower" it. The Johannine group could not let this text stand without relating it to the Gospel event. Thus the paraphrase in verses 6-13 reproduces the dualist expressions, but indicates that Jesus is in fact the Light (9-10); above all, it specifies

that the reaction of the "world" to the Light was to reject it, not to overcome it (compare *parelaben* in 11, vs. *katelaben* in 5). A second re-reading, in verses 14-18, shows no traces of this problematic, which seems to have been rendered inoperative by events. This passage has been purified of the old Jewish vocabulary, and shows traces of hellenistic influences and even of an anti-gnostic reaction; it undoubtedly belongs among the latest written parts of the gospel.

In addition, the content of the passage is not simply Christological. It picks up themes that were the subject of doctrinal reflection in other apostolic circles. We may mention the antithesis of Moses and Jesus or of Law and eschaton, which sums up the history of salvation (17); the difference of value between "vision" (14) and hearing (cf. 18) as forms of religious experience; and, last but not least, the Christological title of "Only Son" (14, 18) which is the Greek equivalent of the title "Beloved" that is used in the synoptic tradition.

2) The prologue of the fourth gospel is metrical and otherwise of a quite special character. But the kind of development we have found there is not restricted to it.

Advice given in view of coming persecution is a central part of the "farewell" discourses. In 15:18-19 and 23-25 the advice is built upon the hate-love antithesis which is characteristic of the religious expression of the communities of Palestinian Judaism. But in 20-22 it is based on the vocabulary (*diōkein*--"harry"--etc.) which was current in parallel kinds of apostolic exhortation. A re-reading is all the more likely to have taken place as the secondary text hints at a hardening of the opposition to the disciples (cf. 22) and borrows from the synoptic tradition the motif of persecutions "because of Jesus' name" (cf. 21).

Another example is provided by the washing of the feet. As Rudolf Bultmann has shown, this event gave rise to two divergent explanations.[4] In the account itself (13:2-11), which draws to some extent on the ancient vocabulary of purification, there is a stress on the "impure" condition of Judas over against the "purity" of the disciples (10). But in the later reinterpretation (12-20), the washing is presented, in accord with apostolic exhortation, as the model of service to the community, which must be imitated if one is to follow Christ (14-15). The related allegory of the vine (15:1-10) underwent a similar development. The early version (1-4), which plays on the words *airein* ("prune") and *kathairein* ("trim clean, cleanse, purify"), is pointing to asceticism as a higher way to perfection. The re-reading (5-10), on the contrary, stresses the idea of judgment (6), and this in terms which even the popular translations of the fourth gospel rightly assimilate to the vocabulary of the synoptic sayings on the punishment of the wicked.

3) The most expressive example, however, of the tendency to a lessening of theological particularism is to be found in the themes of the "Paraclete" and the "Spirit of truth". The themes are derived from different veins of Palestinian Judaism (Pharisaic thought and the dualism of the sect communities) and give rise within the same context to three different presentations. The fragments 16:7-11 and 13-14 (which, however, give evidence of having been retouched to some extent) still distinguish between the Paraclete (or "helper, defender") who "will prove the world wrong" (8), and the Spirit of truth who will confirm the disciples in the whole "truth" (13). However, in the parallel passages, 14:16-17 and 15:26, the Paraclete is the Spirit of truth. Moreover, according to 14:26 (which is to be set beside 15:26), the Paraclete--Spirit of truth--is none other than the "Holy Spirit" who is the source of apostolic witnessing according to the whole synoptic tradition.

In summary, the convergence of doctrinal lines is in two phases: the unification of the Jewish heritage preludes and prepares the way for the adaption of the Johannine traditions to the main currents of apostolic thought.

* * *

This first aspect of the fourth gospel highlights, by contrast, another which is central from the standpoint of our present subject. The Johannine group remained faithful, in every phase of its existence, to its proper vocation, which was to assert and, if need be, to define the spiritual content of those values which early Christianity accepted and was proposing to others. The group thereby directly contributed to resolving the religious and doctrinal problems which arose in the Churches toward the end of the apostolic period; it thus set its mark on the life and thought of later Christianity.

The contribution is primarily theological and is varied in origin.

The idea of a spiritualized temple and worship goes back beyond Jesus to the marginal elites of recent Judaism. The fourth gospel makes the idea its own. But, unlike the parallel passages, Acts 7:38-50 and especially Mark 14:58, the fourth gospel justifies the idea by pointing to the transformed humanity of Christ as being in fact the eschatological sanctuary (2:19).

The vocabulary of "exaltation" or "lifting up" is applied to the Paschal event in the prayer and worship and in the Christological reflection of the Palestinian community. By the end of the first century, however, such vocabulary is archaic and relatively rare, despite the re-readings to which it has been submitted. It is nonetheless, in its original meaning, the chief element in the Paschal language of the doctrinal passages of the fourth gospel. In comparison with the parallel term "resurrection", "exaltation" stresses the "spiritual" or "trans-earthly" character of the Paschal event.

The spiritual interpretation of the biblical theme of the manna (1 Cor. 7:1-5) is, in Pauline preaching, simply a parallel to the instruction on the Eucharist (1 Cor. 11:23-24). In John 6, on the contrary, the manna takes preponderance over and explains the Eucharist, for the homily on Christ, the "bread of life" (26-51), takes precedence over the homily on the Eucharist (52-57) and provides both a key to and a context (cf. 58) for the highlighting of the latter by the editors.

The decisive contribution, however, is undoubtedly the idea of salvation that is proposed to the final apostolic generation. Despite its being influenced by gnosis and hellenism, the fourth gospel does not evacuate the eschatological message of Christianity. Rather it highlights the spiritaul content of that message from its own central point of view, and it begins the process by de-judaizing the message, even while keeping the traditional scheme of it. To "see" and "hear" the Son are the ways to "life", which is "communion" with Christ and "knowledge" of God and thereby establishes the "community" of believers. Thus the work of salvation is, in principle, going on here and now. To an end-of-the-century Christendom that might be tempted to exaggerate the role of the coming parousia (the latter was already overdue), the gospel gives answer and recalls to it: "*Now* has judgment come upon this world" (12:31); "An hour is coming, *has indeed come*, when the dead shall hear the voice of the Son of God, and those who have heeded it shall live" (5:25). The aim of the gospel is not hermeneutics. It is rather to show the full significance of the ancient message of the *eschaton* as now being brought to pass.

* * *

The Church is a major element in the eschaton, and the Johannine group highlights the fact, even if it does not offer a particular theology of it. In order to give contemporary Christianity a sense of its unity and especially of its true religious condition, the group presents the Church as the supreme institution which Christ intended as essential for the period following the events depicted in the gospels. To this end, a recent literary procedure is employed, of which wide use is made in certain later texts: the ecclesial acts of Jesus which the earlier tradition located during his ministry in Galilee and Judea are here placed after Easter.

At first sight, it is true enough, the Church is not one of the major topics in the Johannine tradition. In exhortation as in the reflection of the group only vague and sporadic references are made to it. To what communities, for example, is allusion made in the metaphor of the sheepfold? What is the point of the basic allegory of the "shepherd" in John 10: 1-5? More particularly, who precisely are the "other sheep" which are invited to become part of "this fold" (mentioned again in emphatic fashion by the redactor in the supplementary gloss in 10:16)? Are they the hellenized Jews who lived in various diaspora centers before Christianity was preached? Or are they, on the contrary, the pagan hearers on the missions throughout the Greco-Roman world? The embarassment of the exegete when it comes to determining the perspective and especially the ecclesial viewpoint of the fourth gospel is also due to the allusive, occasional, and--be it said once again--disparate character of the texts. The fact of the apostolic mission is in the background of the fragments 10:16, 11:52, and 18:20-21; it may also be envisaged, in its main lines, in 8:35 and 12:20-28. But it can hardly therefore be called the key to the fourth gospel.

According to the redactional conclusion to chapter 20 (verses 30-31), the gospel is addressed to the Christians of the end of the first century, who had witnessed the passing of the disciples of Jesus. The aim is to recall to these people, or to demonstrate to them, the legitimacy of their titles and condition as a Church--this despite the unparalleled value of the gospel events and the experience of the apostolic group. To accomplish its purpose the gospel makes extensive use of a literary procedure that had been applied for similar purposes by Luke and Matthew: it presents the Christian community with its characteristic institutions as being essentially a post-Easter reality founded by the risen Christ in order to complete his work of evangelization. In other words, the gospel locates after Easter, in the period regarded as that of supreme revelations, the ecclesial acts of Jesus which the earlier tradition had located in his Palestinian ministry.

In the synoptic gospels Jesus founds the Church at the end of his life, at the last supper, with the words about the "covenant" that is sealed, or renewed, in the blood "poured out on behalf of many" (Mark 14:24 and parallels; cf. Exod. 24:8). The parallel passage in John is more hieratic; it is to be found in the Christophany to the Twelve on the day of the resurrection (20:19-23). The fragment of discourse (21-23) is a late composition, as are the other gospel texts containing the post-Easter instructions of Christ. In fact, the only thing traditional about them is the materials, themselves disparate, which the redactor uses to express his intention. To indicate only the major borrowings: the word "breathe upon" (22; cf. Gen. 2:7) is drawn from biblical and especially apocalyptic anthropology; connected with the theme of eschatological "re-creation" in the Pauline letters and the Christological formulas of Palestinian Christianity (cf. Rom. 1:3-4), the word is not used elsewhere in the fourth gospel and is related to the Johannine idea of spiritual "renewal". The words "Receive the Holy Spirit" (22) are a fragment from the liturgical prayers used by the group. Finally, the phrases about "forgiving" and "binding" sins are parallel to the "binding and loosing" of Matt. 16:19, except that they are here addressed to all the disciples and stress the pastoral aspect of their mission.

We are not saying that this text, with its heavy concentration of theology, is part of an ordination liturgy. The "disciples" (19) are neither the leaders nor the ministers of the community; as in the passage on the Supper, they are the first-fruits of the community and, by this title, its representatives. By repeating over them the creative act that marked the beginning of the world and by giving them as a group the messianic gift of the Spirit, Christ is raising them to the status of a purified, reformed mankind. The Church is mankind in the eschatological state. In thus noting the anthropological meaning of the fragment, we are not turning it into something Pauline. The fourth gospel does not derive its thought from the same sources as the Apostle; its primary source is Ezekiel (cf. 36:24-28 and parallels), not intertestamental Adamology. Above all, however, the fourth gospels adapts the traditional idea of the new creation to the Christology it presents in 20:31 as object of Christian faith. Jesus is more than the chief part and model of a mankind purified by the Spirit; he is also the author of it, as he was of the first creation.

This late highlighting of a major theme of apostolic eschatology is surely due to the crisis through which Asiatic Christianity was then passing in its struggle with moral laxism and the gnostic heresy. The sending of the disciples (20:21),

which explains the action of breathing on them, is instructive
in this respect. In Luke, Matthew, and the end of Mark, Christ's
commission refers to witnessing and preaching, initiation and
postbaptismal instruction. In other words, it implies that the
Twelve are the leaders in Christian preaching. In the fourth
gospel, however, the commission has undergone a twofold change.
The moment, it seems, is not for missionary action; the major
need is simply to preserve the community. Consequently, in the
Johannine version, Christ's order is to "forgive" sins and
"bind" them; that is, to preserve Christianity in its spiritual
integrity and fullness against dangers from without and within.
Moreover, the order is not now given to the disciples alone; by
way of the Twelve it is addressed to the community that has been
recreated in the Spirit, the community of which the disciples,
as we noted, are simply the first-fruits.

* * *

The stress thus laid on the ecclesial character of the
pastoral function is not something unique at the end of the
first century, even though this was the time when community
organizations and hierarchies were taking shape. The same
stress is found, for example, in the "ecclesiastical" discourse
in Matthew (18:1-35), that is, in a similar disciplinary and
pastoral context. Moreover the fourth gospel does not call in
question the specific doctrinal prerogatives of the disciples
(although unlike Acts the fourth gospel hardly stresses the
simultaneously collegial and monarchic structures of the early
Church). In this area the witness of the fourth gospel is an
original one, with the particularism of the Johannine group
hardly influencing the rereading of the evangelical tradition.

The fourth gospel hardly mentions the college of Twelve
as such or its institution. It is concerned rather with the

religious behavior of the apostles. The "other disciple" (18:15 and parallels), the one "whom he [Jesus] loved" (19: 26), is the perfect disciple: he has the understanding of faith, access to Jesus, tested attachment to him, in short the decisive attributes which make him superior to the other disciples, including Simon Peter. The six fragments--13:23-26; 18:15-16; 19:25-27; 20:3-10; 21:7; 21:20-22) which compare John and Peter are among the most suggestive in the fourth gospel. They all belong, as A. Kragerud has shown,[5] to a single cycle of secondary traditions, the formation of which was undoubtedly rather complicated. In other words, they bear witness to a characteristic reaction on the part of the intimates of the "other disciple", and one that was hardly a passing affair. This is not to say that the Johannine group "substituted" the disciple for Peter at the central moments of the passion,[6] or even that it opposed the representative of the charismatic hierarchy to the representative of the institutional hierarchy.[7] Such antitheses are justified neither by the thought nor by the expression of the fourth gospel. It is the Spirit who equips a man for the pastoral ministry, and does so by raising him to the eschatological condition. The comparison between the disciple and Peter is much narrower in scope. It provides a critical appreciation of Peter, which is very probably based on the testimony of a peer and can be explained only by the special position Simon-Cephas had in apostolic Christianity.

The final page of the fourth gospel, the appendix which is chapter 21, confirms this interpretation. It was composed after the martyrdom of Peter and the death of the "other disciple", and, in its central section (15-19), treats precisely of the service of the community that was entrusted to Peter. Thus it brings the most recent stratum of Johannine thought to bear on this aspect of New Testament ecclesiology. From the exegete's viewpoint certain doctrinal and literary data are clear.

1) To begin with, Peter's investiture with office is deliberately put after Easter. The passage hardly refers to the Christophany to Peter that is mentioned in 1 Cor. 15:5 (compare Luke 14:24); the ancient traditional account of this appearance soon became lost in apostolic Christianity. According to the most probable interpretation, the passage is correlative in its various elements to the other account (Luke 5:1-11) of Simon's calling at the beginning of Jesus' ministry.[8] The theological intention of our passage can hardly be called in doubt. As in the fragment on the breathing on the disciples, ecclesial realities and initiatives are put, on principle, in the period after the resurrection. The call of Peter to be a disciple is part of the gospel event, but his pastoral mission belongs to the period of the Church.

2) There is something more. The account of Peter's investiture strongly recalls the allegory of the Shepherd (10:1-18). In both, the same basic vocabulary--feeding, sheep--is drawn from the same scriptural sources (the prophets and especially Ezek. 34:1-31). The allegory makes it clear that "the good shepherd lays down his life for his sheep" (10:11, cf. 15). The investiture passage uses the martyrdom of Peter to explain his appointment to the service of the community (21:18-19). It wuld surely not be rash to see in these concordances the evidence of a relationship of continuity between the past ministry of Jesus and the pastoral presence of Peter.

A final point to clarify the ideas we have been presenting. The author of the Second Letter of Peter, probably a church leader living at the end of the first century, uses the device of pseudepigraphy and pretends to be Peter in order to recall in an authoritative way the normative value of the tradition. The Johannine group reacts in a different and less daring way. While pointing out the unique nature of Simon

Peter's mission, it raises in definitive form the problem of the relations between the disciple's pastoral activity and the various ministries found in the community. This is surely no small contribution to the theological discussion which occupies us today.

CHAPTER 8

Informal Groups at the End of the Middle Ages:
Rhenish Types

by

Francis Rapp

As the informal groups have been presented to us by the sociologists and theologians, they bear the marks of the contemporary world to such an extent that we cannot discover any kind of direct predecessors for them in the distant past. Since we cannot find identical realities in the two quite different historical periods, we must be content if our research can turn up analogous phenomena. In order, then, to avoid misunderstandings, we shall define straight off the characteristic traits of the communities we shall be discussing.

The communities in question may possess internal structures; but they also may not have had time to acquire such structures, or may not have considered them necessary. What they have in common is that they exist to foster the shared ideals of men and women who are bent on mutual aid.

The purpose of the activity of these groups is to correct a fault or fill up a lacuna in the life of the Church. The defect may have been quite consciously noted by the members of the group, or it may simply have been confusedly, even if deeply, felt. But, whether explicit or implicit, criticism of the ecclesial organism always plays a decisive role in the origin and continued existence of the group.

On the other hand, the groups which we shall be examining in this rapid survey, are not the ones which spontaneously reached the point of radical challenge and then passed over into open heresy. If the members of these groups moved away from orthodox belief, they did not do so intentionally.

They did, however, deliberately refuse or simply neglect to enter the institutions officially approved and favored by the hierarchy. Their work was done at the periphery of, and sometimes completely outside, the framework set up by canon law. For example, the clergy did not necessarily play the leaders within these groups; the laity were at least deeply involved in the life of these communities and in some instances were the real force behind the communities.

We have investigated the groups which fit these criteria, in the history of the Rhineland between Basel and Mainz, with special attention to Strasbourg. The chronological limits we have set to the inquiry are quite wide enough: the beginning of the fourteenth century to the beginning of the sixteenth. The materials provided by the documents of the period suggest that we distinguish three phases within this long period: the first covers the whole of the fourteenth century, during which informal groups are rather numerous; from about 1420 to 1480 these groups disappear; they come to the surface again during the forty or fifty years before the Reformation.

We must first attempt to describe the milieu which, after 1300, saw the development of the groups we shall be trying to reconstruct for ourselves. A first factor in the "context" strikes us immediately: the mendicant Friars who had supplied the Church's answer to the religious aspirations of the preceding period were now at the height of their power. They had numerous convents: at Strasbourg alone there were forty of them, along with seven monasteries of Dominican nuns, two of Poor Clares, and one of Magdalenes. These various religious families fitted perfectly into local society. The leadership of the Dominican and Franciscan houses was in the hands of the sons and daughters of the aristocracy. Material resources were abundant; moral authority, based on a first-rate intellectual formation, was solidly established; the wealthy did not forget their confessors--Franciscans or Dominicans--in their wills.

At the same time, there were serious defects in this fine structure. The poverty of the mendicants was not much more than a legal fiction. News of certain disorders had reached the ears of the laity, and rumors which were not entirely caluminous showed that there had been a disturbing relaxation of discipline. These defects were not much in evidence around 1300 but they grew as the years passed and became more and more public. They were all the more dangerous as important changes in religious sensibility seem to have been taking place. Thus, detachment from material goods, which in the twelfth and thirteenth centuries had been a touchstone for judging the spiritual quality of Christians, no longer had the same dominant place in the hierarchy of religious values. Such detachment was now thought of simply as the probably necessary condition for a more worthwhile kind of experience: the union of the soul with its creator. The only spiritual realities considered authentic and worthwhile were those experienced in the depth of the heart, beyond rites and words and gestures and indeed, according to bolder spirits, almost independently on these externals.

Various factors helped in the development of such aspirations and the accompanying growth of individualism. We may note, first of all, the attitude of religious men and women and of the clergy: they felt unsatisfied by external practices. Moreover, the social elite had at its disposal numerous means of instruction: there were books and sermons in far greater quantity than before to stimulate and feed the meditative prayer of the more fervent souls. There was a final factor: fear, which remained latent or sprang to sudden life in the collective consciousness. It is not simply an anachronism to

speak of a crisis of civilization in the fourteenth century.
In any event, the age had a sense of modernity (using the term
broadly), and the novelty made it dizzy. Catastrophes such as
the Black Death which rolled down the Rhine could only intensify
this existential anxiety. In such an atmosphere every passion
became strong. Discord became more and more clearly felt,
and undermined the imperfect but real harmony which the mendicants had managed to create between popular religious feeling
and ecclesiastical institutions.

Some of the currents which the discord brought to light
were frankly heretical. We shall recall here only one of them:
the Brothers and Sisters of the Free Spirit. They were probably
quite numerous in the geographical area we are discussing, for
the bishop of Strasbourg (in 1317) was one of the first to take
severe measures against their ideas, which had contaminated
the beguines and beghards. The pantheism which promised its
adepts a fusion of the soul and God had complete scorn for the
means of sanctification offered by the Church and especially
for the sacraments. It was impossible, therefore, to profess
this doctrine and not break away from orthodoxy.

The status of the Waldensians was less clear, and this
ambiguity allows us to bring them in here. At Strasbourg
people called them the *Winkler* [those who carry on their
activities in corners, that is, in obscurity]; the Waldensian
community at Strasbourg came into existence before 1330, if
we may trust the testimony of one of the members. The Inquisition harried the Waldensians, and intensified the persecution
after 1350; in 1399 the Waldensians of Strasbourg were arrested,
and their testimony has survived so that we are in a position
to draw a rather accurate picture of their beliefs. The testimony shows that many of the accused were not aware of their
break with the Church. They claimed, in fact, to have inherited

a mission given two centuries earlier by the pope to two men
named Waldo; the latter had been commissioned to restore the
faith which at that time was subject to grave dangers. In
the community's accounts of the history of their movement
nothing was said of the condemnation issued against their
founders; the later generation could therefore believe that
the commission given by Rome had never been withdrawn.

Moreover, the activities of the group did not make an
autonomous Church of them, one completely separated from the
Roman Church. The Waldensians of Strasbourg met to pray and
to read and comment on the Scriptures. The houses where they
met had the significant name of "schools". The Prefect, who
visited the various communities from time to time, heard the
confessions of the simple believers and imposed penances, but
did not celebrate the Eucharist; the Waldensians received
communion from their parish priest. If they did not have the
opportunity to confess to one of the Prefect on a visit to
Strasbourg, they confessed to a priest before approaching the
altar. Thus the orthodox Church and the Waldensian community
lived together in a quasi-symbiotic condition. In these circumstances it was possible for Waldensians to think, in good
faith, that they were effectively contributing to the regeneration of the organism whose defects and superfluous rites they
criticized but whose sacraments they frequented. They sought
advice and received penances from the Prefect, whom many regarded as true priests; these holy men had through mortifica-
tion and prayer reached the point at which God became a friend
(the Waldensians sometimes called their ministers "friends of
God"--*Gottesfreunde*), and were in a position to lead their
disciples to the same heights. After all, did not the rest of
the faithful choose directors of conscience from among the
mendicant Friars, yet the secular clergy did not bitterly

reproach them for this preference? Could one not go to the chapels of the convents and hear preachers pitilessly denouncing the vices of the clergy and the superstitions of the laity? It is certainly true that not all the Waldensians believed they still belonged to the Roman Church, and the Inquisition made it its duty to enlighten all Waldensians on their true situation. Nonetheless it is clear that until 1399 Strasbourg was the home of a group, which, situated on the borderline between open heresy and complete orthodoxy, shows clear affinities to the present-day "base communities".

The "Friends of God", to whom the history of German spirituality has given deserved celebrity, manifested all the characteristics which we listed at the beginning of this essay. Contrary to the view that long prevailed, the Friends of God never formed a society with well defined structures; they were not an anticipation of the Nocturnal Adoration Society. But the bonds between them were strong enough. They all cherished the same ideal, for they wanted Christianity to be an imperious call to perfection, and they tried to live it in their own hearts as a personal encounter with Jesus Christ. Saint John, the disciple whom the Lord loved, was their model, and union with the creator, even if it remained beyond their reach, was always what they had in view. Moreover, the best known among the Friends of God--Tauler, Suso, Henry of Nördlingen, and Marguerite Ebner--are the great names of Rhenish mysticism.

What we know of the interior lives of the Friends of God, we know from the writings, letters, sermons, and treatises composed to communicate the fruits of rich experience and laborious thought to others who wanted to follow their example. The exchange of letters, which took up where visits and long conversations left off, seem to have been all the more necessary to

the life of the group since the members did not all live in
the same place but were scattered along the Rhine from Basel
to Mainz and on the Swabian plateaus, and felt isolated among
tepid and superficial Christians. The Friends of God felt
deeply the indifference and neglect to be found in many of the
faithful and the carelessness and laxity of some priests. They
did not question the principles underlying ecclesiastical organization or the theological foundations of the Church's teaching office, but only deplored the defects of the individuals
who made up the Church. Moreover, they feared that the huge
number of defects and sins would draw down God's wrath on sin-
ful mankind.

The Friends of God thought of their community as the ark
that was ready to welcome the elect and save them from the
deluge, or, to use another of their favorite images, the
community was the last solid column of the temple. In their
eyes, the future of Christianity depended on their prayers and
works, but the prayers and works themselves were simply those
which the Roman Church provided and recommended. The Friends
did not reject any rite or practice; they did condemn the
mechanical and purely external repetition of rites and practices, and devoted all their energies to turning acts and words
into the sincere expression of inner conviction and feeling.
Nor did they at all scorn institutions. Their devotion to the
Eucharist imposed on them a respect for the priesthood. Many
of them wore the religious habit, while convents such as Saint-
Jean-du-Marais-Vert and the Augustinian house at Strasbourg
served as bases of operation where they could be sure of finding experienced and loyal advisers.

If the Friends spoke with some disdain of the Parisian
doctors and their scholasticism, it was certainly not because
they themselves were ignorant. On the contrary, there were not

a few trained theologians among them, while the lay Friends--
bankers like Rulman Merswin, and members of the upper bourgeoisie
and the nobility--almost all belonged to the social elite and
were certainly well-read people. It is, in fact, tempting to
see in the disdain an attitude favored by the better educated.
At any rate, there was no categorical rejection of ceremonies
or institutional framework or sacred science. In the eyes of
the Friends, however, the quality of spiritual life was more
important than status as defined by canon law; the advice of a
genuinely pious father of a family carried more weight than the
admonitions of a cleric whose morals were suspect. Highest rank
of all was given to the wisdom of a "Friend of God" who had been
tested by years of prayer and meditation. The community was, in
fact, made up only of high-minded souls. It may even be that
the devotion of some of the Friends was cast in the aristocratic
mode; the difficulties experienced after 1350 by the patrician
class, which was progressively excluded from posts of political
power, were favorable to the development and success of this
kind of spirituality. We need not pass any judgment on the
action of this group, for the only task we have set ourselves,
however, that it is largely owing to them that we possess some
of the classical texts of medieval spirituality.

We may now turn to the passage of the flagellants through
our region and to their influence upon it. In some respects
the flagellants represent a complete antithesis to the Friends
of God. The latter, as we have indicated, belonged to the
upper levels of society; the former, on the contrary, chiefly
drew men and women of modest estate. The Friends were interested
only in the interiorizing of religious life; the flagellants,
on the contrary, sought salvation in the frenetic and spectacular repetition of a penitential practice. The Friends' activity
was contained within the noiseless murmur of their meeting-places,

and their quiet work flowed on continuously throughout the second half of the fourteenth century. The flagellants appeared suddenly and for a relatively short time, preceded, accompanied, and followed by outcries, moans, and the whistle of their whips, first in 1261, then in 1296, and finally, and chiefly, in 1349.

Despite these contrasts, however, each movement has its place within the framework we described earlier. The flagellants, too, had a great purpose: the divine wrath was threatening to descend upon the world, and the Lord's arm must quickly be stayed. In 1349 the Black Death was the affliction which the expiatory processions were intended to end. The flagellant groups cannot be called "informal", however, for their activities were regulated by detailed rules. Moreover, the penitents lived together for only a short time, thirty-three and a half days (the number was symbolic, recalling the years Christ spent in the work of our redemption), and what created the unity of the group was simply the will of the members. Their purpose implied sharp criticism of the Church or at least of ecclesiastics, who had not been able to save mankind from the wrath of God and who were too soft on violations of the law.

Official institutions did not succeed in channeling this current of piety in which fear was such a strong motive. Priests were indeed accepted as members of flagellant bands (though a Strasbourg chronicler observes that not many educated clerics sought admission), but they were excluded from the committees which directed the groups. Laymen, therefore, intended to keep control of the movement. The rites they practiced and the lamentations they chanted owed a good deal to official ceremonial, but they used the borrowings to make up an original whole. They did not avoid entering churches, but the flagellations took place outside of consecrated buildings, in the open fields or in the public squares. One cannot but think that in an age when the populace was limited to passive presence at religious

services, the kind of "wildcat liturgy" which the flagellants
had invented answered an obscure need for active participation
in cultic acts. The inspiration which the penitents thought
they were obeying, and the mission they thought they had, came
to them directly from God. A letter had fallen from heaven,
they claimed, and told them what to do. The hierarchy could
not accept such a claim. Even if the flagellants had not
committed the excesses which they did in fact commit in some
places, they would have been condemned; the condemnation came
in 1350. They submitted, partly, at least, because the fever
which preceded their coming on the scene had broken. Very
soon there was no trace of them at Strasbourg, and the con-
fraternity which the Church authorities approved for those who
wished to engage in penitential flagellation lasted but a
short time.

For the greater part of the fifteenth century the documents
and chronicles show no trace of communities with the characteristics which we indicated at the beginning of this essay. Even
the heretical enclaves seem to have died out. When arrested by
the Inquisition at Strasbourg in 1458, Frederick Reiser, a
Waldensian who had become a priest and then a Hussite bishop,
admitted that the cause to which he had devoted his life was
losing its vitality "like a slowly dying fire".

This fact requires an explanation, and we shall try to
give one. After 1430, even though the general reform sought
by the Council of Constance did not take place, Christendom did
at least experience a restoration of discipline in some of the
religious orders. In Alsace, or more accurately at Strasbourg,
the recall to a strict observance met with unquestionable success,
especially among the Dominicans. The movement had positive results. On the one hand, the new austerity heightened the prestige

of the reformed houses. On the other, these same houses were extensively influenced by the spirituality--the "modern devotion"--diffused by the Brethren of the Common Life and the Augustinian Canons of Windesheim. This kind of prayer, which was very methodical yet also rich in affectivity, was closely related to that practiced in the meeting-halls of the Friends of God; in general, indeed, the Bretheren and the Canons had inherited much from the Friends. The laity likewise felt the effects of the return to a strict observance. They kept up regular contacts with those of their relatives who had made their profession in the reformed congregations. Letters, books, and pictures came from the cloisters. Devotional confraternities brought together the friends and benefactors of these communities and initiated them into the spiritual exercises practiced in the monasteries of strict observance. Thus, between the aspirations which we have seen at work in men of the fourteenth century (and which had not died out in the course of the fifteenth) and the models of religious life which the "reformed" monks and nuns provided, there was a kind of harmony.

The harmony did not last until 1500. From about 1480 on, the movement to strict observance slowed down, and became ever more costly by way of compromises and coercive measures. Good example had lost its contagiousness. Moreover, the ecclesiastical world as a whole still suffered from the serious abuses which preachers like Geiler of Kaisersberg (who occupied the cathedral pulpit from 1478 to 1520) denounced unsparingly. The hope of a general improvement grew weaker and gave way to discouragement. We can hear panic in the cry of Geiler, in a sermon of 1508: "Each of us must bury his head in a corner and try to work out his salvation alone. Christendom as a whole is beyond reform!" Printing made books much less expensive, especially after 1480, and led to their wide diffusion, but the books were not the kind to allay the disquiet. Along with breviaries and edifying treatises, the bookstore shelves contained much less orthodox works, for example, bold programs of reform, which ecclesiastical censure, in weak and delayed form, could not cause to vanish. The German translation of the Bible put the inspired texts into the hands of the laity, who did not always seek advice from the clergy on how to interpret them. Finally, in this increasingly stormy atmosphere, economic and social developments played no small part in increasing the trouble: the sudden shifts in the price of grain and wine caused a gulf to open between lucky and unlucky speculators and between rich and poor.

The ones hardest hit by the economic changes were the peasants. They were therefore the most desperate and bold in trying to change their condition. Between 1493 and 1517 conspiracy followed on conspiracy and pointed ahead to the great revolution of 1517. The archives still contain large numbers of documents, attestations, and depositions which reveal the intentions of the conspirators. As the years passed and the anger of the rural masses deepened, the plans of the revolutionaries who dreamed of overturning the established order seemed to become more and more expansive.

The changes sought were radical and concerned the Church as well as society generally. In fact, the revolutionary plans came to look more and more directly to the Church. One is almost inclined to say that the political program of the "Bumpkins" became progressively sacralized. In order to promote the overturn and simplification of both the ecclesiastical organization and the secular administration, the peasants formed the *Bundeschuh* movement, by 1502 at the latest;[1] their basic principle was divine justice. The law of the Lord, they said, condemns the iniquities under which the lower classes, and especially, the peasants, had suffered for so long. Clerics and monks were the objects of open attack; these avaricious and vain men were betraying the gospel they claimed to serve. The plans put in motion were a curious blend of practical realism and wild-eyed prophetism. They expressed the millenarian dream of the city of brotherhood, built upon the ruins of a Babylon that would be destroyed by the cataclysms of the Apocalypse.

In trying to explain the vitality of a current of ideas that had long since been condemned by the hierarchy, we may point out that in the countryside the ecclesiastical organization of the masses was rather loose, while the personnel engaged in pastoral work was most often of mediocre quality. Among the "mental furniture" of the rural masses pieces of heretical origin often had a place, coming into the area by very complicated journeyings. John Wycliffe's postulate concerning the law of God, for example, had travelled a long way before reaching the banks of the Rhine, passing through Hussite Bohemia and the throngsswho surrounded the visionary shepherd of Niklashausen in Franconia. Some of the conspirators surely knew that rather curious program for social reorganization, the *Reformatio Sigismundi*, while the "Hundred Chapters", written at fever pitch around 1518 by the anonymous "Revolutionary of the Upper Rhine", shows such striking parallels to the cherished hopes of the *Bundeschuher* that we are almost forced to admit the existence of a connection between the conspirators and this ecstatic visionary. Yet these various elements, almost all of which fall outside orthodox doctrine, were amalgamated in the peasant mind with traditions that were wholly conformed to Catholic faith. The necessity of a priestly ministry, in particular, was acknowledged without reserve, and a good priest was idolized. The little clandestine groups which dreamed of a just society and a holy Church did not necessarily have any intention of breaking with Rome. In fact, there are documents which enable us to assert the contrary. If these people were heretics, they were so unwillingly and unwittingly.

The desired renovation required a foregoing revolution. It was not at all any catastrophic upheaval that the humanists had in mind, but they did aim to restore to the Church the purity that marked its earliest days. In heaping sarcasm on the heads of the ignorant and vice-ridden clergy their intention was not to blacken the Church. It was rather in order to draw the attention of contemporaries to the depth and extent of the evils which the protesters thought they could cure. Instruction and education were the remedies they prescribed and attempted to apply. Sebastian Brant, Jakob Wimpheling, and their competitors, disciples all of Geiler and, through him, heirs of John Gerson, had the best intentions toward the Catholic patrimony. There is in them no trace of the moral libertinage and the airy intellectual manner that marked so many representatives of the Italian Renaissance. They wanted to spread knowledge, understanding, and respect for the "sacred literature", that is, the Scriptures and the writings of the Fathers. For the most part, they were more prudent than Erasmus and had no wish to issue a blanket condemnation against the works and methods of the Scholastics. Continuity was almost as important to them as change. Until about 1510 all these men were not gathered into any organization but were united by the ideal they served. To strengthen their friendships these "Friends of God" and sacred science wrote each other long letters, exhanged manuscripts, dedicated their books to one another, and spent a lot of time in conversation. After 1510 they formed brotherhoods (*sodalitates*) at Schlettstadt and Strasbourg; these groups were a combination of literary club and devotional coterie. They did not fit at all into the framework envisioned by canon law. Moreover, they were made up both of laymen, like Brant or Beatus

Rhenanus, and priests, whether seculars like Wimpheling or regulars such as Paul Volz, the Benedictine abbot to whom Erasmus had dedicated the second edition of his *Enchiridion militis christiani*. After 1515 the influence of the Erasmians was in the ascendant, and gradually the circle accepted the still more corrosive criticisms of Ulrich von Hutten. Clearly heretical ideas made their appearance in the writings and resolutions of the new generation of Alsatian humanists. These elements were not sufficiently numerous and strong, however, to cause the whole group of literary men, who continued to accept Wimpheling as their guide, deliberately to break with tradition. To become convinced of this, we need only think of the violent "We cannot!" which the elderly master from Schlettstadt opposed to the upheavals in religious organization and beliefs which occurred after 1525. Beatus Rhenanus, like his model, Erasmus, refused to subscribe to the Reformation. Some members of the literary brotherhoods--and not the least important of them--indeed entered enthusiastically into the ranks of Luther's followers, but the community as a whole did not take this path. The work of renewal which they had undertaken was to be carried out within the tradition and in communion with the Roman Church.

The religious revolution begun by Martin Luther effected a complete change, and that on both sides of the gulf which henceforth separated the rival confessions, in the conditions under which "informal groups" could arise and develop. One kind of relationship between official hierarchic institutions and spontaneous popular movements had seen its day and disappeared.

We are finished with our rapid excursion into the past. Let us glance back over the data we have noted and brought together. The harvest is poor enough, but that can hardly surprise us. We must observe, first of all, that the convictions and practices of the declared heretics whom we have excluded from our purview are relatively better known, since the Inquisition took the trouble to draw up a precise description of them and has left us treatises on the heresies as well as minutes of the interrogations to which they subjected the heretics. Moreover, within orthodoxy the juridically acknowledged and favored congregations have left the historian very many more texts, rules, constitutions, property deeds, and legends than have the "informal groups" with their necessarily blurred outlines and brief span of life.

In addition to these considerations which directly affect methodology, deeper reasons were at work to limit the number and importance of the base communities which were the object of our research. The transformations which the Church had experienced in the Gregorian period and which shaped it for a long time to come, had not simply deepened the laity's "thirst for God" and fostered the formation of popular religious movements. They had also brought in their train the establishment of an institutional structure which, down to the end of the Middle Ages, was to become ever more complex and rigid. Only with difficulty could the movements which arose after 1100 develop outside this framework; if the movements did not run in these established channels, if their promotors did not found or adopt an "approved religious order", then the movements almost inevitably passed first into schism and then into heresy.

In such conditions the informal groups could not long survive as such. If they did not become religious congregations, they became heterodox sects. Within the geographical and temporal space we surveyed so rapidly, we noted that twice, first in the fourteenth century and then between 1480 and 1520, there was discord between the models of religious life which were proposed by the recognized religious orders, and the felt needs of the popular soul, and that this lack of harmony manifested itself through the appearance on the scene of a new kind of community. On the first occasion strict observance and the modern devotion made it possible to reduce the discord. On the second occasion, however, solutions were not discovered until too late, and medieval Christendom tore itself apart.

CHAPTER 9

Informal Groups in the Reformation Period:
Rhenish Types

by

Rodolphe Peter

Three things favored the development of informal groups in sixteenth-century Strasbourg, the city of which we shall chiefly be speaking here.

1) The spread of the vernacular Bible.[1]

The first German Bible was printed, as we know, at Strasbourg in 1466 in the shop of Johann Mentel from Schlettstadt. The translation was a medieval one, based on the Vulgate, and not very good. In addition, the book was costly: the folio volume sold for twelve florins, which was two months' earnings for a workman. Yet the Bible found buyers, so many that four years later the Strasbourg printer, Heinrich Eggestein, hoped to make a good profit by putting out a second edition. In 1485 a new edition proved necessary; it was published by Johann Gruninger, and this time was accompanied by 109 engravings. I have mentioned only the three printings at Strasbourg. In all, this pre-Lutheran translation went through fourteen printings from 1466 to 1518, at Strasbourg, Nürnberg, and Augsburg.[2]

Enthusiasm for the vernacular Bible only intensified with Luther's translation. In the letter to Pope Leo X which he prefixed to his book *The Liberty of a Christian Man*, Luther wrote: "I acknowledge no fixed rules for the interpretation of the Word of God, since the Word of God, which teaches freedom in all other matters, must not be bound."[3]

Preaching by example, Luther translated the New Testament into German in 1522, while staying in the Wartburg. On returning to Wittenberg he settled down to translate the whole Bible; it would appear only twelve years later, in 1534. This translation from the original languages, with its clear and expressive style, became extraordinarily popular, the more so since improved technology enabled the printers to lower the prices, and since they offered parts of the text as well as the whole Bible.[4] The New Testament cost one and a half florins in 1522, or the sum a housewife would spend for two rabbits.

A member of the Zorn family of Plobsheim provides a typical example of how the faithful sought to satisfy their thirst for knowledge of the Sacred Scriptures. This man wanted to acquire a Bible in 1530, when Luther's complete translation was not yet on the market. He therefore bought whatever parts of the Lutheran translation he could find and filled out his collection by turning to the second best that the booksellers were offering. His Bible, preserved in the Bibliothèque Nationale and the Université de Strasbourg,[5] includes the Pentateuch, the historical and poetic books, and the New Testament, all in Luther's translation; the prophetic books in the version made by the dissenters, Ludwig Hetzer and Hans Denck; and the apocryphal books in the translation by the Alsatian, Leo Jud, Zwingli's assistant.

2) The importance of corporations in the old-time free city.[6]

The population of sixteenth century Strasbourg was about 22,000; of these 3500 were burgers, divided into twenty corporations. Each had its meeting-hall where artisans and businessmen discussed their professional concerns. They talked about the news from the great fairs of Frankfurt and Lyons, and acquired an initiation into the political life of the city. Each corporation was headed by fifteen deputy magistrates, elected by their peers. The deputies, three hundred in all, represented the sovereign people, which was consulted each time a decision of importance for the city had to be made. These were the men who proposed, and even imposed, the application of the program for religious reform during the 1520's.

Special mention must be made of one corporation, the market-gardeners, who were the most numerous, the most restless, and socially the least well-off of all the groups. This corporation had almost 600 members. A contemporary geographer, Sebastian Münster, in commenting on the chief cities of the Holy Roman Empire, notes the presence of the market-gardeners as one of the curiosities of Strasbourg: "At Strasbourg there are several hundred gardeners who earn their livelihood by growing turnips, radishes, onions, and cabbage; these vegetables turn out better there than anywhere else in Germany."[7] Because of their numbers, the market-gardeners were subdivided into three groups: one was located in the Sainte-Aurélie section, another in the Faubourg-de-Pierre, and the third in the Krutenau.

3) The spirit of mildness, not to say tolerance, that characterized Strasbourg at that time.[8]

The imperial free city welcomed men and ideas; consequently all kinds of refugees, bold innovators, and men inspired by extravagant doctrines all streamed to it. One such, and not the least of them, Sebastian Franck, relates that "crimes which elsewhere were punished by death here drew only a flogging."[9] Strasbourg owed this liberal outlook chiefly to its civil government, and especially to the commanding figure of Jakob Sturm who for twenty-five years (1527-1553) determined the domestic and foreign policy of the city. Though a sincere convert to the Reform, he was completely free of the dogmatic spirit, and his humanistic attitude counteracted the exclusivity faith inspires. However, it must be admitted that when disciplinary measures were required, their application was often difficult because of the connivence given some heterodox preachers by elements of the populace.

* * *

Let us look more closely now at the informal groups to be found in Strasbourg during the Reformation period.

To begin with, there are the evangelical groups themselves.[10] On March 13, 1524 the market-gardeners from the Saint-Aurélie sector informed the magistrate that they had chosen Martin Bucer as spiritual direction of their corporation. They stated "that they had no desire to dismiss their curate or deprive him of his income, but that on the other hand they could no longer stand having the old songs sung at them; they were therefore ready to undertake the support of someone who would faithfully preach the Gospel to them and lead them, their wives, and their children along the path of true faith in God and sincere love of neighbor." The parishioners of Saint-Pierre-le-Jeune pledged the same support to Wolfgang Capito. The magistrate found an expedient for letting them have their way. But when all the parishes pressed their right to the same freedom, the magistrate consulted the 300 deputies in the summer of 1524. The sovereign people decided that, given the absence of the hitherto competent ecclesiastical authorities, the magistrate should himself proceed to install preachers of the Gospel in the seven parishes of the city. This represented, of course, a total overturn of the ecclesiastical order. Here the Reformation occurred by the will of a populace that wanted to follow the Gospel alone. The initiative came from below: from the people which boldly exercised its sovereignty in the religious sphere. The universal priesthood which Luther was preaching had begun to make itself felt. Then the support of the magistrate gave institutional form to what had, on the part of the people, an informal and wildcat character.

We can see from this example that, apart from some humanist circles, the evangelical movement came to birth among the people. Franz Lau's statement that "the Reformation was never the work of a committee" holds true for the whole of the Holy Roman Empire. In fact, on most occasions, those in authority did not favor the movement of reform but checked its expansion. It was only in some of the imperial cities that the Council, either immediately or after brief hesitation, simply yielded to the wishes of the people and thus gave the Reformation a quick victory by the shortest path. The most striking example of such a response is Nürnberg, but the same thing happened in Strasbourg, Konstanz, Memmingen, and, in North Germany, Magdeburg.[11]

This Lutheran ground swell, however, which swept Strasbourg into the camp of the evangelical cities, also brought with it various other heritages. The religious aspirations of the Waldensians and the Hussites and the social protests of the *Bundschuher* were still alive in certain strata of the population. The evangelical movement satisfied these people on some points but not on others. Heterodox theologians from outside were able to exploit this situation. The ideas to which they drew many in Strasbourg centered on two points which are characteristic of all the sectarian movements of the sixteenth century: the priority given to the direct inspiration of the Holy Spirit, and the importance allotted to social ideology. All these movements maintain that a person can obtain faith without the mediation of the Scriptures, since the latter are but a witness to faith. The Holy Spirit can bestow upon the believer new revelations, which may even go beyond the Scriptures. The other central idea is represented in the effort to turn the Sermon on the Mount into a law. People wanted to return to the apostolic age, especially in the following respects: adult baptism, community of the saints, equality of all members, mutual material help, negative attitude to the state. Thus the heterodox movements of Strasbourg, too, gravitate around these two central points which at times are in harmony and at times in conflict. The accent is put now on the one, now on the other, but both are always present, whether the groups in question are trying to shape society in accordance with their own mysticism, or are taking refuge in mysticism after having failed in this world.

The groups which at Strasbourg coexisted with the evangelical group can be divided into three categories of varying importance: the anabaptists, the enlightened, and the spiritualists.[12]

The first group found its recruits among the poorist social classes and was numerically the strongest. It underwent constant influence from outside due to the various leaders who passed through the city: Andreas Carlstadt, Balthasar Hübmaier, Wilhelm Reublin, Martin Cellarius, Hans Denck, Ludwig Hetzer, Michael Sattler, Jakob Kautz, Pilgram Marbeck, and Johann Bunderlin, to name but some, in the order of their appearance on the Strasbourg scene.[13] But the anabaptists also had spokesmen within the city and sympathizers in the most varied circles.[14]

The best way to understand anabaptism is to regard it as an attempt to transplant directly into contemporary reality the religious ideas of early Christianity, without paying any heed to the historical circumstances and cultural situation in which these ideas saw the light. As their name indicates, the anabaptists allowed infant baptism no value at all. The idea of a popular Church that would embrace the multitudes was not only foreign to them but anathema; only those could be part of the Church who by exemplary life and personal profession bore witness to the fact that they were saved. Only then, and with full consciousness of the act to be done, they asked for baptism and confessed their faith before the whole congregation of believers. Among themselves they shared possessions to a large extent and submitted to a strict discipline which provided, in extreme cases, for the excommunication of unworthy brethren. In a very obvious rejection of the civil powers and of all established authority, they refused to take an oath and opposed war. Some of them preached the final restoration of all things and the final salvation of all men.

The support-base for the anabaptists of Strasbourg was the meeting-halls of the market-gardeners, especially that of the Krutenau, at the sign of the fox, along side the church of Saint-Guillaume. There the group was inspired by one of its own number, Clement Ziegler.[15] As a simple tenant farmer, Ziegler first took care of the garden belonging to the nuns of the convent of Saint-Nicholas-aux-Ondes, and then of a piece of land, about five acres in size, belonging to the Knight of Endingen in the Robertsau. "I am but an uneducated peasant," he said; "let no one object to my speaking, but simply listen to the word of God." But in ten or so pamphlets and memorials, all of which he signed "Clement Ziegler, gardener at Strasbourg", he showed that he had extensive knowledge of the Bible, even if his exegesis was freakish at times. He knew that Origen had defended the doctrine of apocatastasis (universal restoration); he was acquainted with the Moravian Brethren, and mentions Luther's writings with respect. He also quotes anecdotes drawn from the history of the Church and which he probably got from Caspar Hedio's *Chronicon*.

Ziegler continues to speak of himself as "a simple soul", but he is not unaware of the promises Scripture makes to the poor and the poor in spirit. He is a propagandist and wants to arouse in the people an interest in spiritual and political problems. "The simple man is not to be left out of account. The cowherd must know God's will no less than the emperor, the barber no less than the bishop."[16] He shows that the New Testament acknowledges neither popes nor cardinals, neither tyrannical overlords nor crushing rents, but only Jesus, the friend of the poor and lowly, not of the rich and mighty. We are all equal, all of us being brothers in the eyes of Christ, our only Saviour, and of God our Father. The time has come for all men of good will to form a truly fraternal community, in which all equally enjoy this world's goods. Again, the Bible does not have even the word "sacrament", and it is time to denounce the abuses that have attached to this notion and still bring a handsome income to many. Baptism depends on faith and without faith has no value. Infant baptism is not justified, it is even contrary to Scripture. The important thing is that God himself baptizes us with Spirit and fire and that we gradually attain to the knowledge of Jesus Christ, to faith in the Gospel, and to the fire of love, "so that finally we are so fervent and inspired that we want the outward sign of water baptism as a witness to our dedication to Christ and our readiness to endure all, even death, for his name's sake."[17]

For Ziegler, the holy Supper brings us into intimate communion with the eternal Christ, the Christ who is Spirit. But the authentic reception of the body of Christ does not depend on words pronounced by someone else, but solely on the faith of the communicant. Without criticizing the rite of the Supper,

Ziegler asserts: "If a man keeps meditating in his heart on the truths of the Bible, if he is aware of the price God has paid for his salvation, and if he is stirred by a burning desire to do God's will, then, then whether his job be to cut wood, clean stables, or mow the field, he really communicates with Christ, even though celebrant, altar, and every other external sign be lacking. It is the Spirit that gives life; the letter without the Spirit is dead."[18]

Ziegler was not content to preach Christian freedom, as he understood it, only to the market-gardeners of Strasbourg; he preached it as well to the peasnats in the Obernai area, whence he himself seems to have originally come. The first unlawful assemblies of peasants at the beginning of 1525 in the villages at the foot of Mont Sainte-Odile were directly related to his preaching. But although he was teaching them to fight only with the sword of the word,[19] extremists did not interpret him in this way. As we know, the movement was crushed a few months later at Saverne and Scherwiller. Thus brutally awakened from his dream of social renewal, Ziegler had to admit that the Kingdom of God would not be built by human hands. From 1526 on his message became a more spiritual one. He no longer sought to form a Christian society but became the champion of the eternal salvation of all men.

The blow to Ziegler in the peasant uprising did not lessen his prestige among the market-gardeners in the northern section of Strasbourg. In fact, those of the Robertsau, about 150 families, wanted him for their pastor in 1528,[20] on the grounds that during the last epidemic to sweep through their area Ziegler alone, and not the appointed parish priest, visited the sick.

Other anabaptist meetings took place in the Rue du Faubourg-de-Pierre, under the direction of a Georg Ziegler, a tailor by trade.[21] Investigations by the magistrate and subsequent questionings uncovered numerous other cells of the movement, for example the one under the leadership of Rudolf Claus, a carter, at the Aspe Restaurant, on Rope-Merchants Street, behind the work-shop connected with Notre-Dame.[22] We learn that the meetings began with a prayer for enlightenment, followed by bible study during which each one spoke in turn.[23] Rebaptisms at the end of these meetings were rare. Such ceremonies took place out in the country, and especially in the woods between Benfeld and Rossfeld,[24] on the occasion of important gathering due to the occasional presence of a leader of the movement at large.[25]

The special success of the Strasbourg anabaptists around 1550 is due to the fact that neither Bucer nor especially Capito were clear in their own minds during the 1520's on the necessity of infant baptism. It was only around 1530 that Bucer and then Capito came to realize the importance of this sacrament for the life of the Church as the Body of Christ.

* * *

The enlightened made up the second informal group in sixteenth century Strasbourg. Their leader was Melchoir Hofmann.[26] A native of Hall in Swabia, and a furrier by trade, Hofmann appeared in Strasbourg in 1529, won some disciples, explained the Apocalypse to them as "the key to the whole of Scripture", and published seven pieces of writing, all of which show a marked millennarianism.[27] Hofmann sees three stages of spiritual resurrection: one in apostolic times, the second in the time of Huss, and the third in his own time. Strasbourg was the city chosen by God for the establishment of the new Jerusalem. After Hofmann had gone on various journeys into

Friesland and Holland, a friend urged him to return to Strasbourg, predicting that he would spend six months in prison there but then, through his disciples, would spread his teaching all over the world. Hofmann eagerly obeyed the call, and returned to Strasbourg with the fondest hopes, for, according to his calculations, 1533 would be the year for the inauguration of the Messianic kingdom. As soon as he arrived, he began holding regular meetings in the Fossé-des-Tailleurs, behind the Dauphin, in the house of a goldsmith named Valentin Duft, and preparing his disciples for the great events to come.[28] In addition, he did not spare the preachers of the city but proclaimed to anyone who would listen that "Bucer had hidden the light from the people of Strasbourg";[29] moreover, he rejected several points of doctrine that were commonly preached: the two natures of Christ, predestination, and infant baptism. For these attacks the magistrate decided to put him in prison nine weeks after his arrival. Hofmann was overjoyed, as he saw the predictions being fulfilled. Meanwhile, groups of visionaries and enthusiasts were springing up on all sides, not only in Strasbourg around prophetesses like Barbe Rebstock, the wife of Hans Kropff,[30] but also in the surrounding villages, for example at Illkirch where Lienhard Jost, a shoemaker, and his wife Ursula, were strong supporters of Hofmann's ideas.[31] Far from being disheartened by the delay of the parousia and by the capture of Münzer, Hofmann hardened his position. In new memorials written in prison he claimed to Elijah returned to life in anticipation of the terrible day of the Lord, and he encouraged his disciples not to be troubled by the persecutions which might come upon them.[32] It was only after Hofmann's death in his Strasbourg prison around 1543 that the movement lost its force.

It is worth noting how far the politico-social ideas of Hofmann could lead. One of Hofmann's disciples, Nicholaus Frey, thought he could use Hofmann's writings to justify bigamy, which he interpreted as the kind of spiritual marriage which would be practiced in the last times. Frey was put to death for adultery in 1534.[33]

Finally, it is a curious fact that the people whom Hofmann stirred up were essentially from the lower middle class from the businessmen and artisans of the city.

* * *

We come to a third informal group: the spiritualists. Characteristic of them is an indifference toward the Church, from which they expect no help for their religious lives. The only things important to them were the direct inspiration of the Holy Spirit and the direct contact which they believed could be established with God. These people were deeply individualistic and acknowledged no obligation to belong to a Church, and no duty to establish a Church for the sake of other men. They were therefore naturally opposed to any attempt at ecclesiastical organization, being unable to understand its deeper necessity or its practical usefulness. At Strasbourg the uncontested leader of the spiritualists was the amiable and attractive Kaspar Schwenckfeld.[34] A native of Schlesien, he was a man of somewhat ambivalent and haughty temperament, but his sincere piety and theological culture set him above and apart from the other leaders of the group. He stayed at Strasbourg for four years, from 1529 to 1533, and appeared there again briefly in 1534, but his influence long survived his presence; this was due in part to the interest roused by his writings and in part to the attraction his ideas had for influential circles in the city, as well as to his continued epistolary contacts with his disciples there.

Schwenckfeld had managed to form a group made up of the ladies of the Strasbourg middle class, among them Katherine Zell, wife of the pastor of Saint-Laurent de la Cathédrale.[35] The latter remained his friend even after the estrangement between him and the preachers of the city. The preachers had accused Schwenckfeld of avoiding their churches and of speaking sarcastically of their sermons. Schwenckfeld's answer put the finger on the real conflict between him and the preachers: "If he were requiring too great a perfection from Christians and thus narrowing Christ, the preachers for their part were broadcasting Christ too much and making him too common."[36] What mattered for Schwenckfeld was the regeneration of the believer, and that could come about only through enlightenment by the Holy Spirit; such enlightenment, however, did not necessarily come by the external means of word and sacraments.

It is of interest that in the meeting-houses of the Schwenckfeldians spiritual conversation was accompanied by songs that were taken from the hymnal of the Moravian Brethren rather than from that of the established Church. In every city where Schwenckfeld stayed for however short a time, his passing left its trace in a collection of songs that displayed a more individualistic piety than did the Lutheran hymns. Thus, for example, we find Katherine Zell overseeing the publication of an adaptation, by Michael Weisse, of the songs from Czechoslovakia.[37]

At the end of the sixteenth century the Schwenckfeldian tradition will be carried on at Strasbourg by the fine poet and distinguished teacher, Daniel Sudermann, to whom we owe, among other things, the adaptation of Tauler's song, "Es kommt ein Schiff geladen".[38]

In addition to Schwenckfeld, in the same spiritualist line but more militant in his style, we have Sebastian Franck.[39] He was at Strasbourg in mid-1531 and gave his *Chronica* to Balthasar

Beck for publication.[40] The work caused an uproar, for in the last part of it, under cover of ancient events, Franck defended the heterodox movements and free thought; in the process he even co-opted Erasmus for his side.[41] The book was prohibited and Franck was expelled from the city.[42]

* * *

We can now see that communities of many kinds--anabaptist, millenarian, and spiritualist--were numerous in Strasbourg and attracted a good part of the population, including quite often the better elements in the parishes. Some were looking for a Church of professing Christians from which doubtful Christians would be excluded; others were not looking for a Church at all and preferred to allow the Spirit to act freely; almost all rejected the official Church because of their religious convictions. The official Church was thus confronted with a powerful movement, the origins of which in part were a good deal older than the Reformation and had traditionally drawn off a not negligable part of the population. As long as the Catholic Church was present in Strasbourg it was easy for it to defend itself thanks to its dogmatic and disciplinary weapons. But as soon as it was replaced by the Churches arising from the Reformation, the heterodox had a field day until these new Churches should in their turn acquire a firm set of doctrines and sufficiently strong institutions. In point of fact, little was done along this latter line from 1523 to 1533, that is, during the first ten years after the introduction of the Reformation to Strasbourg.

Moreover, as we saw at the beginning of this essay, the civil power refused to use coercion in matters of faith. It agreed to apply stern measures only on two occasions: the condemnation to death of Thomas Saltzmann in 1527 for well-known antitrinitarian blasphemies, and the condemnation of Nicholaus Frey in 1534 for adultery.[43] In a petition to the magistrate on October 16, 1532 the ministers loudly complained of the boldness of the sectaries "who had no qualms about preaching their errors openly."[44] Some weeks later, Bucer shared his fears with his friend Ambrosius Blaurer: "Pray for our Church, for the heretics are unbelievably active in trying to destroy it. We have been mistakenly easy on them, and the result is that they have made so much progress that we can neither support the evil situation nor find a way to remedy it."[45] Capito wrote in disillusionment to the same correspondent in 1534: "After all, the Strasbourg printers do a better business in sectarian books than in ours."[46]

What was to be done about the situation?[47] To put an end to the uncertainties and fluctuations which were inevitable in any system that simply reacted to particular cases, the reformers decided to determine the official beliefs of their Church and to give the Church precise rules and regulations. They convoked a synod in 1533, with the cooperation and under the direction of the magistrate. For, in Bucer's view, the carrying out of the Christian ideal was not the business of the Church alone; the first duty of the state, too, was to foster true religion by providing the Church with the necessary means of action. The synod took the whole situation for its agenda, and definitively decided on the broad lines of ecclesiastical organization. The next year, in 1534, the magistrate issued an "Ecclesiastical Ordinance" which gave legal force to most of the synodal decisions.[48] Simultaneously with the appearance of this ordinance, Bucer published the first official catechism of the Church of Strasbourg.[49] Thus the results of the Reformation were codified in both the administrative and the spiritual spheres.

* * *

The act of construction was thus carried through successfully, but it showed certain practical defects.[50] In the area of discipline, in particular, the measures taken never functioned as Bucer would have wished. Thus the ministry of the elders or churchwardens (*Kirchenpfleger*) never acquired the importance Bucer wanted it to have. Like the elders of the early Church, the churchwardens were to see to it that due order was observed in all that went on in the parishes, in regard to the profession of the faith, the moral life, and administration. But the way in which the wardens were recruited and appointed prevented the institution from working. The elders, three to a parish, were appointed by the magistrate; one was a counciller, another a deputy magistrate, and a third a well-known burger. The Church had no say in the choice, which was guided less by religious or ecclesiastical considerations than motives of domestic politics. In fact, the names of the elders as shown in contemporary documents are almost always those of the men who were the leaders in Strasbourg politics. Among them there were indeed men with deep concern for religion,[51] but how many citizens, well-known as substantial merchants or well-off artisans, would not have hesitated to compromise their social or professional relationships by censoring the religious ideas or moral conduct of their fellow-citizens? The churchwardens had no desire to be regarded as the kind of elders found in the early Church; their administration was poor; and the magistrate was unwilling to surrender something he regarded as a right of office: the right to excommunicate.

Realizing that his efforts were not achieving the desired results, Bucer ceased relying on the magistrate and advocated an entirely new course of action. Here he was an innovator, for this time he attempted to solve the problem of discipline exclusively by means of the Church itself. In three papers of 1546 and 1547, Bucer called for the establishment within each parish (*Gemeinde*) of a community (*Gemeinschaft*).[52] To put an end to the confusion caused by the informal groups, he was recommending the formation of informal groups within the Church. He agreed with the sectaries that the Church cannot exist without discipline. Therefore he sought to create cells of committed people who would freely submit to discipline and would have no ambition except to be the leaven in the mass. Here we have "the little Church within the Church", so much so that when Spener would launch his idea of the *collegia pietatis*, he would cover himself with Bucer's authority by republishing the latter's third paper in 1691 and again in 1692. There is thus a clear dependence on the historical scene of what would later be called pietism.[53]

The question remains whether the community of professing Christians will manage to transform the Church of the masses, or whether the unity of the Church will not be undermined by having two distinct ecclesiological entities, really two Churches, one made up of the masses, the other of professing Christians, and both in the same place. As it has developed historically, Protestantism has known the two forms of Church; in their action and reaction they have had their moments of fruitfulness and their moments of tension.

CHAPTER 10

Informal Religious Groups of European Origin
in the United States
during the First Half of the Nineteenth Century

by

Julien Freund

Many Europeans in the last century thought of America, that is, the vast area of the present-day United States, as a promised land which would provide a refuge from European society with its fixed political, economic, and religious organization, with its mentality, traditions, and geographic and spiritual divisions. The West was the land of adventure for the men with strange dreams; it was the land of good fortune for those who thought themselves condemned to live in poverty; the land of religious freedom for all who yearned for a new faith, and for the heterodox whether they were millenarists or simply dissenters. At the end of the seventeenth century and even more during the eighteenth, the new sects which were oppressed by the official Churches of Germany or England had already sought refuge across the Atlantic. To name but a few typical groups, there were the Quakers who under William Penn's direction established the present-day state of Pennsylvania; the Moravian Brethren who founded the community of Bethlehem in Pennsylvania, which today has become a great center of arms manufacture, and the Shakers, under Ann Lee, who settled in the Niskayuna Valley near Albany. There is room for extensive study of these little known American religious communities and their social, religious, and millenarist conceptions.

234

The movement to America only grew during the first half of the nineteenth century, because to the religious sects there were now added the experiments of such European social reformers as François-Charles Fourier, Robert Owen, and Etienne Cabet, whose disciples saw America as the ideal place for creating a new society. It is evident that the theme of a new society, so much on people's lips today, is not of recent origin; people have been dreaming of such a society for a century and a half. How many experiments America has seen!--and all have failed. Of the 232 communities known to me, 91 did not last more than ten years, 59 lasted only five, 50 only two, and 32 but a year and a half. A few rare exceptions managed to endure over a century, especially the Ephrata community, the Shaker community, and the Harmony community, all of which will concern us later on.[1] If we look for the moment only at the quantitative side, we will observe that there were about ten communities deriving from Robert Owen, about thirty from Charles Fourier, two attempts at communities deriving from Cabet, to say nothing of communities that were purely American in origin and in no way dependent on European ideologies, such as Brook Farm, Hopedale Community, Mountain Cove Community, and the most famous of all, the Oneida Community. The study of these various communities is important not only for history and religious sociology, but also for economic sociology and the history of the various types of communism.

The preceding data has been given for several reasons. To begin with, they help understand the context of the informal groups which we shall be studying. America during the period in question was a vast testing-ground for social experiments that were religious or socialist in origin, and usually both at once. It is true enough that the United States have been

the promised land of capitalism, but before this form of
economy became predominant, people had tried other ways,
especially socialism. Because of stereotypes which create an
intellectual blind spot, we have trouble now in grasping the
importance of the socialist current in the United States during
the nineteenth century. Yet most of the great names in American
literature and many journalists as well accepted the socialist
ideology. I am even inclined to believe that one reason for the
rapid growth of capitalism at the end of the century was the
failure of attempts at socialist organization, for the failure
left a deep mark on American intellectuals. In fact, some
communities managed to survive only because, once aware of the
obstacles to a life in accord with authentic socialist principles, they shifted over to the capitalist system. It is even
the case that a number of American economic societies originated
directly in the socialist communities. If we want a proper
understanding of this period of American history, I think it
is basic to realize that for the communities in question
socialism was not simply an economic system, but also a morality and a life-style connected with religious practices, and
that in consequence it was not only a principle for organizing
the life of the community as such but also an experiment that
marked the personal life of each member.

In the second place, it would be a mistake, sociologically
speaking, to separate the attempts to find a new religious life
from the attempts to shape a new economy. I will not discuss
here Max Weber's well-known thesis, except to say that one
could extend and supplement it by showing that not only does
it help explain the relations between Calvinism and capitalism,
but it also has a more general value, inasmuch as one could
show other kinds of relationships between economics and religion,

even if these took a different direction than the Calvinism-capitalism relationship.

Finally, although the religious groups went their own ways with their experiments, relationships existed nonetheless between communities that were inspired by socialist economics and those whose inspiration was essentially religious. This was especially true of Owen's communities and those of Rapp's Harmonists. Many other instances could also be cited.

We shall restrict our study to groups of European origin; of these we shall choose those that seem most typical.[2]

* * *

In the eighteenth century the informal groups which sought refuge in the United States were of Anglo-Saxon origin, but in the nineteenth they were mostly German and sometimes Scandinavian.

1) The best known of the communities was the Separatists (as they were called in Germany) or Harmonists (their American name) or Rappists (from their founder, Johann Georg Rapp, born at Iptingen, Württemberg, in 1757). Georg Rapp was a weaver who had taken part in the religious disputes (pietism, millenarianism) which were rife in the country areas of Württemberg; he soon left the official Church and founded his own sect. At this period his teaching was essentially millenarian in character, being marked by a rejection of the civil powers and of military service. To escape the persecution leveled against the sect, he decided in 1803 to go to America. He himself went on ahead with his sons and two other members of the sect, and bought a 5,000 acre tract of land in Butler County, north of Pittsburgh; the rest of the sect, about 600 persons, mostly peasants and manual workers, followed in 1805.

The problem of economic organization quickly proved urgent. Back in Württemberg the sect had been able to get along without too many economic difficulties and on a very informal basis, because each member had his own home. The situation was entirely different in America when 600 persons of little means had to live together in a state of insecurity on land that was almost entirely uncultivated. In a covenant of February 15, 1805, Rapp turned the sect into a community in which each member turned all his possessions over to the new organization. The basic principle to be followed was equality and harmony; this accounts for the name Harmony Society which was soon adopted. Under the influence of a new inspiration the community decided in 1807 to live as much as possible after the fashion of the early Christians. Up to this point, despite the community of goods, the members had lived in their separate families. Now they abandoned marriage and chose celibacy, with men and women living separately in different buildings. Those who rejected the reform left the group.

Despite this change the community prospered quickly. In 1814 it sold Harmony and took up residence on 20,000 acres in Posey County, Indiana; the colony was given the name New Harmony. Economically, the community continued to prosper. For reasons, however, of climate and of diseases that decimated the membership, Rapp sold the acreage to Robert Owen, who wanted it for a communist experiment along his own lines. The sect returned to Pennsylvania in 1824 and settled not far from the original Harmony, in a new colony that took the name Economy. The place became an important commercial and even industrial center, although it received a setback in 1831 when a new member, a German adventurer named Bernard Muller who called himself Count Maximilian von Leon, rebelled against the authorities. He challenged Rapp's authority, and demanded in particular a return to marriage. The community was divided on the issue; a referendum was held, and 500 members sided with Rapp, about

250 with Leon. The minority then received the sum of 105,000 dollars and established another community not far away, but it was threatened with extinction after only a year; the members scattered after a vain attempt to take over the mother community which was still under Rapp's control. After Rapp's death in 1846 Economy in its turn was endangered, because the prohibition against marriage made it impossible to recruit enough new members. On this account the community had to rely increasingly on outside manpower. Yet the community continued in existence until the beginning of the present century when the two last survivors finally willed the whole operation, in 1908, to a single young heir.

We must note, in regard to religious teaching (in addition to the indications already given), that the sect continued to evolve after leaving Germany. When it first came to the United States, the sect was simply a dissenting form of Württemberg pietism with the accent on milleniarism and opposition to established authority. Once established in America, and especially after the inspiration of 1807 due to which the structures of the colony were modified, the sect came close to the Shakers in its teaching. In this conception God is a dual figure, containing both the masculine and feminine principles; but the unity of the two principles was broken by the sin of Adam in consequence of the separation of the feminine principle. This accounts for the belief that celibacy is more pleasing to God than marriage. The original milleniarist expectation of the Harmonists now became concretized as the hope of a new coming of Christ on earth to establish a kingdom of happiness for all mankind. Unlike the Shakers, however, the Harmonists made the community as such, and not the family, the basic unit of organization.

At Economy the members lived in groups of four to eight people in separate houses, each group (composed solely of men

or of women) thus forming a distinct household. The economic
structure was communist, but the communism was of a rather
capitalist variety. By this is meant that although the individual members accepted the discipline of a strict sharing
of possessions, the community as such was very rich, not only
because it owned the splendid lands on which the colony lived
but also because it possessed a large fortune in shares in coal
mines, oil wells, saw-mills, and other enterprises. It was this
fortune that enabled the community, despite its ever decreasing
numbers, to survive into the early twentieth century.

With the Harmonists can be compared the Zoarists, a
community established by another pietist dissenter from Württemberg, Joseph Bäumeler, in 1817, at Zoar in Tuscarawas County,
Ohio. The principles accepted by the two groups were similar:
sharing of goods along with a large capital in the form of
shares; life-style like that of the early Christians; celibacy;
refusal of military service; etc. However, beginning in 1828
marriage was permitted (Bäumeler himself married), but sexual
relations for any purpose but reproduction were forbidden.
Marriage was only tolerated and the community continued to
regard celibacy as a superior state and one that was more in
accord with Christian principles and the community of possessions.
The sect had another peculiarity, at least until the change
legitimizing marriage: it had two kinds of members. There
were members with full rights, and there were novices. The
latter group passed through a one-year period in which they
still kept the right to individual ownership, although they
deposited all their money with the community as a pledge; otherwise they lived like the other members. If after their novitiate
they still wanted to live with the community, they entered into
a contract with the sect, gave up all personal possessions, and
were accepted as full members. If they wanted to leave instead,

they could do so, and received back their monetary pledge in full.

At the end of the century the community became shaky by reason of financial maladministration, and finally the 222 members decided to dissolve it in 1898 and to divide up the 350,000 dollars still left of their capital.

2) The origin of the Bethel and Aurora communities was quite different from that of the communities we have been describing thus far. Bethel and Aurora were founded by a Prussian immigrant named Keil, who was a tailor by trade but passed himself off as a doctor in America. When he came to the United States in 1838, he first attended the Methodist Church but soon left it to start his own sect which was made up for the most part of German immigrants who had not been able to integrate themselves into American society. Keil bought 2,000 acres at Bethel in Shelby County, Missouri. The community there was augmented in numbers by followers of Bernard Muller ("Count Maximilian von Leon") after their split from Rapp's community had proved a failure. The community's land holdings also increased and the community built a saw-mill, a distillery, and a textile factory, although agriculture continued to be its chief occupation. Internal dissension led Keil to hand leadership of the community over to his assistant. Keil and some other members then went westward and founded a new community, named Aurora, on 18,000 acres in Oregon. The new colony quickly became larger than the mother community, with about 1,000 members to Bethel's 500.

Unlike the Harmonist and Zoarist communities, religion here played a less significant role. Keil was indeed the leader of a sect, but he also accepted members of other sects, imposing on them only the obligation of attending a Sunday service which Keil himself organized. The communist structures

were also less rigid. In fact, the basic principles of the two
types of community were different. At Bethel the community as
such owned all the shared possessions, but each family had its
own house and certain possessions assigned to it. In 1850 a
number of members demanded their share in the common possessions
and the profits the community had made; as a result, a general
division was made, with every member receiving his or her share.
The majority then put their shares back into a common fund,
while the others sold off their shares to outsiders and left the
community. The result was an anomalous situation in the village
of Bethel since a community-based system now existed side by
side with independent holdings by individuals. This state of
affairs contributed to the deterioration of Bethel, once Keil
had left for Oregon. Keil learned from the experience and
while maintaining a community of goods and services, had all the
holdings of the Aurora community legally registered under his
own name. He could thus run things as he chose, with a council
of four. He died in 1877 at Aurora. In 1880 the Bethel community
which had been in a decline for some years was dissolved; in
the following year Aurora was also dissolved because a successor
could not be found who would be able to administer the common
possessions; the latter were then divided up among the members.

3) The style of the Inspirationist sect was different
again from either of the preceding types. It too originated
in Germany. The Inspirationist movement was already known in
Westphalia in the seventeenth century and in Hesse in the
eighteenth where its leader was a Lutheran pastor, E. L. Gruber.
It received new vital impulses in the Strasbourg area at the
beginning of the nineteenth century, thanks to the influence
of the Strasbourg illuminist, Krausert. Soon two other illuminists, Barbara Heinemann, a Strasbourg servant-girl, and Christian
Metz, a German, gathered disciples all along the Rhine. According to their teaching, God would continue to act as he had with

the first generation of Christians and give the world messages through the mouths of prophets. The growth of the "Communities of True Inspiration" finally disturbed the official Churches. In the face of persecution some members of the sect took refuge first at Marienborn, where they made a first attempt at an economic community, then in the old monastery at Arnsberg, and finally at Engenthal. It was in the last named place that Barbara Heinemann married Georg Landmann, a member of the sect, and lost her gift of inspiration, so that Christian Metz was left as sole leader of the community. Weary of persecution, in 1839 Landmann decided to go to America. Four illuminists went ahead and bought a piece of land near Buffalo, New York, and founded the Ebenezer Society. About 800 members joined them the following year. As other members continued to flee Europe, the property quickly became too small. Under an inspiration given to Christian Metz they trekked westward and settled at Amana, Iowa, not far from Iowa City and Marengo. In 1849 Barbara recovered her gift of inspiration. The community flourished and continued to do so after the death of Metz in 1867 and of Barbara in 1883. But once they were gone, there were no more illuminists.

As in the other communities we have been describing, the members of this one were chiefly farmers and manual workers. In addition to agriculture, their principal activity, they established saw-mills, tile-works, soap-factories, and even a printing-house. Of all the communities we have mentioned Amana was undoubtedly the most prosperous; it was also the most numerous. Around 1900 it had a population of more than 3000, living in various villages: Amana Center (about 500 members), East Amana (about 100), West Amana (about 200), South Amana (about 200), Middle Amana (about 400), Upper Amana (about 800), and Homestead (about 200). The community had

other special characteristics. First of all, it had a gift
for organization: it had a school next to the large meeting
hall, its own railroad station and post-office, and a hotel for
visitors. It employed about 300 farm workers who did not belong
to the community. This organizational sense is probably due to
the fact that, unlike the other sects, this one had already
tried experiments in communal living before leaving Europe for
America. The constitution which regulated the community had
been drawn up as a result of inspirations given to its leaders;
the following are its main principles:

a) community of goods and shared labor, but no common
life except for meals which were taken in common in the dining
hall of each village. Each family lived in its own house; the
houses belonged to the community but the furniture did not.

b) austerity, which was practiced in a somewhat fanatical
spirit, although as time passed the rules became more flexible.
Thus in time the prohibition against music was lifted.

c) celibacy was recommended and marriage only tolerated.
A man was forbidden to marry before his twenty-fourth year,
and if he married a woman from outside the community, he was
excluded from the community for a time, even though his wife
intended to join the sect. A strict separation of the sexes was
practiced in all affairs of daily routine. Further obligations
were the reading of the Bible and manual labor for all, although
young people with ability could continue their studies in the
American universities.

d) each village kept its own books and therefore a degree
of autonomy. The whole community was ruled by thirteen trustees.

e) each member was allowed a certain sum for personal
needs, in the form of a credit in his name. In this way he
could buy various things he wanted in the community stores.
He could not simply make an independent disposition of the

money allowed him. The sum was, clearly, more important to a young man doing his studies outside the community.

In practice, the community was made up only of Germans, because no one could share in the community worship unless he knew German. There were three categories of members: the elders, the ordinary members, and the novices and children. For lack of recruits the membership kept diminishing after the First World War, and in 1932 the constitution was changed to make the community more of a cooperative; communal elements were played down, and individualist aspects heightened.

4) We may also mention the Swedish community at Bishop Hill, Illinois. Its existence was constantly threatened by internal dissension. The sect in question was a pietist one founded around 1830 by Eric Janson, a Swede. Back in Sweden the sect had tried to return to the ways of the first Christian community by establishing a common life. The hostility of the official Church caused the community to emigrate to America in 1845; here Olaf Olson, a member of the sect, had bought some land at Bishop Hill. Despite financial aid which a brother of the founder brought from Sweden in 1850 and which enabled the community to extend its land holdings, the group split in two: the disciples of Olaf Olson wanted to maintain the principles of the community, while the followers of Olaf Janson (the above-mentioned brother of the founder, who had been physically attacked by a member of the sect) wanted to dissolve the community and divide up its holdings among the members. In 1862 the community ceased to exist. Its principles were those of the other communities we have seen: preference for celibacy, community of goods. But the principles were hardly applied in practice, because the general assembly held each week constantly gave rise to disputes. This experiment must therefore be listed among the ephemeral ones.

We must also be content to say a few words about the Hutterites who came to America in 1875 after journeyings which led them, in the course of several centuries, from Transylvania to Wallachia and then to Russia which they abandoned finally out of opposition to military service. Originally, the Hutterites were not informal groups; they developed into such as a result of the countless difficulties they met with before being able to establish themselves in America and at Tabor, South Dakota, in particular. What is notable about them is that after having been forced by circumstances to abandon their original common life and even having converted to Catholicism during their stay in Hungary, they recovered both their first religion and their early life-style. Here we have a rare case in which a sect abandoned the communist style and later regained it; the Hutterites did so in the form of the *Bruderhöfe* (shared households) which they established in America. But this last remark requires qualification: it was only the Hutterites from Huttersdorf that went back to communal life; those from Huttersthal and Johannesrück kept the system of individual farms. The former received financial help for their undertaking from the Amana community. There are still some Hutterite communities in Canada which live according to the rules drawn up more than 400 years ago: common life in a common house in which each family has a dormitory but no other personal possessions, whether furniture or clothing.

* * *

If we want a sociological understanding of this migration of informal groups from Europe to America, we must keep several points in mind.

1) All the groups developed toward the communal lifestyle; some went as far as a full-fledged communism. (One or other group [the Inspirationists and the Swedish Pietists] tried this life-style in Europe, but unsuccessfully.) This general fact raises several questions.

a) Were the groups better integrated in America than in Europe? It does not seem so. When they established their communities in America, they remained apart from American life, except in some aspects of their economic activity, just as they had lived apart in Europe. The only difference was that in America they could freely practice their religion and were rid of the pressures that made their life burdensome in Europe. What is noteworthy, in fact, is that in America they did not try to attach themselves to any larger religious or ecclesial organization but retained a closed circle of beliefs and life-style, allowing their faith to die out as the community itself died. That is what happened to the Harmonists and Zoarists and to the followers of Keil and Janson. The same thing will very likely happen to the Inspirationists of Amana. In other words: As in Europe, so in America they refused any integration with a larger society; they continued to be isolated groups.

b) Why did such groups evolve in the direction of a communal life-style? There are several possible explanations which are not exclusive of one another. During the period in question, most of the reformist groups were hostile to the new industrial society which was coming into existence, and the notion of community—in the various forms of communionism, the Fourierist phalanstery, etc.—seemed to offer a solution to their social problems. The same explanation seems to hold for sects which were not only anticonformist in spirit but had always had a tendency to form closed communities.

In addition, there is the fact that the members of these
groups, scattered until then in the villages or cities where
they had their homes, now suddenly found themselves brought
together on a ship and, after debarkation, thrown together in
difficult, and sometimes wretched circumstances. To this extent
they were already a community, and their sense of isolation in
a foreign land could only reinforce the feeling. They had come
together, and they would remain together, for they now shared a
common destiny. It would, however, be wrong to attribute
their community spirit solely to these circumstances, even
though the latter played an important psychological role. For
it is a fact that the will to community existed before their
departure for America, inasmuch as, with the exception of Keil's
group, they sent emissaries and scouts ahead to America in order
to buy land for the projected community. Moreover, for most of
the groups, the idea of forming a community like that of the
early Christians, that is, a religious motivation, was part of
their intention at the time they landed in America.

In any event, I think it necessary to look for a deeper
explanation in the fact that their very informality contained
a thrust toward community. We may explain what is meant by
applying Ferdinand Tönnies' categories of community and society.
If sects and informal groups lived on the periphery of society,
with the more or less avowed or formulated purpose of breaking
the social bond which they found burdensome precisely because
it was something established and already fully formed, the
reason is that they were trying to discover or rediscover a
different style of personal relationships which they could regard as more authentic. For most of these groups the community
was the place where such separations and rebellions could become
a reality, where aspirations could be fulfilled and freedom
from the social yoke be to some extent realized. This interpretation seems confirmed by the fact that it can also be

applied to the informal groups of the Middle Ages and the Renaissance and to contemporary marginal groups such as the hippies or some of the little coteries to be found in Paris. However rationally organized society may be, indeed perhaps for that very reason, it is also the place of damnation because intimacy, faith, trust, and ultimately security have all been lost. When everything is established, defined, and marked out in advance, what room is left for spontaneity and the will to create? I simply ask the question here, for I am aware that it can be rightly argued that creativity needs to accept restraints and rules. It may be, then, that a phenomenology of creativity is impossible.

c) The preceding question seems all the more pertinent as, apart from the Amana community, which was remarkably well organized, all the communities declined after the death of their founder. So too, when the leader left the mother colony to found another, the former slowly declined. Thus it can be said that once the inspiring leader was gone, the communities drifted, despite their constitution, as if an informal group found itself unable to accept routine. Moreover, most of the communities we have examined had several successive constitutions due to new inspirations received by the founder; this seems to indicate that a charism was required even while the leader was still alive and present. The communities seem to have survived only because of constant innovations, although the survival supposes that the leader in charge had sufficient authority to impose the innovation. In other words, an informal group continues to exist only because of the qualities of its leader and it goes under when the leader is gone; moreover, the group has but a very ephemeral existence if the founder lacks personality, as may be seen by the numerous failures of American communities in the nineteenth century. The Amana community provides an indirect confirmation

that the more informal the group, the more need it has of a
strong authority figure, since he is the form without which
it cannot perdure. A community usually experiences a very
intense life for a short time, and thus gives the impression
of greater authenticity than society at large enjoys; but the
community also usually lacks the juridical and other mechanisms
which would give it the continuity a society has. When a rule
of life is subordinated to the caprice of inspiration, it cannot provide stability.

d) Is communism a formula which works only for small
groups, that is, communities with a limited number of members,
but not for large-scale societies? In answer it can be said
that, up to now at least, the history of communist efforts
shows only small communities succeeding in applying communism
on a more or less long-term basis. For large scale societies
communism continues to be a goal for some future day, a utopia--
unless, of course, we confuse socialism and communism, as is too
often done even by the best economic theorists. Of its nature
communism is a closed economic system, and it is probably for
this reason that it works only for a closed society. Communism
indeed has other aspects than the economic, for it is a whole
life-style, but from the economic viewpoint it is primarily
a system of internal management that can be adapted to any
system whatever of external economy, including the capitalist
system of our day, just as in the Middle Ages and the Renaissance
it fitted into the whole surrounding economy, agrarian, commercial, or manufacturing. In other words, the possessions of the
community may consist of personal goods and real estate or of
goods produced by the members, but the overall wealth can be made
productive by saving, investment, or shares in external economic
ventures, without the internal community of goods being at all
affected.

The groups we have been studying were all preoccupied with
another problem that occurs in almost all communities of
communist orientation, in whatever historical period. It is
the problem of sexuality: Shall there be a sharing of wives,
or shall celibacy be the rule? These are the logical alternatives. Because the groups in question were deeply Christian,
they chose celibacy. All of them considered marriage as a
system less in keeping with community of possessions, because
it introduced a rival unit, the family. The history of communist attempts is very instructive in this area. A sharing of
women has been a matter chiefly of theory, and the rare practical applications of it have quickly foundered. The only communistic communities that have lasted have been those based on
celibacy and a consequent regulation of sexuality. Thus there
seems to be a logical affinity between communism and sexuality,
in the direction not of greater freedom but of greater constraint. The communities we have examined do not belie this
statement, for their practical experiments with communism have
led them all to give preference to celibacy and even to modify
their constitutions so as to make it obligatory, in order to
preserve their unity.[3]

2) All these informal groups have had a religious basis.
The communities grew out of a sect whose own existence up to
that point had been completely informal. The communities we
have examined, with the exception of Bethel and Aurora, sprang
from pietism. The latter, along with anabaptism, is the form
of Protestantism most open to prophetism and millenarianism,
and responsive to the special charism of the inspired individual.
Yet millenarianism played a less important role in their origins
than it did in such eighteenth century sects as the Shakers.
At any rate, we have here a problem of filiations and correspondences which has occupied the interest of religious sociology
since the days of Ernst Troeltsch and Max Weber.

What chiefly concerns us here is the way in which these sects conceived the relation between the temporal and the spiritual. Typically--and the communities we have examined fit the pattern--they have generally adopted a negative attitude to the political sphere but a positive one to the economic. In a way this is quite understandable. Religious conviction may initially bring together very disparate individuals, but a community cannot perdure unless it can guarantee its membership a degree of material security. The decline of many communities, that of Bishop Hill, for example is due to material difficulties that could not be resolved because of the internal dissensions they created. Consequently the internal solidarity of these communities was due as much to the material well-being they afforded as to the religious convictions which had given rise to their existence.

What is more surprising is that, unlike groups based on egalitarian but non-religious doctrines, such as the teaching of Babeuf, the communities we have been studying were not content with a "decent livelihood" but attempted to become as flourishing as possible, even by putting the whole of the community's wealth into a capitalist system whose political orientation they rejected. At Amana the sect even became a springboard for the social ascent of the membership. It is true enough that these communities did not play a key role in the general transformation of the economy, but neither did they reject or fight against that transformation, despite the asceticism being practiced within the membership itself. Concern for authentic religious communion, for scrupulous purity, and for moral worthiness meant a rupture between the life of the community and the life of the rest of society, but the break did not affect the economic sphere.

The attitude of the groups to the political order is perhaps more complicated. They did not refuse politics as such;

on the contrary they accepted it, at least implicitly, inasmuch as, given their informality, they could not continue to exist without some minimum of protection and general order. Moreover, it was in order to find in freedom a greater security that the sects left Germany and came to America where they established their communities. But the communities did not give preference to one political regime or orientation over others; they were not centers of rebellion. What they rejected were, in essence, certain concomitants of the political order: violence and military service. On the other hand, they paid their taxes. Their attitude was grounded in the principle that it is better to obey God than men. The words "it is better" sums up their position rather well: once the community offered its members the possibility of obeying God, why spoil the system unnecessarily by introducing the element of obedience to men? In point of fact, under guise of self-administration and at times of a closed economic system they believed that they were submitting to God's will in accepting as a norm the inspiration given to their leader. Therefore they had no need of any authority outside the group, once the "Spirit" had manifested himself directly to someone within the group. In the last analysis, however, the communities contained within themselves a substitute for the political order: a directing officer and, usually, weekly assemblies during which the life of the community was discussed.

3) Some elements in the make-up of these communities suggest that they are parallel to monastic communities: for example, the novitiate, the internal magistracy and strict discipline, celibacy, the welcome given to a brother from another colony of the sect as though he were a member of the community. It is tempting, therefore, to look upon the communities as a "secularization" of monastic life, or inversely, in

Max Weber's phrase, as a "clericalization of lay life". But, remarkable though the analogies are, we cannot really give them the same meaning in both cases. The outwardly similar manifestations are connected in each case with specific differences; thus the fact that monks belong to a Church gives the life of a religious order a different meaning than the life of a sectarian community has; so too the importance of the laity in a sect has no parallel in a monastery whose members are usually only priests and others with a parasacerdotal vocation. In addition, most of the analogies we have pointed out are not peculiar to religious orders and sects, but are to be found in every closed spiritual community, whether or not it be religious.

Much more specific to communities based on a sect is the fact that they challenge authority in society, even though within themselves they may have allowed their founders (Rapp or Keil, for example) an almost autocratic power. From the viewpoint of society at large these communities are antiauthoritarian formations. This, not only because the communities have no interest in the political order or even in anything that goes on outside themselves, but also because they came into existence through schism within an established Church whose authority they refused any longer to recognize. They came into being through a breakaway and an act of self-isolation, even in regard to the rest of those who share a common Christian faith. Characteristic of these communities, then, is the will to achieve autonomy so as to protect some special belief or sometimes just one aspect or interpretation of a generally accepted belief (even though the latter itself may have been proper to a relatively small group). The communities in question thus represent a threat of anarchy by their refusal of the generally accepted rule.

* * *

If we look at these communities from the perspective of the whole phenomenon of sectarianism in America, we must say that, however original they may have been, they have counted for little when we consider the preponderant influence of the Quakers, the Methodists, the Baptists, and others. Nonetheless our sects do bear witness to the general spirit that animates the American mentality and American civilization. In America sectarian religiosity played a basic role, despite the separation of Church and State, since in some regions, for example at New Haven, connection with a sect was "a prior condition for acquiring citizenship". It is, of course, rather surprising, that a situation apparently so anarchic (because of the autonomy and exclusivity of the religious groups) should produce the cohesion needed for so vast a nation.

Nowadays, of course, the sects are clearly losing their importance, and the fact of belonging to one no longer guarantees civic and social respectability. But the general spirit to which the sects gave rise lives on in new forms, for the United States continues to be the promised land for informal groups of every kind: religious, ideological, ethnical, and so forth. These groups continue to display an anti-authoritarian attitude, such as is today attracting many young Europeans. The sectarian spirit survives in the little informal groups of students and other young people who, while decrying capitalism and imperialism, think they have discovered another America: the America of the sects. Europeans will soon be only imitators.

PART III

Theological Reflection

CHAPTER 11

Informal Groups in the Church:
A Protestant Viewpoint

by

Roger Mehl

The appearance in recent decades of informal groups within the Church and on the periphery of the Church is doubtless not a completely new historical event. Pietism had already produced its devotional circles and Methodism its "classes", and these creations have had their modest prolongations down to our own time.

What is new is the motivations at work. These make it clear that a crisis is at hand for ecclesiastical institutions, for the Church itself, for the Church-world relationship, and for theology. Our effort here will be to specify these motivations and to gauge their theological value.

The term "informal groups" obviously derives from sociology. The groups themselves do not all accept it but prefer other names: base communities, underground Church, etc. The name "base community" expresses the desire to find what the Church so rarely provides: the experience of brotherhood and community. The name "underground Church" brings out more clearly the semi-clandestine and revolutionary nature of the groups. But the sociological name is also very meaningful. For, in fact, these groups are protesting against the *form* of the Church, against the Church as *established* and *institutionalized*, the Church which manages its relations with other kinds of institution (especially power) by dealing as one possessor of power with another. The protest of the informal groups is part of a general movement of radical challenge that is typical of overorganized modern society. In this movement institutions are seen as essentially oppressive and alienating and as paralyzing every attempt at innovation and, as far as the Church is concerned, any evangelical daring.

In this opposition to institutions there is undoubtedly some naivete or latent anarchism. The anarchism moreover will not stand the test of time. Thus in West Germany informal Protestant groups form well-organized networks and often set up parallel institutions in opposition to those of the established Church.[1] But we can hardly blame the informal groups for this relapse into the institutional. After all, they find themselves in a situation that is somewhat analogous with that of the groups who paved the way for the sixteenth century Reformation. At that time there was a lengthy period when the Reformation was a more or less underground movement within the Church,[2] and when the idea of organizing their protest was absent. This idea came only later on when the break had been accomplished. Even then the institutional aspect did not play a decisive role in the new ecclesiology. This aspect was passed over in silence in Lutheranism and reduced to a strict minimum in Calvinism. Like our present-day informal groups, the Reformers distrusted institutions. In their eyes, to have the Church it was necessary and sufficient that the Gospel be correctly preached and that the sacraments be administered in conformity with the Gospel; in short, that there be a ministry of word and sacrament. But the very success of the Reformation and the need of protecting itself against the "leftists" of the day (the *Schwärmer*, or enthusiasts, or visionaries) obliged the Reformers to surround this ministry with a whole institutional framework. Soon came the

age of what Emile G. Léonard has called "the establishment".
Thus the blanket denunciation of the institution is typical of
all new beginnings in the Church.

The protests of the informal groups are levelled at two
particular aspects of the ecclesiastical institution: the
hierarchy and the parish. This particularization is, in my
view, much more important than their undiscriminating attack
on the institutional as such.

The hierarchy, which in Protestantism is made up of a pyramid of assemblies or councils (each of them having at their head
a president or possibly an elected bishop) has, in the eyes of
the informal groups, the defects of every representative regime.
For it involves from top to bottom a process of selection which
is based on cultural and social norms and leads to the establishment of an ecclesiastical class (analogous to a political
class) which is slow to renew itself, excludes women and young
people, is characterized by prudence rather than daring, and is
based on tradition rather than the Gospel. This hierarchy with
its gradations, fixed rules, and incense-boats gives the impression
that it exists for its own sake and not in order to be at the
service of men. Even if there be no specific link or direct
interest, the hierarchy is nonetheless on the side of order and
thus of power. Thus the ecclesiastical establishment is united
with and supports the political establishment.

A Church which is on good terms with those in power and at
least accepts the latter's value-system can certainly not be
the Church of the poor, the oppressed, and the abandoned. It
is useless for its hierarchy to affirm the Church's neutrality,
for this very neutrality tends, consciously or not, to avoid
embarrassing those in power and thus is already an act of
political allegiance. Thus by its very structures the Church
continues to stand by the Constantinian arrangement.

Furthermore, every hierarchy in the Church is an *episkopē* or overseership, to which a ministry of unity is entrusted. The will to preserve unity, or, if need be, restore it serves as an excuse for excluding from the precincts of the Church the discussion of any burning question (including political and social questions) that might cause division. Instead of being, as the first generation of ecumenists believed, a leaven of renewal, the quest for unity has become in fact an excuse for preserving the status quo, within which unions may indeed be effected but unions which are interested only in eliminating past disputes (an easy job, since no one is concerned with them any more!) and have no vision for the future. That is, the people united feel no anguish about the injustice in the world and the suffering of men whose dignity is flouted. Thus the criticism of the ecclesiastical institution also embraces ecumenism to the extent that the latter proves to be simply a series of polite conversations and summit meetings.[3] The informal groups have their own ecumenical vision, but it is not that of official ecumenism, which they consider hopeless. Theirs is a "wildcat" ecumenism in which confessional barriers are joyfully ignored and bold commitments in behalf of peoples victimized by war or oppression are easily possible.

As for the parish, the criticism of the informal groups is directed essentially against its introverted nature. The parish is a marginal society and is content to be such; it practices a kind of self-consumption. At its best it seeks to build itself up and draw sharply the boundary line between itself and "the world". In social composition it is made up chiefly of elderly people, children, adolescents, and people who are not part of the active population, or of men and women who are active enough but are looking to the Church for security. They want the Church to be a refuge where they can find shelter from the struggles of the world, live a purely individual life of devotion, and cultivate an abstract interior life. The parish thus turned in on itself, its pastoral ministry taking the form of a timeless kind of preaching and a care of souls that is interested only in the little problems of individuals and married people, is, in the eyes of the informal groups, doomed to perish. Only an authentic involvement in the struggles of our time might save it, but the parish is clearly incapable of such involvement. It is all the less capable since it counts among its members hardly any workers, militants, or students; in short, the social categories which offer hope for the future are missing from the parish or have abandoned it.

I think it only honest to acknowledge that these various criticisms have a solid basis, even when they are excessive or have become a caricature. The disgraceful situation which the informal groups are condemning is undoubtedly a danger that must be taken seriously. The task of the theologian, as I see it here, is not to offer a defense of the Church as it now is and as it has been shaped by long exposure to the ongoing secularization of the world in which the Church exists, or even to correct errors in the judgments made. His task is rather to determine whether the critiques, though legitimate in their concrete content, may nonetheless be overshooting the mark they set for themselves and thereby losing sight of the reality of the Church.

1) The institutional aspect of the Church is not an unfortunate historical mistake or a holdover from the Constantinian period, but is connected with the Church's very nature. It is true enough that the Church is first and foremost an *event*, the action of the Holy Spirit as it gathers together, around and in virtue of preached word and sacrament, all those whom the same Spirit inspires to acknowledge in the man Jesus the Son of God who died on the Cross and rose from the dead for our salvation.

But precisely because the Church is basically an event, and an event that is constantly repeated, it also unceasingly becomes a body gathered together under the authority of Christ. Properly speaking, the Church does not have two aspects: it is not at times an event and at times a body (the body representing a kind of "falling back" in the Bergsonian sense). Rather, the event manifests itself by giving rise to a body, and the body is structured and visible, even though the event which constitutes and reconstitutes it is itself invisible and mysterious. This is how the Letter to the Ephesians describes the Church when it links the event (Christ who gives life and growth to the body) and the structure needed if the various parts of the body are to receive life: "Through him [Christ] the whole body grows, and with the proper functioning of the members joined firmly together by each supporting ligament, builds itself up in love" (4:16). There is no room, then, for separating event from institution, since the event creates the institution; the event institutes the Church as a structured body. The Church, as the event in which Christ, now risen and raised to the Father's right hand, gives himself a body on earth, cannot be an informal kind of thing.

But we must be careful here not to play with words. The instituted form of the Church is not to be confused with the different models of organization and hierarchy, a great variety of which can be found in the history of Christianity. These models--be they presbyteral-synodal, episcopal, synodo-episcopal, pontifico-episcopo-synodal--are, as I see it, only the sociological means by which the body of Christ becomes an historical reality. There is a great deal of discussion today about whether there is an ecclesiology to be found in the New Testament, and whether this ecclesiology is one or many. I think that, although it is not prominent, a New Testament ecclesiology does exist, one that is deeply rooted in and subordinate to Christology. But the New Testament also shows various kinds of ecclesiastical structures. The differences between them and the fact of their coexistence show that all of them are relative. What is not relative is the fact that the Church is an organized body, a structure given life by the ministry of word and sacrament. What is and always will be relative, what belongs not to the "being" but to the "well being" of the Church is the sociological expression given to the body by means of a more or less sharply defined hierarchy and an organization. But to say that this expression is relative is not to say that it may or may not exist. Not only must hierarchy and organization exist; they must also change in the course of history, not directly in response to changes in society but in response to the requirements of the ministry of the word if this ministry is to be adapted to a changing society.

The merit of the informal groups in the Church is to put us on guard against any ecclesiolatry, that is, any absolutization of the forms whose function is to give historical expression to the reality of the Church as a body. The danger of the informal groups is to absolutize an informal character that has in fact only provisional value as a critique of a hierarchy that has become hardened and inflexible, and to swallow the myth that sees in institutions the permanent means of oppression and the principal source of alienation. The lack of a sense of relativity has led in the past to sectarianism. I am not at all sure that the contemporary informal groups are not in danger of making the same mistake.

The desire to be an underground Church, moreover, seems to me very dangerous. Clandestinity is not a mark of the Church but of subversive political groups. The Church as body of Christ, whatever be the juridical status (or lack of it) granted it by the state, is always a public reality. This public character, which enables the Church to broadcast itself, is even, according to 1 Thessalonians 1:2-11, the vary basis of evangelization. The Church preaches the Gospel first and foremost by what it shows itself publicly to be to the eyes of all, and not by leading an underground existence. As applied to the Church of the Good News the notion of an underground Church is a contradiction. In West Germany some informal groups accept the notion of an underground Church because they think that to exist in this fashion will enable them to break down ecclesiastical structures from within. Here we are confronted with an operation that is political in character. You may pass varying judgments on the operation, but the latter cannot claim justification in view of the nature and mission of the Church.

2) The classical or traditional parish is the second target of the informal groups. The parish thus understood can be defined as a geographical grouping of the faithful for the purpose of showing forth the reality of Christ's body through gatherings on Sundays and at other appointed times; these gatherings are led by ministers who are specifically assigned to this parish and act in its regard as guardians of unity in faith, as teachers, and as spiritual guides. Two defects in most parishes are immediately evident. One is that the geographical boundaries are most often arbitrary, in the sense that they do not coincide with a genuinely human area and that consequently the bond which is supposed to exist among the faithful has no natural basis. Moreover, the parish assembly does not make possible the formation of a community. The communion in word and sacrament, however intense it may be, has no follow-up; it is not translated into any shared project, simply because, once they leave the church, the faithful do not meet again until the next gathering in church, whether on

the next Sunday for some or at some more distant date for others, and because if they do meet again they do not recognize one another.

The second defect is that the parish systematizes the duality of sacred and profane. It is, in effect, offering a shelter for all who, as the saying goes, "have spiritual needs" and regard themselves as "harmonious souls" (in the Hegelian sense of the words). But these fine spirits continue to lead a secular existence that is unchanged, except perhaps in the limited sphere of personal and familial life. They leave the area of the sacred and return to the area of the profane which obeys its own laws and has nothing to do with the Gospel. They fulfill their "religious duties" in the ghetto of the parish, thus spending a moment in establishing their security, and then they return to their "business". In other words, the parish community is an artificial community. It is often nothing more than a simple audience, a "statistical group" (M. Halbwachs) that, formally considered, is hardly distinguishable from the group formed by moviegoers in a theater.

An informal group is obviously superior to a parish: not only is the informal group smaller; it is also not made up of everyone who comes along but only of people who have sought each other out and chosen each other in view of a definitive objective, people who have committed themselves to a costly involvement and have, at least tacitly, promised to be militants. They take the Gospel seriously, in the sense that they think faith ought to be incarnated in and find expression in a life which rejects the duality of sacred and profane and looks upon the economic and political areas as integral parts of a single existence. Formally speaking, then, an informal group resembles a cell of a political party. It is highly motivated, whereas the parish, apart from the little nucleus of people who are responsible for its running, is only vaguely motivated by the desire to preserve a tradition that offers security.

The parish has come to realize that it is an assembly lacking in inner dynamism, and has therefore attempted, sometimes successfully, to extend its influence by way of smaller and more militant groups with definite limited goals (helping the elderly; teaching migrant workers to read and write; scout movement; ecumenism; etc.). The difficulty is that these groups are dependent on those who direct the parish (pastor and presbyteral council). The latter, however, are often led by prudence to put restraints on the initiatives of the smaller groups and to insist on the latter having an ecclesiocentric character. The result is that here again the Church-world relationship is falsified. On the contrary, to the extent that the informal groups continue to be concerned about the future of the Church, they are preoccupied, intensely so at times, with making the Church-world relationship what it should be. In this they are accepting, whether they know it or not, a motive which has been normative for the World Council of Churches ever since its inception. They are passionately concerned that the relation between Church and world should be entirely different from what it has been in the past, when it was the relation between two powers which supported each other in defending a certain order and a certain ideology. The aim of the informal groups is to show their contemporaries that Christians are their companions on a journey, men who want to be united to their fellows in living to the full the human adventure and to shed light upon its meaning. Thus the informal groups look for the significant points in the political and social struggle in order there to show their solidarity with all who are fighting for social injustice and international peace.

In such circumstances it is rather difficult to justify the existence of the parishes we have described, these refuges which offer security and whose witness is essentially turned in upon itself. Nonetheless that is precisely what we are here undertaking to do. But we must first make it clear that we are not attempting at all to deny the blatant defects of the parishes; on the contrary, we are convinced the parishes must undergo a profound transformation in structure and mentality.[4]

There is, however, a deeper and abiding justification for the parish, and it consists precisely in the fact that it is a local, geographically limited collection of people. For this means that the parish includes men and women of every social condition, cultural level, and socio-professional category and that these people have not chosen each other, since the fact that they are contained within the same parish community is due simply to their happening to live where they do. (We are aware, of course, that here and there there are parishes made up of people who choose to belong to them, especially in the large cities; and that there are also parishes which cover a social homogeneous territory, for example, a residential section, but this last kind of parish is simply a regrettable anomaly.)

This kind of purely contingent community I consider highly significant in view of the Church's nature. In the Church, Paul tells us, there is no acceptance of persons, and he often rejoices at the thought that the Church brings together people as different and distant from each other as Jews and Greeks, men and women, slaves and free men. All through the letters of Paul we catch glimpses of this diversity. A given parish might not have had many rich people, but it had some. The social and cultural level of the Pauline Churches was not very high (the Apostle speaks out against a number of vices which are usually not those of well-bred people; cf. Eph. 4:32), yet they seem to have relied on well-placed individuals for protection, meeting-places, and probably financial resources.[5] Such a variety in social composition, which is assured precisely by the geographical character of the local Church, makes the latter an image of God's people as a whole and represents a victory over social determinisms and cultural selectivity. The common denominator in the Church and in the parish is not a selection and choice of the members by one another but faith alone as expressed in baptism. Those who may be separated by every other consideration are brought together in a shared allegiance to the Lord.

As Dietrich Bonhoeffer has pointed out in his book, *Life Together*,[6] the Christian community is not to be built on the kind of foundations that elective affinities, likeness of condition, or natural sympathy can provide, but solely on the acknowledgement and acceptance of the love with which we have been loved. By reason of the contingency involved in its make-up, the parish is the only place where this kind of community can be sought and where we can learn to bear one another's burdens and to listen to one another despite our varying origins and the opposition that may exist between our political and ideological commitments. Here we have what makes a parish truly rich. The wealth, it must be admitted, is often not put to use, but it is nonetheless really there for the different ministries of the parish to take advantage of it. And it is in this conflicting and incoherent diversity that the body of Christ must take concrete form.

The informal groups are concerned to establish a new relationship between the Church and the world, to dismantle the barriers between them, and to stop speaking of the Church as having an inside and an outside. But amid this legitimate concern the groups forget an essential aspect of the Church that is already visible in the community formed by Jesus and his disciples. That is that before sending the disciples out on their mission to the world, Jesus first drew them away from their natural, familial, and professional milieu, and even from the politico-religious party (Pharisee, zealot, perhaps Essene) to which they belonged. And each time that he sent them on a mission, he later drew them back and gathered them around himself. Insofar as the community of disciples gathered around Jesus is truly the prototype of the Church, Jesus' way of acting means that the Church too is constituted by the twofold movement of withdrawal and going forth. That movement, which will never end, gives the Church its permanent structure. There can be no question, then, of obliterating the boundary line between Church and world, but only of crossing it. The parish in its withdrawal may forget the complementary movement toward the world and thus cease to be missionary. But the informal group, for its part, turns outward to the world and forgets that the Church must establish itself as an authentic community of faith that is distinct from the world. It would be easy to show in both Jesus and Paul this twofold thrust: the Church as a community separated from the world, refusing to conform to the world's ways, and even, on certain points, refusing contact with the world--and the Church as a missionary community that goes to meet men and travel the road with them.

* * *

The distortion which the celebration of the Eucharist almost inevitably suffers can serve us as a proof of the informal group's inability to take the place of the parish. We may turn, for an example, to the "wildcat Eucharist" celebrated by a group of pastors, priests, and laity from both confessions on Pentecost, 1968. The group was a typical informal one, centered wholly on social justice and political involvement in the name of the Gospel. It had no organization; militancy substituted for structure. Its members did not break off from their own Churches; they were not trying to be the nucleus of a new Church. The group did not challenge the authority of the ecclesiastical leaders, but informed them of the group's action (although after the fact). Nor did the group try to invent a new model for the Eucharist. For the liturgy of this holy Supper the group drew rather on the sources common to the two Churches. Not only did they have the clearly expressed intention of celebrating a genuine Supper of the Lord, but they celebrated it in conformity to the Scriptural prototype.

There was then no doctrinal problem, at least from the viewpoint of Protestant theology: the group celebrated a true Eucharist, not a simple agape, as some critics have suggested. It is true, of course, that the Catholics in the group wittingly disobeyed canon law, and the Protestants the discipline of their Church. But from the Protestant viewpoint this disobedience did not touch the substance of the sacrament, since discipline plays at best a subordinate role and is not on the same level as the "notes of the Church", which were respected in this case. We may add that, in our opinion, even acts of disobedience in disciplinary matters can have ecclesial value, to the extent that they are a challenge to prohibitions whose theological nature is highly problematic; this is the case, for example, with prohibitions against intercommunion, which are prohibitions against the visible manifestation of the unity of Christ's body.

Why then did the Eucharist on Pentecost, 1968, leave others disturbed? Why can it not serve as a model for the unity we await and hope for? Solely because those who shared in that Eucharist chose each other in a selective way and because the selection depended on political agreement. Thus the choice was also exclusive. The participants claimed indeed, later on, that if someone representing the opposed camp had come forward, they would have admitted him to communion. In fact, no one like that was present, and the absence was not due to chance! During May, 1968, and perhaps even earlier, the participants had been conducting an experiment in brotherhood in regard to the political and social struggle, and wanted, since they were Christians, to put on the experiment the seal of communion with Christ. They were thus trying to give their political brotherhood a spiritual prolongation and perhaps a spiritual basis. Nothing could be more legitimate! They forgot only one thing: all are called to the table of the Lord who gives his life for all, and only one condition is required of them: that they recognize the body of the Lord. We are not allowed to add any further criterion: the dividing line passes between those who acknowledge the Lord who gave himself up for our sins, and those who do not. Those who share in the Lord's Supper cannot claim any special title for so doing; they are all simply pardoned sinners who come precisely to receive assurance of that pardon. Therefore the informal group which celebrates the Eucharist suffers even in this celebration from the selectivity that controls their origin. They revive the pietist heresy by discriminating between the pure and the impure.[7]

It might seem that the same criticism could be directed against the specialized groups to be found in the Church, which on the occasion of some meeting or some congress, ask that the Holy Supper be celebrated for them. After all, these groups too, by reason of their objective (social, pedagogical, missionary, ecumenical) have selected their members from the Church at large. In fact, however, there is a fundamental difference here: the celebration is organized with the knowledge of the Church or parish, with its approval, and often with outsiders sharing the Eucharist with the group. What we have here is a particular ministry within the Church, and one that involves no exclusion on principle.

The Eucharist of Pentecost 1968 reminds us of a characteristic goal of most contemporary informal groups: the political goal. That is what differentiates them from the pietist conventicles whose aim was conversion or the reawakening of individual piety. In pointing out the contrast we are not passing any unfavorable judgment on the contemporary groups. In fact, the latter are reminding the Church of two basic truths, one anthropological, the other ethical.

They are reminding the Church, first of all, that the man toward whom the Church exercises its ministry is a concrete and undivided human being, not an abstract individual considered only in terms of his private life. The groups are protesting against the privatization of faith which is a corollary of the Church's becoming marginal to society at large. Man is man only if he is taken first in his relations with other people, and then in his properly social dimension. To forget this fact does not make it disappear, but it does introduce into our view of man a duality which is disastrous for his spiritual growth. If then the informal groups take up a position that is marginal in regard to the Church, their purpose is not necessarily to effect a break with the Church; it is in order to take over a part of the Church's ministry which the Church itself fulfills very inadequately because it has become marginal and because it encourages the privatization of faith, thus condemning itself to lose its grasp on the real, undivided human being.

In the ethical sphere, the informal groups with their concern for the political and the social remind us that there is no genuine service of men, no *diakonia*, in the real order unless this service consents to make use of what Paul Ricoeur calls "long relations". By this he means relations which do not go from person to person but require relay stations and the mediation of social and political institutions. It is true, of course, that we discover love in "short [or direct] relations" and that these relations always serve as a norm. But it is equally true that we cannot effectively put this love into practice except by means of "long [or indirect] relations".

The informal groups are thus performing an invaluable service for a Church that has allowed itself to be limited to the spiritual and to consider men only as "souls". The groups are helping the Church to overcome the pietism that is deeply rooted in its tradition and subtly encouraged by the secularization of society at large.

However, three remarks are in place which I consider basic.

a) No Christian anthropology can let itself be forced into a choice between "private" and "social" man. This choice, which the informal groups often seem to be urging, is impossible. In the real man there is a reciprocity between the personal and the social, as Georges Gurvitch has taught us. There is a ceaseless exchange between the inner life and the public life of man. Our inner difficulties have important repercussions in our political and social involvements, just as these involvements can help us overcome our inner difficulties.[8]

b) There must indeed be a connection between faith and political commitment, but the connection is not a completely transparent and univocal one. Between faith and political commitment various motivations necessarily and legitimately come into play. Between the Church's creed and our particular political choices there is no clear and unquestionable link (except perhaps in times of serious crisis when things become extremely simplified, as, for example, under Nazism). That is, the Gospel does not justify us in saying that reformism is Christian or that the revolutionary stance is Christian. In certain German theological circles of twenty years ago, which in many respects were really informal groups, a slogan made the rounds: Accept German rearmament and you deny the three articles of the Apostle's Creed. That sort of proposition I regard as completely unacceptable.

c) In their dedication to politics the informal groups seem to put orthodoxy and orthopraxy on the same level or even to attribute greater importance to orthopraxy. That attitude can indeed find justification in some of Christ's sayings: "None of those who cry out, 'Lord, Lord,' will enter the kingdom of God but only the one who does the will of my Father in heaven" (Matt. 7:21). The informal groups are pointing to the yawning chasm that may exist in the Church between saying and doing. In point of fact, however, neither saying alone nor doing alone can claim to be the whole of faith. Only the man who both hears the word and obeys it has faith. The dilemma: orthodoxy or orthopraxy, is a false one.

The conclusion we come to is simple and clear. The Church would be gravely at fault if it did not listen seriously to what the informal groups have to say, even if they say it in the arrogant tone of radical challenge. The Church would be no less to blame if it simply followed the informal groups all the way.

CHAPTER 12

Informal Groups in the Church:
An Orthodox Viewpoint

by

J. D. Zizioulas

The existence of the informal groups, even though they have appeared only in Western Christianity, is not without its importance for orthodox theology, especially in the present ecumenical context. On the one hand, the phenomenon raises the general problem of the ecclesiological nature of such groups, and, on the other, serves as a reminder of some basic ecclesiological principles that are often forgotten.

In short, the groups do not simply force us to ask what ecclesiological recognition they are to receive from the Church. They also have a critical role to play, and in my view, we ought to give special attention to this aspect of the situation.

The informal groups show such a variety that it is very difficult to speak of them in a blanket way. However, it can be said that the questions the groups pose directly to orthodox theology have to do with these general areas:

a) First, the structure of the Church. To what extent can existing institutions, the diocese and parish in particular, be regarded here and now as a suitable expression for the Christian faith of a living Church? This question is suggested by, for example, the spontaneity of the informal groups.

b) Second, the nature of the institutions within the ecclesiastical structure. To what extent do the various functions or institutions in the Church, as they continue to exist in their traditional form, express the spirit of the Gospel and, in particular, the spirit of this community? This question raises the essential problem of the hierarchic character of ecclesial functions and ecclesial authority.

c) Third, the relation of the Church to the world and to history. Many informal groups are concerned with the political order and believe that the Gospel has political consequences and that the Church exists in its true essence wherever there is political action. What is the relation between the Church and the course of history? To what extent does the Church make history and to what extent is it an eschatological reality? These questions are independent of the challenge which the informal groups represent for ecclesiology.

In attempting to answer these questions we shall be turning to three important subjects. (a) The Church as community. Here we shall present the Orthodox conception of the Church in order to determine what form of community is ecclesial and what conditions a community must meet to deserve the name "Church". To anticipate: the structure of the Church must be seen in the light of the Eucharistic community which has a central place in the Orthodox tradition.

(b) The Church as communion. Here we shall be raising the question of the Church's functions, authority, hierarchy, etc., in light of the meaning of communion and, in the last analysis, in view of pneumatology, which is so important to the Orthodox Church.

(c) Finally, we shall examine the relation between the Church, on the one side, and the world and history, on the other, in order to determine the extent to which, from the viewpoint of Orthodox ecclesiology, the Church's intervention in the world and her efforts to solve the world's problems protects her eschatological character. Here we shall seek light from another aspect of Orthodox ecclesiology: from eschatology in relation to the Eucharistic character of the Church, which, as we have already noted, is so important in Orthodox ecclesiology.

After explaining these basic points we shall try to draw some conclusions on the place of informal groups in the Church--always, of course, from the viewpoint provided by the basic principles of Orthodox ecclesiology.

I. The Church as Community

Orthodox ecclesiology approaches the mystery of the Church primarily from the angle of the local Church, that is, the concretely existing community. Such an approach is not purely sociological but theological in character, and its starting-point is the paradox created by the use of two biblical images for the Church. The first image is that of the "People of God", an image which dominates the Bible throughout the Old and New Testaments. In this image the Church is understood as a community dispersed throughout the world and therefore as a community "on the way", that is, in constant movement and expectation. On the other hand, this scattered people of God is not abandoned to its diaspora. Its destiny is to find its ultimate completion in one place and in a single body that is now taking shape. Here the image of the "Body of Christ" enters on the scene and creates the paradox we mentioned.

The image of God's people can easily be understood on the basis of Old Testament thought, but the image of the Body of Christ has meaning only in the light of Christ's person. The images differ because in the person of Christ the unity of God's people, which had been expected at the end of time, has already manifested itself as a reality. The *eschaton* is henceforth a fulfilled *eschaton*, and the people of God is not simply dispersed: it is also united.

This paradox of God's people being both dispersed and united is at the very center of biblical Christology and, through this Christology, also enters into ecclesiology. It is amazing to see how aware the early Church was of the paradox and how the structure of the local Church was affected by it.

The paradox we have described is the same as the paradox of the "one" and the "many" that we find in Christology. We are all familiar with the idea of Christ as the "one" (the "only one") who identifies himself with Israel in its entirety, the People of God in its totality. That same idea is basically present in the consciousness of Christ himself when he speaks of himself as the Son of Man or as the Servant of God. Each of these titles is based on the paradox of the single person who incorporates the "many" into himself to such an extent that some exegetes have been led to speak, in this context, of a "corporate personality". In thus identifying himself with the "many", Christ has become the basis for the paradox. In him the people of God is both "many" and "one", dispersed and gathered together.

Out of this paradox the Church as a community was born, and it must reflect the paradox in its life. When the New Testament writers chose the term *ekklesia*, their clear intention was to express the "gathering together" of the people of God, not its dispersion. The Church was no longer simply the "many" in the "One", but also the "One" in the "many": the "many" united to the "One", and the "One" spread abroad in the "many".

My reason for insisting on the image of the "One" and the "many" is not simply because I think it the really primitive and central Christological image. I insist on it also because by way of it we can get at what really links the structure of the local Church to the mystery of the Body of Christ.

The incorporation of the many into the One is connected in the New Testament with the Eucharist. The ecclesiological consequences of this connection can be seen clearly in the writings of the first three centuries.

The consequences are to be found essentially: (a) in the terminology applied from the very beginning to the Eucharistic community: the latter was called "the Church of God" and, even more strikingly, "the whole Church"; (b) in the composition of the Eucharistic community, which set the Church community off from non-ecclesial communities; (c) in the structure of the Eucharistic community, which was regarded as the expression and image of the Church itself. The last two of these three points are of special interest here.

To gather in love so as to form a community was not something peculiar to Christians in the period of the New Testament. We tend very often to forget that the idea of community was widespread among the Jews with their synagogues and the pagans with their fraternities (*collegia*) in which love and solidarity played a very important role. But Christians gathering together into communities "in the same place" were not imitating either the synagogues or the brotherhoods, for their unity was something special. What is the specific point of difference? The question is a very important one in every age, even today, for the answer enables us to verify the truly ecclesial nature of an ecclesiastical community.

It is evident that the Christians who gathered into a community differed from non-Christians by their faith in the person of the Lord who was the living center of their community. A further impressive fact is that the Eucharistic community differed in its composition from both the synagogues and the brotherhoods. The synagogue community was based on race (even though the religious factor was extremely important), and the brotherhood community on profession, but the Eucharistic community by its nature transcended all physical and social divisions. Neither race nor age nor profession nor social rank could be the basis for establishing a particular Eucharistic community. The Eucharistic community is, on the contrary, the supreme expression of the Church's catholicity; it is a catholic act of a catholic Church.

The same "ecclesiology" must find expression not only in the composition but also in the structure of the Eucharistic communion. A structure which does not express the mystery of the Church but exists solely to achieve an administrative or moral purpose is ecclesiologically unacceptable. The early Church very quickly provided the model of ecclesial organization. In so doing it applied genuinely ecclesiological norms and took as its basis the Eucharistic gathering, in which the "People of God" of a certain city assembled "in the same place", around a "single altar" and under the presidency of the one bishop who was surrounded by his college of presbyters and aided by the deacons.

If we look carefully at this disposition which very soon became the basis for the permanent structure of the local Church, we become aware that it reflects the idea of the Church as the people of God who are gathered in one place and incorporated into the one Body of Christ. We may leave out of consideration the varied symbols to be found in the early literature and note that the presence of the presbyters as a college and not as isolated individuals (as they were later taken to be) was seemingly related to the idea of the Twelve, seated on their thrones to judge the world on the last day. The presence of the presbyters at the head of the Eucharistic gathering was intended as an image of the final unity of God's people on the day when the world would be judged by its attitude to the "little flock" and to "my least brothers" (Matt. 25:31-46). We must not be content, then, to think of the presbyters as a holdover from Judaism, but see that their role in the Eucharistic gathering was like that of the judges on the last day, for they seem indeed to have acted as a *synedrion* or council that dealt with all the problems affecting those believers who had a right to communion (cf. Ignatius of Antioch, the Didascalia, etc.).

But the people of God, the New Israel, the "many", must be understood as united in the One who has identified himself with them, the Lamb of God who lies on the Eucharistic table. Here we have the ecclesiological significance of the bishop as he stands at the head of the Eucharistic assembly. By the one Christ "the multitude" is saved, returns to God, and becomes the priest of creation, offering the latter anew to its Creator. So, too, in the Eucharist the people of God, united in one body, offers itself and creation to God through the hands of the bishop, who thus becomes the "image of Christ". The decisive pre-eminence of the bishop in ecclesiology is due to the place he has in the Eucharistic gathering and not on any juridical office.

To carry out his function, the bishop was assisted by the deacons who stood beside him. The very role of the deacons was a revelation of the mystery of the Church, in the sense that through them the people and through the people the whole world was brought to the bishop. The deacon's function was not only to lead the people to prayer but also to present to the bishop the elements of creation and the world which the people had brought to church in order that these might become Eucharist at the bishop's hands. The deeper meaning of all this is to show the relationship of the mystery of the Church to the whole of creation and to everyday life, for these are redeemed along with the people of God by the blood of the one Christ, are offered by that people to the Creator, and become Eucharist in the hands of the one bishop who is leader of the Eucharistic community.

Today this structure exists in changed circumstances, and the problem this change gives rise to is always with us. I am referring to the creation of the parish. When I say "creation of the parish", I mean that a new Eucharistic structure came into existence: the Eucharist without a bishop, without a college of priests, and, in many cases, without deacons.

How then are we to understand the parish in relation to the local Church and, ultimately, to the mystery of the Church? Two answers, it seems, may be given to the question.

a) We may regard each presbyter as leader of a Eucharistic community and therefore of a local Church. This amounts to identifying the priest with the bishop as far as the latter's most specific function (leader of the Eucharistic gathering) is concerned. If we accept this view, there are serious consequences for structure and for ecclesiology. Structurally: we abolish the presbytery as a college, and we abolish the deacon. Ecclesiologically: we end with the conception of a priesthood with three degrees, that is, three of the same nature, and the Eucharist becomes the communion of individuals with Christ, not the image of the Church in its eschatological unity. If we want to maintain that the priest is the individual leader-celebrant of a Eucharistic community, we must admit that our Eucharistic community no longer reflects the mystery of the Church as we described it above.

b) We may also regard each Eucharist celebrated with a presbyter as a simple extension of the one Eucharistic gathering under the bishop. The purpose of the extension is merely to facilitate communion for those who cannot share in the bishop's celebration. The purpose is not to create a full-fledged

Eucharistic community. Now, if we look back to the origins of the parish, we can see that this second explanation is the one that fits the facts. The *fermentum* ("leaven") in the west, the *antimension* ("instead of a table" [a portable altar; later a cloth, under the corporal, on a consecrated altar]) in the East, the commemoration of the bishop's name during the Eucharistic Prayer, are some indications that in setting up the parish the Church did not intend to set up new local Churches but only to make communion easier for those who did not come to the cathedral church. But this intention was later forgotten, and the local Church therefore ceased to reflect in a direct way the mystery of the Church as we have described it. That is why we find ourselves in such a theological quandary today.

The Eucharistic community which forms the basis of the local Church's permanent structure is sent out into the world as a missionary community each time the liturgy ends. The gathered people of God are declared "sent" (*missa*) and are scattered abroad in the world again until the next meeting on the Lord's Day.

In thus going out into the world the local Church carries with it the various charisms of its members. These charisma may give rise to their own appropriate structures, so as to enable them to give their witness to the world. This is how the monastic charisms, for example, have a place in the life of the Church, as do all kinds of missionary activity. But such charismatic structures can never claim to be self-sufficient or independent. If they are to reflect the mystery of the Church, they must be always related to and dependent on the basic structure that derives from the Eucharistic gathering. In returning to the celebration of the gathered Church, each bearer of a charism brings with him the elements of his own life or the gifts of creation which have been entrusted to him, as well as the fruits

of his mission, if there be any. All of these become Eucharist
along with the people of God itself, which is called together
and given a structure in the Eucharistic assembly.

II. The Church as Communion

The structure of the Eucharistic community and consequently
that of the local Church in general reveals the mystery of the
Church's "oneness" in the person of the one bishop. But that
structure also manifests the "multiplicity" of the people and
the variety of ministries. The idea that the local Church is
a "multitude" (*plēthos, polyplētheia*) is common in the literature
of the first centuries (cf., e.g., the Acts of the Apostles and
St. Ignatius of Antioch). The idea is also universal that there
are numerous ministries in the local Church; St. Paul gives a
list which indicates the large number rather than a systematic
description. The multiplicity of the people and the multiplicity
of ministries are correlative.

We usually overlook the fact that the Holy Spirit is not
only a power that unites; he is also a power that "divides".
When Paul says that the one Spirit "divides" ("distributes"--
diairoun) his charisms or gifts, he is alluding directly to the
mystery of the many personal existences in each community. The
Holy Spirit unites precisely when he divides, for every charism
and therefore every ministry (there is no ministry without a
charism) is strictly linked to a particular person yet also
manifests the unity and unicity of the Church.

Here we are confronted with the idea of the person. The
person, as distinct from the individual, is properly thought of
only in communion with others. In bestowing his gifts "on each
of them" (Acts 2:3), the Holy Spirit links the ministries of

Christ to persons and thereby strengthens the unity of Christ in the Church. Ordination therefore unifies by dividing, precisely because it turns each ministry into a relational entity. It is in this perspective that we must view the Church's hierarchy. The personal character given to each ministry through the rite of ordination also attaches the note of specificity to each ministry: "Are all apostles? Are all prophets? Are all teachers?" (1 Cor. 12:29). This is because specificity is a basic element in the notion of the person. And it is this element of specificity that brings about hierarchy through ordination. The ministries of the Church are necessarily hierarchic, not in the sense of a moral or axiological classification, but in the sense that specificity attaches to the relationship which each person is given, through ordination, within the structure of the Church. Such a conception of hierarchy is identical with the kind of hierarchy to be found in the life and communion of the three divine Persons, for here the hierarchy is not to be defined by ontological or objective criteria of value or moral quality but precisely by the specificity of each divine Person.

* * *

Such a way of understanding the ministries and their relation to the mystery of the Church as communion (*koinonia*) in the Holy Spirit found its earliest expression in the structure of the local Church by means of two conditions required for any ordination. One condition was that ordination must take place during the Eucharistic gathering of the local Church. The other was that it was accomplished by the laying on of the bishop's hands. The significance of the first condition is that it expresses the conviction that no order or charism or ministry is intelligible apart from or independently of the community. Ordination to a ministry does not consist simply in the bestowal of a charism through objective sacramental channels that can be viewed in isolation (by inquiring simply whether the minister of the sacrament is validly ordained, etc.); otherwise a bishop meeting the necessary conditions could ordain in his office! Ordination to a ministry means rather that a particular member of the community is given a specific personal relation to the community and within it (therefore: no ordination except for a particular Church). The significance of the second condition named above is that all ministries and charisms must become one and pass through the One who took the many into himself to make them one without destroying each personal existence but on the contrary affirming it as relational and part of a communion. This is precisely how the Church looks upon the person of him who presides over the Eucharistic gathering: the bishop.

Such, then, is the perspective in which we must understand the hierarchic structure of the local Church. In this perspective the local Church is not a pyramidal structure with one person, the bishop, at the apex or even above the community. The local Church is rather a community in which each ministry or order has its proper place within a communion of persons.

It follows that the element of authority which is attached to every ministry in the Church is also essentially conditioned by the element of communion. This means that authority does not flow from the ministry as such, as its ontological or moral effect and that it is not the result of some institutional purpose. Rather, authority consists in the relationship within the community that is given to the minister by his ordination. It is not accidental therefore that in the Orthodox tradition every episcopal ordination has as an essential part the specific mention of the community in which he is to be placed. That mention

is part of the very prayer of ordination and therefore (at
least for Orthodox theology, which grounds all the bishop's
authority, administrative included, in his ordination) is
intimately connected with the authority given the ordained
person.

The result of all this is that the Church's structure is
not to be conceived as a source of security. In fact, the idea
of objective security is non-existent in Orthodox theology,
since the latter is dominated by the idea that the reality of
the communion is constantly dependent on the Holy Spirit. This
is why we may say that the problem of authority as *auctoritas*
and of rebellion against this *auctoritas* is to be found chiefly
in the history of western Christianity, since in the western
Church sin has been understood as a rebellion against an
auctoritas and not as a breaking of communion with God.

III. The Church and the Problems of the World

If our interpretation of ordination is correct, there can
be no ministry in the Church except in relation to a concrete
community. The prohibition of such ordinations as were forbidden
by the canons of the early Church still expresses this deeper
meaning. Moreover, the striking similarity between the rite of
ordination and the rite of marriage in the Orthodox Church
right down to the present time is a further testimony to the
close connection between the person ordained and a concrete
ecclesial community. This connection brings home to us the
existential nature of the structure of the Church as a whole,
since all of the Church's ministries link her to a concrete
"here and now" situation.

The purpose of the Church's ministries is to bring about a communion of the world in the life of God by bringing into the world the love of God the Father, in the form of the grace of our Lord Jesus Christ within the communion of the Holy Spirit (cf. 2 Cor. 13:13). This means that through its ministries the Church is a missionary, since it is through her ministries that she brings the world into union with God. The mission of the Church, then, is an *ek-stasis* or going forth of communion. In this going forth, the Church refuses to stand back and be a city set over against the world; rather it has compassion and shares in the life of the world. The result is that the Church is necessarily involved in a concrete situation, with all the problems the situation contains.

The Church, through its ministers, becomes the world's servant and, as befits its incarnational nature, takes upon itself the burden of the physical and cultural life of the milieu in which it finds itself. Indeed it is precisely because this milieu differs from one geographical area to another that the Church is by nature a community: a local community and not simply an over-arching, worldwide organization. But the incarnational relationship of Church to world must be understood eucharistically. The Church does not share the world's life in order to leave the world as it is, but to bring it to God as the body of Christ, that is, as baptized and transfigured. It is in this that the prophetic role of the ecclesial community in the world consists; that prophetic role, in the perspective we have been sketching, is less one of confronting the world than of raising up and transfiguring the world from within.

Such a conception of the Church-world relation clearly means that the problems of man in the world are also the Church's problems. The division of creation into "sacred" and "profane", which has prevailed for centuries in the West, is wholly alien to Orthodox ecclesiology. The daily sorrows and daily burdens of man, as well as all of his political, economic, and social problems, are not somewhere outside the Church's door, because the individual, as a member of the Eucharistic community and a sharer in the divine Eucharist, brings his whole life with him into that communion.

This close relation between the Church and the world's daily problems, however, can be looked at in different ways. The Eucharistic and eschatological approach which Orthodox ecclesiology prefers does not allow a morality view of the Church-world relation. By this I mean that since the Church does not stand over against man but rather shares sympathetically and Eucharistically in the world's life, it cannot provide the world with moral rules for handling its various everyday problems. The Church offers the world, not a rigid, autonomous set of moral precepts but a sanctifying presence that does not lay insupportable burdens on men's shoulders but calls the world to "the freedom of the children of God".

When the Church-world relation is thus conceived, it is clear that while the Church fully shares in the world's problems, its task is not to provide concrete solutions for these problems nor to adopt or suggest a particular policy or set of tactics. We must insist, however, that this attitude does not mean indifference to the world's problems. For, while not providing concrete help in a particular case, the Church continues to inspire men by its presence in the midst of their concrete, real circumstances. It seems that in the New Testament period the Church did not adopt a policy of striving for the abolition of slavery, but this does not mean that the Church was not responsible for the gradual, progressive abolition of slavery in the course of time.

The participation of the Church in man's daily anxieties and problems is always linked to an eschatological vision of history. The Church cannot apply merely historical measurements to history and its development. The very nature of the Church requires that she bring to history the presence of God's kingdom, the presence of the *eschaton*. Human reason is always trying to impose a program upon history, but the Church's task is to react against this rationalism (which is the Church's greatest historical temptation) and to link everything to the Holy Spirit. The Church cannot become simply another power at work within history but must always present itself as an "earthen vessel" (2 Cor. 4:7), as power "in weakness", and as an absurdity to reason and even to morality.

IV. Ecclesial Community and Informal Groups

What has thus far been said will suggest that a number of elements of Orthodox ecclesiology can be related to the basic motives and aspirations of the informal groups. Consider, for example, the attempt of these groups to make the Church be "here and now" in an existential situation and in the form of a community, with its basis less in historical, objective ways of expressing the faith and structure of the Church and more in the personal forms of charism and communion. Such an effort seems aimed at a highly pneumatological ecclesiology, such as we find in Orthodox theology. May the informal groups, then, be considered by Orthodox theology as a "kind of Church"?

To answer this question, we would have to study more fully several aspects of the informal group phenomenon. This, however, we cannot do here. We must therefore limit ourselves to raising some basic ecclesiological questions.

a) The first concerns the idea of the Church as eschatological community. As we have already noted, a pneumatological vision of the Church leads to the idea that by the descent and energy of the Holy Spirit (Acts 2) the *eschaton* penetrates into history. By this I mean that the Church faithfully preserves the past and the forms it has inherited from the past, but must constantly set them in the light shed by the future. The future in question is that future which God has prepared for his world in Christ and of which the Church receives a sacramental ("in mystery") foretaste in the Eucharist "until the Lord comes" and manifests that future fully in his parousia. In consequence of this pneumatological vision, the criteria for ecclesiality may not be derived solely from history but must depend also on this eschatological dimension of hope and expectation which the Church embodies in our world. This kind of ecclesiology is very far from giving rise to the false hope, the opium, of a "social gospel" according to which history leads, and is led by the Church, toward perfection in the form of progress or revolution. On the contrary, ecclesiology as understood in the Orthodox tradition brings the *eschaton* into history in a dialectical way, that is, as an unending struggle between Christ the Conqueror and the Devil (such a struggle as we find in monastic asceticism in the Orthodox tradition). This dialectical character prevents history from becoming eschatology and eschatology from becoming history, while at the same time guaranteeing the existential confrontation of the two. This point is very important, for only in its light can we pass judgment on the many problems raised by various movements in the West, including the informal groups.

From our point of view, the informal groups seem to embody a quest for the eschatological dimension of the Church. One of the forces that motivates and sustains these groups is a reaction against "historicism", whether in the form of "dogmatism" or in the form of "institutionalism". "Historicism" prevents the Church from incarnating, in and for the world, the dimension of hope, expectation, and change--a dimension to which ideological or revolutionary movements outside the Church give far better expression in our day. Nonetheless it is also precisely here that we must be critical of the informal groups. For, whatever be the influence of various political or sociological forces in the genesis of the informal groups, the different Christian theologies at work in the groups ("theology of revolution", or of change, or of development, or generally "social gospel" theologies) have one thing in common with these non-ecclesiastical political and ideological currents: they all assert and look for the future or the *eschaton* in a purely historical form. To identify the *eschaton* with history in this way is ultimately to eliminate the *eschaton* as God's kingdom, as God's "visitation" of and "dwelling" in the world; it is to secularize God and to historicize his eternal life and his kingdom. Thus, although the groups look for the *eschaton* that it may give history a dimension of hope and the future, they are really looking only for a moral improvement of historical existence. The informal groups, therefore, can hardly avoid being subject to criticism when they create an ecclesial community on a moral basis.

Here we run into the problem of defining ecclesial identity. The problem may be stated thus: How "recognize" the Church as an eschatological community within history?

In the perspectives of Orthodox theology as we explained them earlier, the answer is that no form of improved historical existence can constitute a "church". The only form of purely "ecclesial" eschatological presence is that which manifests itself in the Eucharistic gathering where the scattered people of God comes together and renews its taste for the life of God in Christ. Apart from this Eucharistic gathering the Church cannot be "eschatological" in an "ecclesial" way. Only by applying this Eucharistic reality can the members of the Church in the world, individually or in groups, experience the eschatological dimension as a dialectic involving Christ and Antichrist as a struggle against the devil in which only hints of Christ's victory can be gained but not a complete transfiguration of history in God's kingdom before the parousia.

It was something of this kind that Eastern monasticism intended to demonstrate through its monastic communities, just at times when the Church's eschatological sense seemed to be weakened (in the Constantinian period, for example). But the monastic effort could not have the incarnational result which the Church, as eschatological community in history, achieved in its Eucharistic gatherings. That is why monasteries have never been regarded in the East as Churches. Only the bishop-centered Eucharistic assembly, for reasons already explained (Part I), is privileged to represent fully the eschatological dimension of the Church in history. Consequently, it is in Eucharistic form that the ecclesial identity of the eschatological community is manifested in the life of the Church.

b) The second question suggested by the informal group phenomenon concerns the catholicity of the Church. To be "Church" a community must take upon itself the burdens of the world, as Christ did. This occurs when the Church takes concrete shape as a localized reality. Here we see the Church's existential nature, which derives from a pneumatological vision of the body of Christ. For the Holy Spirit builds up the body of Christ "here and now", just as he makes Christ "personal" and alive in a concrete way. On this account, the Church shares in the agonizing problems of the world in which she lives. It also impels her to make part of her own life the expressive forms proper to the concrete culture of the area in which she lives, and not to derive these from elsewhere. For all these reasons the local Church has a predominant role to play in ecclesiology as the Orthodox tradition understands it.

In this conception of the Church there is still another element: for the Church to be a Church it must incarnate in itself not one part or some parts but the whole of its milieu. And that is what makes the local Church catholic: the fact that she absorbs and transcends the divisions created by the social and even the natural life of men in the region where she exists. If the Eucharistic community as we have described it (Part I) is in the supreme sense "ecclesial", this is because in the Church all the divisions created by natural and social life (divisions of age, profession, race, secular interests, etc.) are transcended and transfigured in unity. Inversely, as soon as the Eucharistic community is based deliberately on only some of these factors, it ceases to be the Church. (I would even go so far as to say the Eucharist ceases to exist, but that would only raise numerous objections.)

May we not suggest that the informal groups fall under this judgment, inasmuch as, by reason of their very nature, communion within their communities is based on the common interests of the members? In such communities what organic, constitutive place is there for little children who have no conception of contemporary social problems, or for those who belong to a political group which the majority of the members oppose, or for the elderly who do not "understand" the younger generation, or for the rich and the "privileged" of society who do not belong to the "base" on which the community is erected? Is not this kind of exclusivity, resulting from natural and social divisions, a negation of the Church's catholicity in a given geographical area?

Another aspect of this problem of catholicity is the relationship of a local community to the other ecclesial communities around the world. For a local community to be a "Church" it must be identical with and in communion with the other Church--communities of the world. In a bishop-centered Eucharistic community this unity is expressed by the fact that the bishop is "recognized" by the other bishops, that he has been ordained by at least two other bishops, and that he offers the Eucharist "for the Catholic Church throughout the world". If we prescind from the case of a schism (which is an abnormality in terms of catholicity and which ecclesiology has not, to my knowledge, fully explained), no local Church can be considered a "Church" unless it is "acknowledged" by and in communion with the other local Churches. In the light of this ecclesiological principle, which allows no Church to be simply indifferent, what is the ecclesial character of the informal groups?

A parallel theme is that of the Church's apostolicity, that is, the charismatic, sacramental bond between any ecclesial community and the Apostles and early Church. This theme, like that of catholicity, suggests our third question.

c) A third and final question concerns the Church's structure. All that I said earlier in Parts I and II shows, I think, that the reaction of the informal groups to institutionalization has a substantial basis from the viewpoint of Orthodox ecclesiology. The context of communion in which pneumatology located the structure of the Church cannot justify a defense of the historical forms of ministry in the Church, simply on the grounds that they are traditional. But there are other grounds for defending them, which are not a matter simply of respect for tradition and inherited institutions. What is significant for us here is that these reasons involve the dimensions of communion and eschatology in which the informal groups are so interested.

As I tried to show in Part I of this essay, if a community is to be ecclesial, it must manifest our unity in Christ as transcending all the divisions of everyday life. It is precisely to this purpose that the *one* bishop in each Church serves by offering the *one* Eucharist and *ordaining* all the ministers himself. We also pointed out the significance of the presbyteral college, the significance of the deacons as representing the Church-world relation, and, above all, the significance of the people, without whom a community cannot be called "Church". Consequently, there is, at least for Orthodox ecclesiology, an ecclesial structure that is as basic to the image of the Church as the Church itself. St. Ignatius of Antioch was very explicit, saying: "Without this the Church is not the Church."

In this matter two questions may be asked. The first is whether a certain structure must necessarily keep the shape history has given it. The second is whether such a structure can remain unchangeable when social conditions, etc., are changing so rapidly in the transition from rural to industrial society. I know that the informal groups must have raised these very questions very seriously, for most of the groups owe their origin to the fact that the parish can no longer express the Church in modern society.

In a theological reflection, such as that in which we are here engaged, our chief interest must be limited to the consequences which a change of structure, for historical and social reasons, may have in ecclesiology. But even in approaching matters solely from that direction, I am forced to conclude that I cannot discover any other structure for the Church but the one I have expounded, that would express and represent the structure of the Church as I have described it. Of course, if you presuppose that some other structure can indeed express or at least not essentially alter the mystery of the Church, then there would be no objection to its replacing the old structure. I would point out, however, that if historical necessity and social change are pushing us, as many people claim, to a transformation of structures, that is not the first time this has happened in the course of history. But it is important to be aware that such structural changes as have occurred from time to time in the past (fourth century, Middle Ages, etc.) are what accounts for our changed consciousness of the mystery of the Church; from that change we are still suffering and we ought on no account cause a still greater change. It would be a tragic paradox if a phenomenon such as the informal groups were to lead to new changes in the mystery of the Church on the grounds of new historical pressures. Why a paradox? Because the informal groups have arisen precisely from the desire to recover basic elements in the mystery of the Church which have disappeared because of historical and social pressures at different periods of history!

* * *

All that I have said represents a positive as well as a negative critique of the informal groups in the light of some basic principles of Orthodox ecclesiology. Our main position is that from the viewpoint of structure the ecclesial potentiality of any individual or group in the Church depends on their participation in the holy Eucharist. In this context we understand the Eucharist to be, as we have indicated, not one sacrament among others, but the community that gathers "in one place" to offer and communicate in the body of Christ, and thus most perfectly images forth the Church in the world. This is why we believe the Eucharistic community must be essentially one in each local Church and why the bishop is therefore essential to any structure that is to deserve the name "ecclesial". To be linked to the bishop is thus a condition of any ecclesiality.

From the viewpoint of the ecclesiology we have described we think there is no way of evading or setting aside the application of this principle to the informal groups. And this not for historical reasons or on institutional grounds, but because the concept of "Church" belongs to that one community which effectively brings to pass in the world and in history communion in the Holy Spirit and God's loving plan for his creation.

The informal groups, therefore, cannot substitute for or ignore the parish and the diocese. The more important thing, however, in my opinion, is that the informal groups can make an essential contribution to the reform both of diocese and parish. That is their true role, and it is a role that can well be called "charismatic", that is, something like, though quite different in content, to the role which the monastic communities have played in the East or the highly significant movement of the "fools for Christ" in the Byzantine Empire. It is clear enough that the diocese and the parish of our experience are not the ideal diocese and parish which we described earlier. The informal groups stress the dimensions of communion and of the Church's existential presence in the world (elements which have for various reasons become less important or even wholly absent from our idea of the Church). Perhaps the presence and witness of these groups may serve a para-Eucharistic charismatic function that might lend the groups a certain ecclesial character.

CHAPTER 13

Informal Groups in the Church:
A Catholic Viewpoint

by

Yves Congar

It is appropriate that I begin by indicating the conditions under which I shall attempt to handle the topic assigned to me. I am the last speaker. I do not rise last because I want to, or under any illusion that I can pronounce such a wise and comprehensive judgment on the whole business that it will be the final word. On the contrary, the fact that I speak last has its problems. Everything worth saying has probably already been said. When I was preparing my paper, I did not know what others might say before I spoke, and so I risked repeating other men's thoughts. Moreover, the subject of this colloquium has been dealt with freqently in the last three years, at times in such an excellent way as to discourage further attempts to go over the same ground. On the questions to be raised and the conclusions to be drawn at least three or four of my fellow theologians have already said all that is essential from a Catholic point of view.[1]

One further remark. In becoming acquainted with the literature on our question, I found myself confronted with enterprises that were sometimes flighty yet often required heavy commitments of inner energy and way of life. What an abundance of ventures we find! I have the feeling a dictionary compiler must have as he sets about combing contemporary poetry for examples of words: he must want to beg off the task Bernanos says: "We admire the services, the commissariat, the military police, the officers, and the map-makers, but our hearts are with those who give their lives." Here I am just one of the map-makers. But, of course, if the map does not correspond to the terrain, the map is wrong and the terrain is right. In addition, things can get quite complicated if the earth itself is moving! Moreover, the theologian is not an ordinary map-maker, for he himself doesn't determine anything. However, on condition that he act with humility, discretion, critical intelligence, patience, and respect, the theologian is the interpreter of a design that has normative, determinative value. In this sense he can refer to a map that exists before the terrain does and therefore pass judgment on the terrain itself.

More than ever we must ask the question: What are we dealing with? The diversity of terms in use forces us to reflect on whether we are faced with a homogeneous datum. People talk of informal groups, base groups, spontaneous groups, marginal groups, wildcat groups, or simply small groups. But they also talk of base communities, small communities, even free Churches (Rosemary Reuther), underground Churches, a second Church or parallel Church. Georges Casalis has even spoken of "floating communities", such as the Mark Community. So we have three or perhaps four substantives and at least a dozen adjectives. Let us review them critically.

"Group" is the broadest term. Of itself it says nothing more than an assemblage of persons who have come together or are coming together. A distinction is made between primary groups, limited in number, in which the members communicate with each other directly and personally, and secondary groups, of much larger membership, in which there is an impersonal

element of organization or structures. "Community", in the
strict sense of the word, signifies that people live together
in some degree, on the basis of some economic sharing and also
share a spiritual ideal which is not necessarily formulated as
a system of ideas. A community cannot do without some structures
or rules, but it goes beyond the level of society (the "Gesellschaft" of Ferdinand Tönnies) and of legislation. If the term
"community" be taken in a broader sense, the togetherness is
of a looser kind, but it is still a matter of life and not just
of utility for production or gain; in this sense we have the
parish community. With the term "community" we can compare the
term "communion" that has been adopted at Boquen and could just
as well be applied to the Légaut Group.[2] Here we have a community
without common life except on occasion. The third substantive is
"Church". This term can be applied to any community that celebrates the Eucharist in union with the legitimate bishop. The
use of the word "Church" may, of course, imply an ecclesiology,
but it may also carry a simply descriptive, sociological meaning.
Its use in our present context can be ambiguous. We shall be
coming back to it later on.

What of the adjectives? "Small communities" is probably
the most general term, since it is purely descriptive--although
there must still be a "community". "Informal" is the adjective
given a certain precedence by the title of our colloquium. We
may ask whether this does not show favor to a particular kind
of group. There do exist some formal groups, those for example
which are integrated into a parish community. I do see, of
course, the legitimate sense of the word "informal". It is
equivalent to "not instituted", if we accept the common-denomin-
ator definition of "institution" as a structure that is relatively
permanent, dependent on some authority, and prior in existence to
the individuals who find in it a model for behavior and the sign-
post for their role in the group. But groups which began as

"not instituted" can become instituted and official. Isn't that what happened to the religious orders? "Marginal" may mean the same thing as informal or spontaneous, but it may also connote a will to remain on the periphery and not be taken over. In any event, the term "marginal", like the term "wildcat", is not applicable to the many groups who want to be part of the Church without challenging her in a radical way and who think of themselves as playing a classical, and even central role in the Church's life by helping her to be a community of brothers.

The expression "base group" or "base community" is preferred by many.[3] It is the most generally appropriate term if we understand it as referring to a group or community that comes into existence, not as the result of a comprehensive pastoral project or some initiative by the institution (Catholic Action or the Third Orders would be examples), but precisely through an initiative from those at the base of the hierarchical pyramid. But we do come across more specialized understandings of the term by equating "base" with those who are without grace and thus constitute the favorite place of God's revelation and gift: the little people, the poor, the exploited, and the oppressed.[4] But often, certainly in the United States according to the results of Rocco Caporale's inquiries, the enlistment in the groups does not correspond to such an ideal vision.

The enlistment does seem to correspond to such a vision in São Paulo where Father Dominique Barbé works, although this does not mean that such people necessarily and as such constitute the substratum of the base communities he tells us about.[5] What the latter involve formally is a beginning or new beginning of the Church in the overall context of a Church whose Establishment is distant and out of touch with a poor population of working men. The problem here, as people like to put it, is "to bring the Church to birth" by establishing a basic group of Christians. In this sense, the name "*base* community" is a very suitable one. *In fact*, then, at São Paulo and probably in many other places, the birth of the Church is taking place in a group of men who are disinherited by society. But is this fact accidental and simply material, or is it a formal element in the very nature of such groups? I am not rejecting the idea that there may be something more than accidental involved, for, after all, "The poor have the Gospel preached to them." But in our own country, many "base communities", where the term is used in the formal sense that such communities represent the re-establishment of a basic group of Christians, draw on the middle classes and cultivated circles; but the São Paulo experience is also repeated among us from time to time.

I shall not undertake to set forth a typology of base groups. But it is worthwhile to advert, even if very incompletely, to their variety so that we may get a better idea of what they have in common. To begin with, there are groups focused on a spirituality of community. Among them are the groups of families such as existed for twenty years before the present-day small-group movement began. We may also mention the Italian Focolari and the groups embraced by Max Delespesse's Centre Communautaire International at Brussels. Secondly, there are missionary communities which aim at the birth or rebirth of the Church in a given place or a given milieu. Thirdly, there are the groups committed to an evangelical life; they may or may not be connected to a religious institute. Such are, for example, the secular institutes of Charles of Jesus or of Father Lataste. A challenge to or an active determination to reform ecclesial structures is not a characteristic of these groups. Their desire is simply to give concrete form to the Gospel summons to brotherly sharing and support, to some kind of voluntary poverty, and to a Christian life of some intensity.

At the far end of the spectrum there is the "underground" group, which is the most critical of all. Between this extreme and the groups already mentioned there is a great variety of people who seek in a limited group for what they do not find in the forms of the Church at large. Here we have the common denominator for all the groups that concern us here. Yes, *all*-- provided we leave aside, not because we look down on them but because they are not part of the homogeneous, worldwide phenomenon we are discussing, the conservative groups set up for the defense of the Church; I am speaking of the groups whose spokesmen in France are, for example, Jean Madiran, Jean Ousset, Pierre Debray, and Bernard Prudhomme. These groups are not really informal groups or small communities, but groupings for action and reaction.

Apart from this last category, then, we can say of *all* the others that they are trying to provide those who feel the need with what the Church at large does not and perhaps cannot give them. "Everything boils down to the inability of the Church to make it possible for those most deeply motivated by the Gospel to live the Gospel within the traditional structures."[6] The goal, then, is to rediscover the Church, and this within the Church but outside its traditional structures; in extreme cases *in opposition to* these structures, but usually only alongside them. The goal, in the last analysis, is a renewal of ecclesiology. If, then, we are to discover the meaning of the groups, evaluate them, and determine the conditions under which the movement is possible, we must go further into the matter of motivations. Like all the contemporary challenges to the Church, that of the informal groups cannot be separated from its motivation; people challenge what no longer offers a valid *meaning* for contemporary man.

We can distinguish two major motives. They are often pursued conjointly; but often, too, one is dominant to such an extent that I think myself justified in considering them successively. Some groups are primarily concerned with revitalizing the internal activities of the Church; others are primarily concerned with accepting the political consequences of the faith.

A. Under "internal activities of the Church" we include essentially: fraternal life in community, the expressions of faith and morality, worship, and the Church's existence in the world as a sign. These questions, especially the first, third, and fourth, are central in the experiments now being carried on among religious men and women.

a) The general conditions of contemporary social life with its fragmentation of existence, its excessive organization, the mechanical uniformity of timetables and of the settings in which men work, and so forth, evidently help create the need a man feels of finding his own identity within a circle of friends who know and accept him and with whom he can exchange and share in a personal way. People feel the same frustration and alienation in the Church: whether in the huge anonymous parishes where they brush against others without knowing them and without exchanging or sharing, or in the formalistic religious communities from which creativity has, as it were, been institutionally banished. People therefore look for Church activities which will not be impersonal but will give expression to what they think and feel, and in which they can truly participate.

The same situation is the setting for what can be called "democratization" (provided the word be properly understood[7]). The demand for democratization, like many others that seem new and almost revolutionary, is a demand for something written deep in the nature of Christianity: that it be a brotherhood, a place where people know and accept each other, where they can call each other by their name and feel that they are fellow-members of a group in which exchange and sharing is the rule. This describes

exactly the small group. The small group allows people to
express themselves in depth and with sincerity. It imposes
nothing; in the small group the only demands are those one makes
on oneself through one's contacts with others. Such demands, of
course, can be stringent. In the small group, a person can be
himself and find his true identity. Thus it does not give rise
to any sense of alienation. It allows one to exchange with and
listen to others, to benefit from the stimulus of their questions
and their fidelity, and thus to enter more deeply into oneself
and to become oneself more truly and fully.

I am of the opinion, moreover, that the need of fellowship
takes different forms in different periods of history. The
twelfth and the nineteenth centuries in the west, for example,
are quite unlike each other in this respect. Our own age is
marked by the need for the small, intimate, warm group, the need
to band together; this, evidently, in reaction to the anonymity
characteristic of the macro-organizations of the technological
era, but also to a Church in which a pyramidal hierarchical
structure and the primacy given to social regimentation are
always in danger of strangling the element of community.

As for religious life, we may think of it either as the
place where small groups take shape, or as itself becoming fragmented and blending with lay communities of shared life (such
communities possibly becoming mixed from the confessional standpoint). Religious can play the role either of animator of a
small group or of the cell out of which a communal group will
grow, as happened with the Poudrière Group at Brussels. In
short: small groups in religious life, or religious life in
base groups. This is the first aspect of the matter that I
shall discuss.

The desire is very widespread--and at least as much among
religious women as among religious men--to have communities in

which the individual can truly experience the fraternal relationship of personal knowledge and exchange with others, without having to bear the weight of the anonymous structures and fixed regulations which are inherent in the large communities of the classical type. The latter had their own balance, and I owe them too much, as do so many of my generation who have won their spurs in the apostolic life, not to proclaim the virtue that was in them. But I must also acknowledge the limitations of a style of life which, at least as we experienced it, belongs to a certain kind of religious world. In these communities and in this religious world, religious life was looked upon as a whole which had a perfect internal coherence, and each sufficiently large community was, as it were, a complete city with well-defined laws and well established ascetical practices. The community provided services to men and the world, and even had its guestmaster for welcoming people; but all of these were as it were functions and projections into the outside world, which did not really affect the nucleus of the community's life.

Now that whole life-style has been challenged to a greater or lesser extent today. Instead of a self-contained asceticism, religious want an asceticism that is intrinsically related to the service of men; this new asceticism can be just as exacting, even more so than the old, and by comparison with it the old seems artificial and rather useless. Religious are trying to discover anew, but in a way that is valid for and intelligible to the men of today, the sign value which religious life ought to have, which it once did have, and which, it seems, it does not have for many today. Religious want the welcoming attitude to be not just a special function of an appointed individual but the openness of the whole community; they want it to be a sharing with those from outside who will cease to be any longer really outside: a sharing at table, study, and prayer. So it goes for other aspects of religious life.

In view of these rather widespread aspirations, I think a distinction must be made. The desire to have small fraternal communities may be an end in itself; that is, there may be simply the desire for sharing and for communion on a truly human scale, and the need to break out of the uniformity imposed by an impersonal rule that fosters individualism and the closed mentality. On the other hand, the desire for small fraternal communities may be functionally connected with the service of men, with entering into their life, with some apostolic task or commitment. The first kind of quest tends to be more linked to an animating personality or a happy conjunction of several such. It hardly challenges the basic tradition of an Institute. Moreover, the kind of community sought is likely to be unstable. It is likely to bring together men and women who each have their own problems, who *cannot* become a part of a larger community, and who quickly run through their limited resources.

The second quest is undoubtedly a more fruitful one. The group is more deeply changed (both in its practice and in its conception of the religious life) by the task it undertakes and by the effort to meet the inherent requirements of the task; in other words, the life of the world with which the group now exists in a symbiotic relationship will affect the life of the group. The result can be radical revisions, even new creations. In extreme circumstances the question would arise whether the identity and grace of the original foundation can be preserved. There is also, of course, the danger of allowing the life of prayer to disintegrate. Yet the Little Brothers of Jesus, to take but one example, seem to be succeeding. Will others, with a different calling and a different grace, succeed as well?

b) In many groups the sharing concerns the faith. The sharing can be, and often is, done on the basis of Scripture,

but the groups are not interested simply in Bible study. The
purpose often is to bring the faith to bear on a situation in
which the ordinary parish is *incapable* of meeting the need.
The people involved in the groups have some general knowledge
of the critical questions concerning the Bible and history and
of the philosophical bases for maintaining the reasonableness
of belief. They talk with unbelievers whose sincerity makes
stringent demands. Does any informed and reflective person
today go along one hundred percent with the official teaching
of "the Church"? Some people find in that teaching something
repressive and likely to cause alienation. The classical form
of that teaching neither satisfies nor interests them. Pastor
Georges Crespy hits the nail on the head when he shows how in
contemporary culture deductive knowledge based on a normative
datum has been replaced by a kind of experimentation, namely,
the rediscovery of a content of personal, living faith by
reference *to the person* of Jesus Christ.[8] What is going on,
then, is a "reconstruction of the faith" or, at the very least,
a re-expression of it.

Something else is involved. People speak of the obscurely
felt need to "justify Christianity".[9] There are several aspects
to this. A critical intellectual justification, such as is
carried out in principle in apologetics, is not excluded, but
it is not really the issue. The aim rather is to make sure, by
the processes and conclusions of personal discovery, that
Christianity really does include the Gospel, the sacramental
life, and the ministry which the Church at large presents under
forms that put people off. These realities have their own truth
and the aim is to rediscover and reformulate it. These people
are looking for a closer connection between what is outwardly
professed and what is really thought and acted on than they
see in the mass of Christians, for they feel the connection here

to be largely non-existent. They are thinking above all of
the area of morality, both personal and social. It is clear
enough that the universal Church and even the local parishes do
not meet felt needs when it comes to birth control, education,
development, peace and armaments, and socialist programs. These
matters are already more or less a part of that expression of
Christianity with which these people feel at home. But these
questions will arise again when we come to the second of the
two categories of small groups which we distinguished earlier.

c) The liturgical need felt by the small groups also
arises initially from dissatisfaction. In large liturgical
gatherings they feel more like spectators than participants;
they attend with others but there is no personal communication.
This can even be the case with small gatherings of ten or
fifteen people in a chapel. For, as Etienne Amory has observed,
these small gatherings do not automatically become "small groups".
To have a small "group" the group must exist because each person
in it knows, accepts, and welcomes the others in their personal
existence.

A further difficulty is that worship follows fixed forms
which do not allow it to make concrete life part of itself,
that is, life as it is lived in the family, at work, in political
society, and in events. The awareness of this fact, along with
the very lively awareness of the royal priesthood of every
baptized person, is the basis for all that is worthwhile in the
current search for a "secular liturgy". This liturgy need not
be the Eucharist, as the Note from the French Episcopal Commission
and the Note of the Belgian bishops on Masses in the small groups
rightly remind us.[10] We must recognize especially the role played
by the word of God as not only studied but heard and received as
the very action of God himself: *opus Dei*. On the other hand,
our base groups are not the sole beneficiaries of the Eucharists

celebrated by small groups or in homes. But a community cannot be built if it does not go on to the sharing of the eschatological Bread.

The Eucharist is both institution and event. It is always celebrated in a local and particular way, and, by its very nature and logic, it always has a universal significance which must be signified in one or other way. So too it is desirable that the connection between the Eucharist and the Church's deaconal function (the service of the little people and the poor) be honored and signified. Even the most intimate celebration, the celebration most adapted to those present, continues to be the celebration of "the sacrifice of the whole Church", that is, it continues to be something that belongs *to the Church* and not to individuals or the group they form.

Moreover, the ordained minister is the president of the liturgy. The contemporary rediscovery of the basic Christian equality of all the faithful[11] must be, and in fact is, accompanied by an awareness of functional differences between Christians. These functional differences are not simply a matter of fact; they enter into the structure of the sacraments. As for the texts being used, I cannot go into the matter here. In some countries, especially Holland and the United States, congregations often use "experimental" Eucharistic liturgies, of which there must be dozens. On the few occasions when I have shared in such Eucharists I have felt very unsatisfied, for they did not express me personally, while the faith or Eucharistic sense of the Church hardly found expression either. Apart from questions of the full Eucharistic faith or of Catholic discipline, such celebrations are valid, it seems, only if they genuinely *express* the life of a Christian community. But then, of course, there arises the danger of particularism, which is especially disturbing when it affects the Sacrament of Unity.

d) What place do the informal groups have in the sign which the Church must offer to the world? There are various answers. Sometimes the group is so intimate that it is a sign only for its members. Communities which practice a high degree of charity and effective brotherly love offer a very powerful sign, all the more so since such communities express the innermost nature of the Church. They become authentic manifestations of the holy or of Christ. But groups that are rather critical and politically committed can be signs of those values so rarely found: freedom and hope. The Church cannot afford to do without such witnesses, for rarely does she seem to men a place of freedom and hope. We must observe, of course, that purity and authenticity are necessary qualities of witness, and, on the other hand, that while a sign of the Church may be particular and partial, it must preserve continuity with the nature, purposes, and means of the Church.

B. Another type of group is primarily concerned with accepting the political consequences of the faith.

The common consciousness of our age is colored in a radical and decisive way by awareness of conflicts and dramatic events which may be very distant in place but are brought home to us through the communications media and may even become a major preoccupation: the Vietnam war, the Third World, the racial problem in the United States, the social situation and revolutionary movements in Latin America, the Arab-Israeli war, opposition to France's government, etc. In fact, it is probably events abroad that first stir the political conscience of Christians. That is to be expected, and we might see in the fact an illustration of Georges Crespy's already mentioned distinction between experimentation and deduction from normative principles. The only thing that can be deduced from the Gospel is rather general principles. That is why, as Bernanos observed, "the Church" condemns aggression but abstains from deciding who is the aggressor. Christians have long been told, "You must get involved!" but the exhortation was based on general principles. I am too well acquainted with the history of social Catholicism and Catholic Action to say that such exhortations were fruitless. But more recently Christians have descovered the political order, and the transition from the social to the political has played a role in some of the crises afflicting Catholic Action among young people. Justification for the transition is possible along speculative and even deductive lines. Such a procedure is valid and even quite important.

It can be shown that salvation is not only "eternal" but temporal as well: "He who denies the present life of man denies the eternal life of God."[12] Christianity is essentially a hope for all men! Theoretical justification both precedes and follows up personal experience. François Biot has interpreted and formulated as follows the personal experience acquired in base groups:

> Christians have long been urged from all sides to get involved in politics. They have been taught in season and out of season that loyalty to Jesus Christ and his requirement of brotherly love for all men will be authentic only if lived out in the reality of daily life and in the building of a just and free world from which all oppression and exploitation has been eliminated.
> Today we are witnessing a kind of reversal of situation: it is no longer "faith and politics" but "politics and faith". The change may seem to be purely verbal but in fact the verbal change points to a change of mentalities and attitudes. When men speak of faith and politics, they presuppose (and the supposition is not necessarily wholly false) that somehow or other the Christian law implies that one must adopt certain political positions, and that in certain circumstances the same law excludes other positions; it implies and excludes because principles

imply consequences. The danger in this mentality
is of thinking that the Christian faith can be
determined in itself before it finds expression
(by way of drawing consequences) in the political struggle. In the same way people thought for
a long time that the Church could exist in itself before having any relationship to what used
to be called, and is still called, the world.
When, however, men speak of politics and faith,
they are recognizing the fact that the affirma-
tion and acceptance of Jesus Christ are not a
prior condition of political action but, on the
contrary, are an interpretation of this action,
with the believer discovering in it a new and
irreducible situation.[13]

The ecclesiological problem here expressed in a calm and
evidently candid way is, to my thinking, a considerable one;
we will come upon it again further on. But what are the
specific facts of the case today? We find them described in
some texts by American writers:

A community of Christians, who by definition are supposed to be committed to the eradi-
cation of injustice and evil, is by no stretch
of the imagination even in the arena of the
struggle. Not only is that true, but it is also
ironically clear that some of the most active
perpetrators of the injustice and evil in our
culture hold high places in the ranks of the
Christian community.[14]

We are burdened with the knowledge of the
moral failure of institutional Christianity.
The failure of the Church in Nazi Germany, the
failure of the Church in America to condemn the
atomic bombing of Hiroshima, and the war in
Vietnam, and its refusal to demonstrate its
verbal support of civil rights, are too evident
to be ignored.[15]

The conclusion drawn from the facts is the succinct re-
statement of the ecclesiological problem already mentioned:

"The function of the Underground Church is to define the Peace and Freedom movements as the true Church."[16]

Paul Evdokimov wrote in 1958: "The Church has the message of liberation, but others do the liberating."[17] The statement may be disputed, but it expresses quite precisely a state of affairs which many Christians today find unacceptable. They will have nothing to do with words that are not followed by suitable actions: "orthodoxy" without "orthopraxy". They denounce the gap between declarations and effective action. They denounce, too, the support given to the status quo and even to oppressive regimes or structures by the practice of the great Churches which delude themselves that they are preserving a political innocence.

It seems clear, however, that the official or hierarchic Church cannot act in the same way as the faithful. The Pope may denounce recourse to arms and the illusory balance achieved by terrorism. Some would like him to do more, yet all recognize that he cannot tear up his draft card or, like the Berrigans, burn the files of a draft board. This is precisely why small groups arise, if not on the fringe, at least toward the periphery of the larger Church. That is the situation we are in today. The groups believe that they are meeting a need which the Church at large does not and perhaps cannot meet. Many small groups come into existence in this way, and more than one is concerned with reforming the basic activities of the Church. In addition, groups of political tendency apply their critical analysis to the Church; they challenge her and hope in this way to force her to develop.

* * *

Ecclesiological Interpretation and Evaluation

We shall proceed as follows in this section of our remarks: (1) We shall refer very briefly to the dangers to which the small groups are open; (2) we shall state the very substantial positive contribution of the groups; and (3) we shall take up the important question of a new ecclesiology, a question already mentioned in connection with such groups as have a political orientation.

1) Dangers. Others have already said all that needs to be said in this area.[18] But we cannot fairly assert and praise the positive contribution of the groups unless we have at least pointed out what is problematic. The basic problem always is to preserve Christian identity and to respect the requirements of Christianity inasmuch as it is a communion. Christianity does not have to be invented as to its faith or its sacraments or the continuation of the Apostles' office in the form of the ministry. In this sense, the Church is *instituted*. We must therefore be aware of the ambiguity in some critiques of the "institution". Even before we advert to the Church, faith, which is the source of the Church, is a communion. This is why the personal experience of faith cannot but be concerned to be united to the faith of others and of the whole Church in its synchronic and diachronic reality. This means communion with the bishop, himself in communion with the other members of the episcopal college and with its head who is, traditionally and really, the criterion and means of the unity in question. Unless we take the words as meant jokingly, we cannot but be disquieted when we hear people say: "The team is my Church", or "I cannot take part in the Eucharist except within our little community." The small group runs the risk of concentrating wholly on *its* problems and losing sight of the real dimensions of questions that have to do with the Church or with society. The groups must avoid isolation, a

pure and simple "among ourselves", and, generally speaking, a fragmentation of the Church.[19] They must avoid getting locked into an attitude of negative criticism or challenge, for all are dependent on the whole and all the others, in love.

2) The theological congress sponsored by Concilium at Brussels concluded in its ninth resolution: "We are seeing today a quest for new forms of community; this fact is very important for ecclesiology." I agree. The positive contribution of the groups is a very important one, provided that Christian identity and communion with others be maintained.

The effect of the existence of the small groups is to relativize the institution. If this relativization does not degenerate into negation or de facto exclusion, it may answer genuine needs.

Vatican II gave expression to the sense that there is a difference between the Church and the kingdom of God. The Church does not exist for its own sake but to lead men to the kingdom, to anticipate it, and to be a sign of it, that is, to be a sign of hope. The kingdom, on the other hand, transcends the distinction between Church and the world.[20] It is the period put to history by the power of the risen Christ; in it are overcome the conflicts and alienations from which mankind suffers but which are also a stimulus to effort and progress. If then there is distance, a space as it were, between Church and kingdom, if the kingdom is the goal of the history of the world no less than of the Church, and if finally, to the extent that the Church belongs within history, it also takes on the appearance of this passing world,[21] then the challenge, in the name of the Gospel, to the Church's historical forms and those of society is justified in principle. The list of charges which it is the Church's duty to keep is being drawn up in part by the informal groups; they do it in a more or less healthy way depending on the group and the circumstances.

In this respect and in others which we shall point out in a moment the groups form part of a series--uninterrupted yet discontinuous--of critical movements. Among these were early monasticism which sprang up within a Church that was comfortably settling down in the world; eleventh-century eremitism; from that point on, the sequence, heterogeneous in some respects but rather homogeneous in others, of more or less anti-ecclesiastical spiritual movements, as well as the spiritual groups of which Messieurs Rapp, Peter, and Freund have been telling us: the Lollards and, on the Protestant side, the "little Churches" of the Pietists, the Methodist "classes", and so on.

We must recognize that the Church at large *cannot* meet all the expectations people have of Christians today, or even all the expectations of Christians themselves. But, conversely, neither can each base community claim to show forth in its life and action all the riches and functions of a Church; these communities are often "and quite legitimately, only one-dimensional and pursue a limited object; they must therefore be open to the rest of the Church."[22]

The institution runs the risk of turning itself into an absolute because of its clerical, pyramidal, somewhat objectivist or mechanist ecclesiology. In this ecclesiology the Church tends to be a great organization run by a hierarchy in which power is concentrated and whose clientele need only follow the rules and observe the practices. Is that a caricature? Barely. It was to resist such a tendency that the lay movements from the twelfth to the fifteenth century arose and the Reformers of the sixteenth. The Church, instituted though it was and is, is also at every moment constantly being brought into existence by God. There is perhaps an excessive appeal by the small groups to the charisms and the Holy Spirit; not everything can be attributed to these, and a good deal can be traced to psycho-sociological conditions

which affect everyone. But the restoration of the charisms and
pneumatology to a place in the vision of the Church and in the
Church's life is an undeniable fact.[23] The limited dimensions
of a community are not a prerequisite for the Church to become
an *event* there ("Where two or three..."), but the Church certainly
does become an event in the communities and especially in the
small groups that make an effort to live by the Gospel. "Revision
of life", a specifically lay creation, has often been the instrument making such an event possible in the Catholic Action groups.[24]

While brought into being by God, the Church is also made up
of men and even, to speak more accurately, made by men. Who would
think of denying this? No one would deny it when it is taken
abstractly. But there is a practical lack of recognition in a
pyramidal, objectivist ecclesiology in which everything is determined from without, from above, and in a materialist way; in
which men are simply a mass, a kind of passive matter; and in
which the Church is not truly a community or communion of persons.[25]
For the early Fathers the Church was a "brotherhood"; it was "the
'we' of Christians".[26] What men are and do in their human lives
which they live by the power of and for the sake of Jesus Christ
is also part of the Church. For twenty years now I have been
deeply impressed by what might be called the re-invention of
Christian man, the re-creation of Christian tissue in the human
substance of men and women. I do not mean, of course, that there
were no Christians before our time! There were plenty of them,
even if a clerical, objectivist system had room for pagans who
attended Mass, abstained on Friday, and supported independent
schools. By "Christian man" I mean a man who has in a personal
way interiorized the norms of the Gospel in his own conscience
and who with a sense of personal responsibility acts accordingly
in his familial, professional, civic, and political life; in short,
I mean a man who has in a personal way accepted his human tasks in
Christ.

It is clear that the base communities, if they be authentic and healthy, are the place where such a Christian man may be formed and find expression. This is why laymen of great spiritual depth and intellectual clearsightedness, such as a Marcel Légaut here at home, are forecasting a renewal of the very substance of the Church by means of small groups which have the necessary spiritual intensity.

> The present crisis of the Church will not be resolved for a long time to come. It seems beyond doubt that the Church will enter a period of extreme decentralization in which she will resemble the scattered local Churches of Christianity's beginning. To be faithful to God in the midst of men she will have to take initiatives that are as varied as the human needs and possibilities to be found in different countries or even in a single place. These initiatives will arise under the impulse of vigorous and tenacious religious individuals, for no preconceived plan will be enough, even if put forward by an authority that is legitimated by very ancient tradition but lacks the suitable charism for which no power can substitute. These initiatives will arise first of all within communities reduced in size but marked by great spiritual cohesiveness; the initiatives will be the fruit of such communities and indeed the very reason for their existence. Though negligible from the viewpoint of society at large, these unorganized but highly organic groups will lead to a wholly new conception of the Church's unity that will distinguish the Church from religions that are to a greater or lesser extent structurally bound up with a political society that gives them their identity and permanence.[27]

With Marcel Légaut we acknowledge the necessity of the Church existing in its own depths and renewing in a radical way its own spiritual tissues. But the Church is under another necessity as well: that of existing outside itself, as it were, and the informal groups may provide one means by which the need is met. I say this on two grounds.

1) It is not enough for the Church to live according to its own categories: the sacral categories of catechesis and celebration or even the temporal categories of works and organizations that carry a Catholic label. Many people no longer have any interest in these things. The creativeness and lines of communication proper to our culture lie elsewhere; men live and are to be found elsewhere. Therefore, as Cardinal Suhard used to say, we must "leave our own house and enter theirs". The Church has, of course, long since found means of launching itself into the world in this way: in the last analysis the sanctification of marriage is one such means, the specialized forms of Catholic Action are another. There are still others which you can think of.[28] The small groups may be looked at from this viewpoint.

2) We meet more and more often these days "marginal" people. They may be believing, religious people who do not "practice" and are not truly integrated into the parishes. They may be people who are searching and feel drawn by Jesus Christ but cannot as yet (and perhaps for a long time to come) accept the beliefs, disciples, and cultic practices of the universal Church. We need, therefore, a threshold Church, a catechumenal Church as it were. There exist, of course, communities for catechumens, but many men are not in the catechumenate in the narrow sense of the term. "Trailbreaker teams" also exist. But there is need of groups in which men who are searching, on the fringes, unbelievers, even atheists, can share with Christians (themselves searching) their questions, their understanding of the meaning of things, their service, and their commitments. We may not strip the Gospel of a trait which is characteristic of it and distinguished it from the Judaism of Christ's time (whether orthodox or Qumranian in style), namely, that it welcomed and brought into the community those who were on the fringes:

Samaritans, tax-collectors, prostitutes, lepers, and so forth. It must be said that the Gospels moves not only from the center to the periphery and from above to below, but in the opposite directions as well.[29] May not the informal groups find here one of their functions in relation to and from the viewpoint of the Church at large?

3) In some statements concerning the underground Church in the United States, in the French "horizontalist" type of thinking, and in some of the programmatic formulations that guide some attempts at apostolic insertion here in France, we find the problem of the Church put in rather radical terms that, in my opinion, deserve serious criticism. A text of Rosemary Reuther may introduce us to this radical problematic: she speaks in it of the underground Church as an entirely new way of understanding the Church as such. "This new way of understanding simply does away with the need for a kind of Church that would think of itself as something more or different than man in the world."[30] I see two related but distinct approaches that would justify this idea.

The first has its starting point in Vatican II whose approach to ecclesiology would supposedly provide several bases for the new conception. (a) Vatican II points out the eschatological distinction between Church and kingdom of God. The kingdom of God is at work in the world outside the Church. "God is acting in human history and giving a meaning to every human action",[31] without the ecclesiastical institution acting as an intermediary.

> Whereas the earlier theology had insisted that wherever the Church exists, there is the kingdom of God, this new underground theology suggests that wherever the kingdom is, there is the Church. The Church as a definable, historically continuous community is no longer important. The Church happens wherever people become friends,

> wherever men and women reach out and bear one
> another's burdens, wherever human community is
> realized and celebrated.[32]

A transfer of a kind takes place, with the Church being desacralized or "ex-sacrated", and the temporal or political being sacralized.

b) Vatican II defined the Church as the people of God. It gave priority and even primacy to the values of Christian life over the values of social organization and authority. It recognized laypeople as full-fledged members of the Church. These changes represent "such far-reaching revisions that we cannot foresee all their repercussions," says Theodor M. Steeman.[33] But Steeman indicates some of these repercussions and they are indeed vast in scope. Thus, there is a people of God that is not enclosed within ecclesiastical boundaries and whose life and action are not determined by the institution because they come from God: "The real bases of the Church are thus beyond the Church, and the Church can never claim fully to incorporate and incarnate within itself the transcendent source of its own existence."[34] In point of fact, however, Vatican II's Dogmatic Constitution on the Church says that, now that the Messiah has come, the people of God are the visible, structured Church to which men may point, and that all other men are in varying degrees and different ways related to this people of God. Steeman, on the contrary, distinguishes between the official or institutional Church and a "Church in general" that is wider than the official Church and in which the informal groups of the underground Church belong.[35] Rosemary Reuther speaks of a "free church": "The free church overruns the false boundaries between church and non-church institutions and thus helps us to see more clearly what and where the church really is."[36]

I have elsewhere quoted the profound words of Paul Evdokimov: "You can say where the Church is; you cannot say where it is not." In a less poetic vein, Cardinal Journet speaks of a Church in process of formation, a Church "in tendency" beyond the visible limits of the Catholic Church. The basic problem is the meaning of the establishment of a "universal sacrament or sign of salvation" as a positive, historical, public institution that is based on positive revelation, on the incarnation of the Word and "what he did, said, and suffered in the flesh", and on the sending of his Holy Spirit at Pentecost. It is true, of course, that between the ecclesial "sacrament" and the spiritual reality of grace there exists both a normal union and numerous separations; this is perhaps the most fundamental problem of ecclesiology and one that, according to a recent study, dominated the ecclesiological thinking of Calvin.[37] Therefore, we cannot say where the Church is not. But *we can say where it is*. The description given by the authors we have been quoting is inadequate.

The second approach taken by the new ecclesiology is the one we have already heard formulated by François Biot and John Pairmann Brown.[38] This approach can also claim a basis in Vatican II but more often it quotes Dietrich Bonhoeffer's description of Christ as "man for others". The words are applied to the Church: a Church for others, a Church in solidarity with men. In some who think along these lines, the qualifier has swallowed up the noun; that is, the Church is simply the "for others", the "in solidarity with men". This is the kind of thing I have been opposed to for years under the title of "horizontalism". The words of Rosemary Reuther cited earlier[39] are a fairly clear expression of it. Here are some others: "We find ourselves very reluctant in the face of any credo that is anything but a collection of hypotheses and the expression of the will to live in accord with love."[40] The Church "is simply mankind, the unitive energy at work in man's history that breaks down all the boundaries of space and time."[41]

We find the same tendency in connection with the faith and its communication. There would be no basis for objection to it if the point being made were simply the lives of men must provide a starting-point or be truly touched or that God never speaks to us of himself without also speaking to us of ourselves. All that is quite true. The disquieting thing is statements that we meet God only in events and in the concrete experience of our shared humanity or that we must no longer appeal to a fixed datum of tradition or rely on a category of the religious as a sphere with its own autonomy and inner coherence. The question that arises is the one J. Guichard raises:

> Is religion the primitive, ideological (in the Marxist sense) form under which a new revolutionary idea or force makes its appearance? Is religion therefore destined to disappear once the revolutionary movement has discovered its scientific basis? Is religion part of 'archeology' or does it have a permanent function distinct from the political function?[42]

To put the same thing in ecclesiological terms: Is the Church simply the meaning or deeper movement of the world, immanent in the world's energies and history? Or--for the purpose indeed of providing such a meaning, since that is part of its mission--is it the result of a coherent set of divine initiatives that are irreducible to the historical, public energies of the natural creation? Is there a *supernatural* order of realities or is mankind the only thing there is? One hundred and thirty years ago that was the point at issue in the Lamennais drama. It may also be the issue, not clearly recognized but real nonetheless, in the new ecclesiology implicit in some small group experiments.

In what would the unity of such a new Church consist? That unity is proclaimed today by men and women who received the faith in the other, older Church and benefited by that Church's structures and certitudes. But what would become of it in the hands of a second generation that had not enjoyed all those benefits--but might well develop a nostalgia for them and want to go back to them?

This tendency, the extreme form of which we have been rejecting, obviously has consequences for authority[43] and for the very sacred matter of mission or the missions. It also has repercussions in the area of the liturgy and the religious life, both of which, we are told, must become "secular".

Now in both areas the call for secularization may have an acceptable meaning. As for liturgy, there is a great debate going on which by itself would provide matter for a colloquium. Those involved in it all start with genuine data and questions: Christian worship is the worship offered by faith, not a ceremonial display; it must absorb real life. On the other hand, the world is saved, objectively speaking, and the Spirit of God is active in it. Jesus has (again, this is quite true) abolished the sacredness that consists in ritual apartness; he has abolished the very category of the "profane". Finally, it is quite correct to insist on the role played by the fraternal community as such in the sign of Eucharistic celebration. But, while agreeing with all these points, we must resist the process of reduction at the end of which the world, as created world, is supernaturalized,[44] so that there is no need of baptizing children since they are already saved and no need of an ordained minister to celebrate the Eucharist since the essential thing is the gathering of brothers: "There are no more specific acts of prayer or worship as distinct from the activities of everyday life."[45] Finally, the very people who tend to think of the

Church as immanent in human history and as source and inspiration of the movement of liberation, issue a radical challenge to the building of churches of any notable size as specific places of worship.[46] Yet such buildings are perfectly in place, for they are, in their own way, a sign that the Church is not to be identified with the inner movement of the world but is an original and specifically different reality.

The question of the secularization of religious life is rarely taken up in books for public consumption, except with regard to the secular institutes, where the secularization has already taken place. In fact, however, these institutes are a "mixture", as Gabriel le Bras used to say, a "fourth type of Christians". We are not speaking here of such institutes, even if the secular form of life which some religious want is objectively the form of life proper to the secular institutes. The intention of these religious is to preserve their own vocation and what they call the "project" of their Order, while striving for it in new forms: *small* fraternal communities living in apartments, in the midst of other men; professional work; openness to others; complete sharing in contemporary culture; being as little "apart" as possible; active association with the struggles of men for justice, brotherhood and peace. In and through such a life style, with the help and inspiration of their brothers, they want to live by the Spirit and bring the Gospel home to men.

In theory there is no reductionism involved in such a program, which has in fact already been put into practice here and there. But the question must be raised in each case and for each Order, whether the Order's reason for existence, the grace proper to its foundation, and the essential structures which purpose and grace imply, are being respected. Similarly, is the distance between religious life and the common, secular way of life, a distance which seems required by the aim of the religious to be completely at God's disposal, being respected? Can religious life be reduced to the vow of chastity or consecrated celibacy?

* * *

By way of conclusion I would like to quote a few words of my friend Henri Denis which he spoke at the most recent Semaine des Intellectuels Catholiques. They express my own personal conviction:

> The centralizing Roman model with its monolithic character is too formal. We may expect the institution to renew its own substance in two essential directions: in the direction of small communities and in the direction of an all-embracing community that will manifest the unity of Christ which underlies all tensions and differences. The issue for the Christianity of tomorrow is to unify these two non-contradictory movements.[47]

CHAPTER 14

By Way of a Conclusion

I

Remarks of Georges Casalis after Yves Congar's Conference

My dear Father, for almost thirty-five years I have been following you with admiration and affection. I remember that in 1936 when I was 19 and you were already 32 (a thirteen year difference we have never been able to eliminate!) I crossed the whole of Paris to hear you preach on "separated Christians" during a Prayer for Unity Octave; the somewhat disconcerting scene was the Sacred Heart Church on Montmartre, but it was not acceptable at that time to recall that it had been built on the blood of the Communards. Since then I have always paid careful attention to what you say or write, and so I have listened very closely to the paper you have just read to us. Now I must admit, my impression is that I have heard an example of what I myself called yesterday "balanced theology", that is, a refusal of the present polemical situation and of all polemical confrontation. The end-result is that I find myself wavering between conviction and disquiet: conviction because by and large I agree with what you have said; disquiet because, if I may so put it, I disagree with all that you did not say.

I am disappointed because the theologians at this colloquium have shown themselves chiefly concerned to justify their respective traditional ecclesiologies and to show how well founded and relevant they are; on the whole, they have refused the challenge offered by the sociologists. And yesterday when I had tried to make those present hear the questions being asked by the informal groups, I was attacked for *my* theology. The theologians were mainly interested in whether I stood in the traditional orthodox line, and not whether the informal groups were challenging *all* ecclesiastical structures, and therefore all the theologies as well!

Despite the reserves which you and others have formulated, I maintain that the cutting edge of the informal groups is represented by those who take for granted the reality of the political order and the risk of politics. With them, I raise once again the questions I hoped this colloquium would help us answer, for in your silence in regard to them I find confirmation that the severe diagnoses of the informal groups have hit the mark. So then:

Are the Churches willing to analyze themselves, or let themselves be analyzed, from the political point of view? What position are we taking, what position are the Churches taking, in the face of the undeniable results of such analyses, which show the Churches to be, almost without exception, on the side of "established disorder"?

Are ecclesiastical structures politically indifferent, harmful, meaningful? I am especially taken aback by the silence of my colleague, Roger Mehl, on this important matter.

Is the Gospel politically neutral? If yes, we must have the courage to say so! If not, we must have the courage to live accordingly!

If, as the recent letter of Pope Paul VI to Cardinal Roy, *Octogesima adveniens*, claims, the paths of liberalism and of marxism are both closed to us, how can we take seriously the call to "play an active role in political life"?

The essential need, in my view, is that we find as well grounded and developed an answer as possible to the two questions

I see at the heart of the challenge our times are issuing to
the Churches, their faith, their apostolate, their service in
the collective and personal spheres. These two questions are:
the Christian interpretation of the political order, and the
political interpretation of Christianity.

We find the first kind of interpretation being practiced
by Second Isaiah who does not hesitate to say of Cyrus, the
Persian conqueror: "Here is *my* servant, *my* anointed one, Cyrus,
says the Lord." Why does he say it? Because Cyrus has destroyed
the Babylonian Empire and rescued whole peoples, Israel among
them. The question must be asked: Where are the Cyruses of
today? Are the Churches condemned to preach: "Thus said the
Lord *in another day*"? Or can they risk saying: "Thus says the
Lord *today*"?

The second kind of interpretation is being practiced by
many Christians and non-Christians who make use of the tools of
Marxist analysis and thereby restore to us an astonishing grasp
of Scripture such as centuries of socio-political conformism
had made us forget. I have already pointed out how such analysis
has brought us to see the politicization (in favor of the powers
that be) of the Churches' teaching. It has brought the rediscovery of essential dimensions of the human, namely, the collective and the historical dimensions, and with it the critique of
that personalist individualism so dear to many theologians. We
might add that it has led to the denunciation of the importance
given to private property in treatises on social ethics, and has
made us at least look carefully at André Philip's challenge:
"socialist, because Christian".

It is evident that the deductive style of theology has led
to an impasse and must once again be set aside. But if, as I
think I understood you to say, you are open to the inductive
approach, why do we hesitate to undertake it? If we refuse that

way, we shall condemn ourselves to having absolutely nothing to say to our world at the end of the twentieth century. It is already clear that in many cases the "great" Churches are leading a completely marginal life, while those which are "marginal" are really at the heart of reality and at the center of the real problems! That is why I stand with the latter.

We must not be like the salt that stays in the shaker and there loses the savor which it preserves only when it risks disappearing into the mass to be seasoned--"the human masses, my neighbor", as Father Chenu puts it in a striking summary of the whole Gospel.

II

Concluding Remarks by Yves Congar

We have reached the time for summing up. That is too bad, for, as our chairman for the day said quite rightly just now, our colloquium--our "speaking with each other"--is just in a position to begin. But the session has its program and horarium, and these offer me the honor and the burden of bringing things to a conclusion.

First of all, let me sum up the colloquium from a formal point of view. The colloquium has certainly been a success and has been most interesting from beginning to end. We owe this success and interest to the care with which René Metz and Jean Schlick organized the colloquium and then, with impartiality and modesty, saw that it went smoothly. We have all learned a great deal. Yet there is also room for some criticism of the sessions.

First of all, there was not enough time for genuine sharing. Obviously, it is quite difficult to decide in advance and to

program the amount of time to be allotted to the discussion.
Sometimes a half-hour may be too much, sometimes two hours are
not enough. In any case, there was no real dialogue between
Georges Casalis and Roger Mehl. The latter's paper dealt with
the small groups as though they must inevitably reject the two
ecclesiological values I agree are essential; institution, not
selectivity. But Georges Casalis, for his part, looked at the
informal groups only insofar as they stand for political critique and political commitment. There was need of dialogue!

There is a more radical criticism. We started off as though
all we had to do in order to give our theme sufficient definition
was to stick the label "informal groups" on it. We added "in the
Church", and I myself have tried to observe this limitation. But
the phenomenon embraces far more than the Church. We may pass
over the sectarian groupings of which Julien Freund spoke to us,
for these are expressly within Christianity. The sociologist,
however, may think that the phrase "in the Church" is already
an evasion of reality, since, as René Lourau remarked to me, the
"informal group" phenomenon is not specifically religious either
in form or in content. In "form", groups of Christians differ
very little from cultural, artistic, or political groups. In
content, groups of Christians adopt a good deal of the groupist,
marginal, anti-institutional ideology that we also find in an
avant garde artistic group or an oppositional group within the
French Communist Party. If I understand him correctly, René
Lourau thinks the only worthwhile approach to the "informal
group" phenomenon is to analyze them in their daily challenging
of society and in their socio-political context.

But would we not then be excluding from our study the very
numerous groups which, while not denying or failing to recognize
the political impact of all we do, come together in order to live
in a fuller and more authentic way the program of Christianity?

There was need, then, to make clear from the very beginning just what we were talking about and what was to be implied in the words "informal groups *in the Church*". Possibly we should have discussed the legitimacy of such a topic.

We have also been led at times to point out the lack of precision in certain terms, such as "institution". I myself offered as one example the phrase "juridico-institutional accessory". The generality and impreciseness of some of the challenges issued was also disquieting. After all, the word "institution" can be made to cover things that are quite relative and very much open to criticism. But it can also be made to cover others for which I personally would not hesitate to give my life! In short, then, our colloquium was not sufficiently focused. We did not even really discuss the value of the different labels given to the realities in question.

In turning now to a summary of the content of the thirteen very substantial papers which we have heard and sometimes discussed, I would see three major points as having been made.

1) The very existence of the groups rests on the experience, sometimes expressed in harshly critical terms, of the inability of the Churches and the parishes to meet the needs of a Christianity that is lived to the full. At times there is the criticism of the Churches for having adapted themselves to cultural models that are now more or less outdated, or to political and social regimes that are to be rejected in the name of justice, human dignity, and the demands of the Gospel. An idealistically oriented ecclesiology does not take sufficient account of all these requirements, which presuppose an acknowledgement of the historical nature of the earthly Church.

At a more radical level, we are to recognize that the whole of Christianity, the whole of the Gospel, is not mediated by the institutional forms of the Church. Things ceaselessly come to birth and develop. But our contemporary experience is not something wholly new. The historians have shown us that it had many forerunners. And what an abundant crop, indeed, of challenges, spiritual movements, and initiatives more or less at loggerheads with the various "establishments"! Theologically speaking, we are forced to recognize the existence and importance of the personal principle alongside the institutional principle of pure docility. What is really involved is pneumatology, as J. D. Zizioulas reminded us in a penetrating way. Still speaking theologically, we are confronted here with a subject that is filled with questions and problems: the relation between creativity and what is already instituted, the relation between Christology and the initiative of the Spirit, the discernment of the Spirit, the relation to the universal community, the sense in which the many initiatives which mark general history outside the assignable limits of the Church can have their origin in the Holy Spirit; and so on.

2) The base groups challenge the Churches. It seems that some Christian values cannot be achieved, at least not without further mediations, in structures that embrace the masses. This is true, for example, of brotherhood which requires that people enter into a personal relationship with each other and call each other by name. The base communities look at things through the opposite end of the telescope from the established structures; that is why they are communities "of and at the base". They question the kind of authority that has predominated in the great Churches, certainly in the Catholic Church, and the manner in which this authority has been exercised. I myself have come to a better understanding of the light that sociological analysis can shed in this area; concretely, in Jean Remy's paper, the idea of "cultural models", the decisive role they play, and the cultural sensibility that corresponds to them, as over against

the kind of rational organization and discourse which prove unable to fit these things in. Or, again, the distinction between (social) "movements" and "organizations". Yet it was not in vain that when Catholic Action began "movements" replaced the older "works"!

But the challenges today issued to the "establishments" by informal groups have taken on a more radical character as a result of *political* analysis and critique. René Lourau and Georges Casalis have enabled us to understand this challenge. It is quite true that the Church is often silent when it should speak. It thinks itself politically innocent and neutral when it is not. It must analyze and criticize itself as a political factor. So must theology. In an exchange here with Georges Casalis, and earlier at the congress sponsored by Concilium at Brussels, I acknowledged my own inadequacy and datedness in this regard. It is partly a question of the generation I belong to. Among Catholics, ever since the divisions caused by the war in Ethiopia, the Spanish civil war, Nazism, and the Resistance, there has been a new discovery of the political dimension and, after the Second World War, a passage from the "social" to the "political" or to the full recognition of the political dimension of the social itself. All that, which reached a kind of boiling point after May 1968, is playing an important role in many small groups. Yet we cannot without qualification reduce the question of the base groups to the political question, even though we acknowledge that all reality, including even the most purely "spiritual" base groups, inevitably have a political significance.

We have heard mention of the fact of a revision of the "Church--world" relationship, and of the criticism, often voiced today, of dualism. In regard to the latter, I would like to see the avoidance of general, imprecise statements. I myself would acknowledge that the criticism of dualism is justified in some areas, but I would reject it as valid at certain levels.

3) If Georges Casalis has brought out the full force of the challenge issued to the Church by the informal groups, Roger Mehl, J. D. Zizioulas, and I have, I think, shown what a serious ecclesiological question the small groups must answer. The point, clearly, is not that the informal groups are taking the place of the Church, although one might have thought it was as he listened to the justification (well grounded, in my view) which Roger Mehl offered for the institution and the parish. I myself probably gave a more positive welcome to the base groups as fitting into the program of the Church at large. The real question that keeps coming up is the question of unity. Georges Casalis himself has spoken of a "ministry of unity", and this--if I understood him correctly--at the very highest level. But we would be in agreement, I think (and not just verbal agreement!) that the contemporary movements force us to look for a unity with new requirements or a new kind of unity that makes room for tensions and a type of pluralism.[1]

The sociologist and historian, as such, address themselves to *facts* and analyze these. There is a lesson for us in this. We sensed it, for example, in Danièle Léger's paper in which preciseness did not detract from freshness. The theologian exercises a critical function; *in principle*, he is always attempting to give bearings. Facts are one of the data he works on, but he applies criteria. The pastor, the churchman, or simply the mature Christian cannot help raising questions and asking the implications of things. To be sure, they must not decide too quickly where things are going. The critique in which the theologian engages must also be brought to bear on himself and his work. People indeed force him to such self-criticism by asking whether his judgment may not be influenced by the institutional, ideological, and political implications both of what he is defending and of the facts which he attempts to judge.

Independently, however, of this critique of our procedures, we must in the name of theology itself respect the open-endedness of and element of mystery in the history of salvation for which Oscar Cullmann has suggested as an exergue the Portuguese proverb: "God writes straight with crooked lines." Karl Barth used to say that we must have the *courage* to theologize, because at times theologizing means going against the current. The courage must be shown toward both the right and the left: courage to accept the criticism of any elements of "ideology" there may be in our defence of principles and to reject either the vague and emotional generality of criticisms leveled at the "institution" or the reduction of ecclesial realities to purely political categories or tendencies in which the questionable is mingled with the highly respectable. I am thinking, under this last heading, of the tendency to judge oneself only in terms of one's own sincerity and one's sense of personal appropriateness. Jean Remy has offered us a significant example of this tendency; it took place in California, but, in this respect, we all live in California. The result of this tendency would be an "a la carte Christianity" that would border on aimlessness or syncretism. Here again, what emotional generalities we find in much contemporary criticism of what the critics call "hypocrisy" and "repression"! Yet at the same time how much authentic generosity and, often, undeniable evangelical spirit we find in so many contemporary pleas and quests!

I am aware that what I have said will be labeled "balanced theology". I accept the label, and hope only that, in speaking last and summing up the conclusion reached by a colloquium which has been and remains the work of all the participants, I have not excessively obscured the rich harvest of these days which, thanks to CERDIC and its director, have brought us together in work and friendship.

NOTES

Notes to pp. 3-39

NOTES TO CHAPTER 1

1. [On the basic meaning of *communauté de base*, usually translated by the somewhat awkward phrase "base community", cf. the remarks below, of Yves Congar in his essay, "Informal Groups in the Church: A Catholic Viewpoint," p. 299.]

2. Erving Goffman, *Asylums: Essays on the Social Situation of Mental Patients and Other Inmates* (Garden City, N.Y.: Doubleday [Anchor Books], 1961).

3. ["Hot" in the pre-McLuhan sense: communities in which people are deeply involved with one another.]

4. Cf. Jean Remy, "Fault and Guilt in the Perspective of Sociology," in Edward Schillebeeckx (editor), *Sacramental Reconciliation* (Concilium 61; New York: Herder and Herder, 1971), pp. 11-25.

NOTES TO CHAPTER 2

1. The *Vademecum du catholique fidèle* (Paris: Ferrey, 1968^2), pp. 9 and 13, seems to invite "faithful Catholics" to build up such networks.

2. Cf., below, the section "Generations, Social Belonging, and Socio-Religious Change."

3. Cf., below, the section "From the Dynamics of Change to the Analysis of Causes."

4. Friedrich Engels, *On the History of Early Christianity*, in Karl Marx and Friedrich Engels, *On Religion* (Moscow: Foreign Language Publishing House, 1957; New York: Schocken, 1964), pp. 329-30.

5. On the opposition between social movement and social organization, cf. Jean Remy's essay in this volume.

Notes to pp. 39-43

6. ["Radical challenge" here translates the word *contestation*. On this term, with its connotations not only of simple "questioning" or "challenge" (though these English words may be adequate translations in some contexts), but of "radical opposition, rebellion, revolt", cf. *Contestation in the Church*, edited by Teodoro Jiménez Urresti (Concilium 68; New York: Herder and Herder, 1971), especially the opening essay by Emile Pin, "Contestation," pp. 13-21, which analyzes the meaning of the word. -- Tr.]

7. I am referring to the sects: militant and pacifist Anabaptists, anti-Trinitarians, etc. Cf. Jean Séguy, "Anabaptisme et réforme de l'Eglise au XVIe siècle," *Christ seul*, January, 1969, pp. 1-16; or George H. Williams, *The Radical Reformation* (Philadelphia: Westminster, 1962).

8. The only scientific description we know of is in Danièle Hervieu-Léger, *La Mission Étudiante (1966-1970): Essai de sociologie d'un développement* (Paris: Ecole des Hautes Etudes, 1971; unpublished dissertation), which deals only with informal student groups. Cf. the same author's contribution to the present book. [And cf. now Danièle Hervieu-Léger, *De la mission à la protestation: L'évolution des étudiants chretiens (1965-1970)* (Paris: Editions du Cerf, 1973).]

9. Cf. Friedrich Engels, *Socialism: Utopian and Scientific*, translated by Edward Aveling (New York: International Publishers, 1935).

10. To the extent that regulative orthodoxy loses its plausibility due to social change, the beginnings can acquire normative value once again and thus give new life to the original utopia; cf. Jean Séguy, "Une sociologie des sociétés imaginées: Monachisme et utopie," *Annales: Economies, sociétés, civilisations*, March-April, 1971, pp. 328-54. Our reflections on regulation in the functioning of utopias and of social groups generally owe much to frequent conversations with Jean-Pierre Deconchy; cf. his *L'orthodoxie religieuse: Essai de logique psycho-sociale* (Paris: Editions Ouvrières, 1971).

11. Cf. Max Weber, *The Sociology of Religion*, translated by Ephraim Fischoff (Boston: Beacon, 1963), chapter 4 (pp. 46-59).

12. Cf. Max Weber, *The Protestant Ethic and the Spirit of Capitalism*, translated by Talcott Parsons (New York: Scribner's 1958), p. 183: "But it is, of course, not my aim to substitute

Notes to pp. 43-47

for a one-sided materialistic an equally one-sided causal interpretation of culture and of history." Cf. also p. 277, n. 84.

13. As we have already pointed out; examples of such occurrences are given in Maria Isaura Pereira de Queiroz, *La guerre sainte au Brésil: Le mouvement messianique du Contestado* (São Paulo: Faculty of Philosophy, Science, and Letters, 1957).

14. Weber also stresses the fact that the prophet exercises his charism gratis, while the priest requires payment. This aspect seems to us secondary in relation to the present situation. But the contemporary challenge (by priests) to the full-time priesthood highlights the fact that the traditional-style priest is economically dependent on the faithful. The desire for economic independence through the exercise of a secular profession is connected, therefore, among other things, with the opposition between priest and prophet.

15. This at least is what Engels wants socialism to do; in his view Christianity became institutionalized when it was taken over by the dominant classes of the Roman Empire.

16. One stage or two, depending on how sharply we distinguish "circle of disciples" from "apostolic community".

17. Cf. the opposition between Peter and John in early Christianity. Sometimes, however, such a "special role" is justified later on by reference to a supposed choice by the prophet.

18. Joachim Wach has seen the importance of the "circle of disciples"; cf. his *Sociology of Religion* (London: Kegan Paul, Trench, and Trubner, 1947), pp. 135-39.

19. A conception that will be reflected in various writings, some of which will become canonical.

20. Cf. Jean Séguy, *Les assemblées anabaptistes-mennonites de France: Etude de sociologie historique* (Paris: Faculty of Letters of the Sorbonne, 1970; unpublished dissertation).

21. Note that Troeltsch's typology is not reducible to a dichotomy, as is only too often asserted. It involves three types (church, sect, and mysticism) which the author calls "pure", and a fourth (the free church) which he regards as dependent on specific circumstances. We will not make use of this fourth concept here.

22. Troeltsch means *"claiming* to have been endowed".

Notes to pp. 47-53

23. Again, the meaning is "*claiming* to have experienced 'the new birth.'"

24. Ernst Troeltsch, *The Social Teaching of the Christian Churches*, translated by Olive Wyon (New York: Macmillan, 1931), p. 993.

25. On this problem cf. Peter L. Berger, *The Sacred Canopy: Elements of a Sociological Theory of Religion* (Garden City, N.Y.: Doubleday, 1967), pp. 160-66.

26. Troeltsch, *op. cit.*, pp. 993-94.

27. Troeltsch, *op. cit.*, pp. 330, 699-700.

28. Cf. Jean Séguy, "Multiplicité et non univocité du phénomène religieux populaire," *Cahiers des études des religions populaires* (Montreal) 8 (December, 1970) 48-55; and "Religion et réussite agricole: La vie professionnelle des anabaptistes français du XVIIe au XIXe siècle," *Archives de sociologie des religions* no. 28 (July-December, 1969), 93-130.

29. For discussion of this point, cf. Talcott Parsons in his "Introduction" to Max Weber, *The Sociology of Religion* (above, footnote 11).

30. H. Richard Niebuhr, *The Social Sources of Denominationalism* (New York: Holy, 1929).

31. Niebuhr, *op. cit.*, pp. 19-20.

32. Bryan R. Wilson, *Sects and Society* (London: Heinemann, 1961).

33. I think I have demonstrated this in my dissertation (above, footnote 20).

34. Cf. Max Delespesse and André Tange, *Le jaillissement des expériences communautaires* (Paris and Ottawa: Fleurus and Novalis, 1970), pp. 51-72, on the Belle Community experiment, where problems arising from the family made their appearance in an evident way. According to information which I have received through personal communications concerning a community established by Mennonites in a large American city, the same kind of problems have arisen there.

35. Niebuhr, *op. cit.*, p. 19.

36. Niebuhr, op. cit., p. 33.

37. The first chapter of Niebuhr's book is titled: "The Ethical Failure of the Divided Church".

38. Cf. Peter Embley, "The Early Development of the Plymouth Brethren," in Bryan R. Wilson (editor), *Patterns of Sectarianism* (London: Heinemann, 1967), pp. 213-43, and Bryan R. Wilson, "The Exclusive Brethren: A Case Study in the Evolution of a Sectarian Ideology," *ibid.*, pp. 287-312.

39. Cf. Charles Y. Glock, "The Role of Deprivation in the Origin and Evolution of Religious Groups," in Robert Lee and Martin R. Marty (editors), *Religion and Social Conflict* (New York: Oxford University Press, 1964), pp. 24-36.

40. Ralf Dahrendorf, *Class and Class Conflict in Industrial Society* (Stanford: Stanford University Press, 1959).

41. Weber provides Dahrendorf with his definitions of authority and power (pp. 165-73). Authority is "the 'probability that a command with a given specific content will be obeyed by a given group of persons'" (p. 166), and power is "the 'probability that an actor within a social relationship will be in a position to carry out his own will despite resistance, regardless of the basis on which this probability rests'" (*ibid.*).

42. On these groups cf. Dahrendorf, op. cit., pp. 179-89.

43. What follows is to be taken as a hypothesis that must be tested by concrete studies.

44. Recall, for example, Henri de Lubac, whose book, *The Splendour of the Church*, was written at the time of his difficulties with Rome.

45. We may see this internalization at work in de Lubac's case; recent conversations with other religious who had difficulty with Rome during the same period convinces me that they still do not grasp the significance of their conduct at the time. Thus ideology can conceal from individuals the functioning of the social system to which they belong.

46. The real stakes in the ideological discussion may have escaped those who took part in them.

Notes to pp. 58-63

47. Once again we must remind the reader that these analyses, which are in any case too concise, do not claim to be anything but a theoretical perspective that needs to be confronted with the facts in a less schematic way.

48. "We do not need a pope in every diocese": this thought was often heard on the lips of priests during the conciliar discussions on collegiality.

49. Once again, this is a hypothesis that would require close scrutiny.

50. The point made in the preceding note applies here as well.

51. The working paper on "ministerial priesthood" which was sent by the synodal secretariat to all bishops in preparation for the synod of September, 1971, began with the words: "The ministry of Catholic priests is today passing through a crisis which in many places is undoubtedly a serious one." On this subject cf. Xavier Charpe, "Avant Synode: Qu'est-ce qu'un prêtre aujourd'hui?" *Informations catholiques internationales*, no. 384 (May 15, 1971) 16-20.

52. Here again lengthy analyses would be in place. Cf. Jacques Sutter, "Mutation organigrammatique de l'Eglise de France," *Archives de sociologie des religions* no. 31 (January-June, 1971). Perhaps the bishops themselves are losing some of their power to these offices, as has happened among the Baptists of the southern United States; on the latter cf. Paul M. Harrison, *Authority and Power in the Free Church Tradition: A Social Case Study of the American Baptist Convention* (Princeton: Princeton University Press, 1959).

53. [Edmond Richer was a sixteenth-century French theologian who propounded an extreme Gallicanism or anti-papal Church-State view in behalf of Henri IV. -- Tr.]

54. Except by way of ritualization of their role (as lay readers, "second [or third?] order" deacons, lay distributers of communion, etc.) or by the granting of participation in pastoral councils whose members are appointed and have no real authority.

55. Georges Gurvitch, *L'idée du droit social* (Paris: Sirey, 1931).

Notes to pp. 64-72

56. The sacrament of penance may be an exception. At least it is practiced in some groups without any private confession of sins or individual absolution.

57. The phenomenon is, in fact, not entirely new; cf. Kathleen L. Wood-Legh, *Perpetual Chantries in Britain* (London: Cambridge University Press, 1965), pp. 303-14 and especially the last paragraph of p. 314.

58. Cf. Pope Paul VI, *Octogesima adveniens: Apostolic Letter to Cardinal Maurice Roy on the Eightieth Anniversary of the Encyclical Rerum Novarum*, May 14, 1971, in *The Pope Speaks* 16 (1971) 137-64.

59. What is said here applies especially to the most autonomous of these groups.

60. The cases in which the Church requires resistance to the established powers are rare and do not invalidate what we say here.

61. Werner Stark, *The Sociology of Religion: A Study of Christendom 1: Established Religion* (New York: Fordham University Press, 1966), especially pp. 5-135. The various Christian rites have attracted little attention from sociologists. On the relationship between liturgy and politics, cf. my forthcoming article, "Liturgia e politica: A prepaus de l'enterrada del general de Gaulle," *Obradors* (Faculty of Letters, University of Montpellier).

62. This state of affairs finds symbolic expression in the fact that most if not all of the groups do not go so far as to celebrate the Eucharist without a priest.

NOTES TO CHAPTER 3

1. Cf. Leon Trotsky, *The New Course* (New York: International Publishing Co., 1923; Ann Arbor: University of Michigan Press, (1965).

2. Cf. Kurt Lewin, *A Dynamic Theory of Psychology: Selected Papers*, translated by Donald K. Adam and Karl E. Zener (New York: McGraw-Hill, 1935).

Notes to pp. 73-93

3. Cf. R. F. Bales, *Interaction Process-Analysis: A Method for the Study of Small Groups* (Cambridge, Mass.: Addison-Wesley, 1950).

4. Wilfrid R. Bion, *Experiences in Groups, and Other Papers* (London: Tavistock Publications, 1961).

5. Unamuno wrote a book entitled *Tragic Sense of Life*, translated by J. E. Crawford Flitch (1921; New York: Dover Publications, 1954).

6. Emmanuel Mounier, *Existentialist Philosophies: An Introduction*, translated by Eric Blow (London: Rockliff, 1948).

7. *Personalism*, translated by Philip Mairet (New York: Grove, 1952).

8. Georges Bernanos, *La France contre les robots* (Paris: Laffont, 1947).

9. Cf. his book, *Feu la chrétienté* (Paris: Editions du Seuil, 1950).

10. Emile Durkheim, *The Elementary Forms of the Religious Life*, translated by Joseph Ward Swain (French original 1912, translation 1915; New York: Free Press, 1965), p. 14.

11. Gabriel Tarde, *La criminalité comparée* (Paris: Alcan, 1886).

12. J. T. Maertens, *Les petits groupes et l'avenir de l'Eglise* (Paris: Centurion, 1971).

13. René Lourau, *Analyse institutionnelle et pédagogie* (Paris: Editions de l'Epi, 1971).

14. Cf. G. Lapassade, *Recherches institutionnelles*, 3 vols. (Paris: Gauthier-Villars, 1971); René Lourau, *L'analyse institutionnelle* (Paris: Editions de Minuit, 1971).

15. Cf. Alain Tourain, *Sociologie de l'action* (Paris: Editions du Seuil, 1965).

16. In his *Logic* Hegel notes that the three moments or phases of the dialectic are really four, since the second phase (that of simple negation) has two faces: one looks toward the positive unity it denies, the other toward the negative unity which in turn denies it. These two aspects of simple negation

in the second moment of the dialectic are, in my scheme, anti-institutional and non-institutional action respectively. However, from the sociologist's point of view non-institutional action is also a first form of counter-institutional action, since it looks for an alternative to existing institutions, even if the alternative does not take a community form as it does in counter-institutional action in the usual sense of the latter term.

17. From this point of view, expressions now popular, such as anti-psychiatry or anti-ethnology or anti-pedagogy, are really not suitable when they refer not to a purely ideological critique being carried on within these disciplines but to experimentation with new procedures in therapy or ethnological work or education. In the latter case it would be more proper to speak of counter-psychiatry, counter-ethnology, and counter-pedagogy.

18. Cf. Jean-Paul Sartre, *Critique de la raison dialectique* (Paris: Gallimard, 1960).

19. Robert Davezies, *La rue dans l'Eglise* (Paris: Editions de l'Epi, 1968).

20. Cf. *Livre blanc des entreprises nouvelles*, published (in mimeographed form) by the Commission Générale d'Evangélisation de l'Eglise Réformée de France, for the National Synod held at Pau in 1971.

21. Henri Gougaud, *Nous voulons vivre en communauté* (Paris: Bélibaste, 1971). Cf. also, in addition to Maertens' book (see note 12, above), the collective work, *L'Eglise souterraine* (Gembloux: Duculot, 1970); Dominique Barbé, *Demain les communautés de base* (Paris: Editions du Cerf, 1970); Bernard Besret, *Tomorrow a New Church*, translated by M. J. O'Connell (New York: Paulist Press, 1973); *Les communautés de base* = *Lumière et vie*, vol. 19, no. 99 (August-October, 1970). Plenty of references can be found in *Répertoire bibliographique des institutions chrétiennes* 69 (1969) and 70 (1970) under the heading "Groupe informel".

In periodicals occasional articles suggest a challenging of institutional Christianity by group Christianity. For example, G. David and S. Larch, "La contestation dans l'Eglise," in *L'homme et la société*, no. 16 (1970) outline three levels of challenge which may not be that much different from the model I have proposed; the authors distinguish three types of movement, which have as their respective goals improvement, spontaneity, and restructuring. The studies of J. P. Deconchy, R. Mandrou,

Notes to pp. 108-140

M. de Certeau, and J. Sutter in *Politique aujourd'hui*, nos. 2 and 12, 1970, are very enlightening.

NOTES TO CHAPTER 4

1. The terminology in quotation marks is that of Louis Althusser, *For Marx*, translated by Ben Brewster (New York: Random House, 1969).

2. The quoted phrases here and in the following paragraphs are from statements gathered from members of the groups in question.

3. Cf. Henri Desroches, *Sociologies religieuses* (Paris: Presses Universitaires de France, 1968).

NOTES TO CHAPTER 5

1. [Cf. Plato, *Republic*, VII, 537, where in the educational program "the detached studies in which they [selected students] were educated as children will now be brought together *in a comprehensive view* of their connections with one another and with reality": *The Republic of Plato*, translated by Francis MacDonald Cornford (London: Oxford University Press, 1941), p. 259; italics added.]

2. Robert Ardrey, *The Social Contract: A Personal Inquiry into the Evolutionary Sources of Order and Disorder* (New York: Atheneum, 1970), pp. 94-95.

3. Ardrey, *op. cit.*, p. 65.

4. Without any discussion Ardrey ascribes to evolution the passage from ape to man. In explaining hominization he allows a good deal of weight to the growth of language, especially of hunting narratives, as well as to the construction of weapons

Notes to pp. 140-161

against distant objects (the bow and arrow). Such considerations are weak, however, and seem at times to beg the question and at other times to be uncontrolled fantasies.

5. On this subject cf. E. Benveniste, "Le langage et l'expérience humaine," in *Problèmes de langage* (special issue of *Diogène*; Paris, 1966), pp. 9-11.

6. Economic groups or newspaper groups, for example, can be powerful bodies that include many individuals. Is this an exception to the ordinary use of the word "group"? No, it is not. An economic union involves, in fact, only a small number of societies (nations). Moreover, the public feels that decisions are taken at the top by a few managers who stand apart from the visible organization and complicated workings of these societies.

Nonetheless, we must admit that the word "group" is embarassingly fluid. If we take "smallness" as a class, it refers to the number of properties, not to the number of beings which possess the properties. A "blood group" includes millions of individuals but it is defined by a single property, that of not causing the clumping agglutination of red blood corpuscles in an individual when he receives blood from someone in the same group.

7. Like all groups, an informal group has a founding father. The latter acquires co-founders as soon as possible. Their purpose is to establish a brotherhood based on equality. But the goal can be achieved only asymptotically, for a short time, and while the members are few. Inequality is natural to societies.

8. Lucien Goldmann, "Pensée dialectique et sujet transindividuel," *Bulletin de la Société Française de Philosophie* 64, no. 3 (July-September, 1970), pp. 73-74.

NOTES TO CHAPTER 6

1. Published at 49, Faubourg Poissonnière ("Témoignage chrétien"), Paris (9).

2. The article quoting me was "De nouvelles communautés de l'Eglise," *Réponses chrétiennes*, no. 37, p. 24. My own article: "L'Eglise des 'petites communautés,'" *Parole et mission* 12 (1969) 533-47.

Notes to pp. 162-177

3. Karl Barth, "Les présuppositions théologiques des structures de l'Eglise," in *L'Eglise* (Geneva: Labor et Fides, 1964), pp. 125ff.

4. Ernst Käsemann, "Unity and Multiplicity in the New Testament Doctrine of the Church," in Käsemann, *New Testament Questions of Today*, translated by W. J. Montague (Philadelphia: Fortress, 1969), pp. 252-59.

5. R. Bohren, "Unsere Kasualpraxis, eine missionarische Angelegenheit," in *Theologische Existenz heute*, no. 83.

6. M. Peuchmaurd, "Qui faut-il baptiser?" *Parole et mission* 8 (1965) 112-32.

7. Cf. Gibson Winter, *The Suburban Captivity of the Churches: An Analysis of Protestant Responsibility in the Expanding Metropolis* (Garden City, N.Y.: Doubleday, 1961).

8. Cf. Peuchmaurd, *art. cit.*, p. 113.

9. *Prédication acte politique* (Paris: Editions du Cerf, 1970).

10. [The New American Bible has "insurrectionist" in John 18:30.]

11. Harvey Cox, *God's Revolution and Man's Responsibility* (Valley Forge: Judson, 1965).

12. Cf. Will Herberg, *Protestant, Catholic, Jew: An Essay in American Religious Sociology* (Garden City, N.Y.: Doubleday, 1955); H. O. Wölber, *Religion ohne Entscheidung* (Göttingen, 1950).

13. Norbert Bellini, "Eglise et oppression," *Christianisme social* 78 (1970) 624-25.

14. Ernst Bloch, *Atheism in Christianity: The Religion of the Exodus and the Kingdom*, translated by J. T. Swann (New York: Herder and Herder, 1972).

15. Paul Ricoeur, "Urbanisation et sécularisation," *Christianisme social* 75 (1967) 333.

16. To use terms which may be found (not necessarily in my order) in the writings of Bernard Besret; cf., e.g., his *Tomorrow A New Church*, translated by M. J. O'Connell (New York: Paulist Press, 1973).

NOTES TO CHAPTER 7

1. Cf. especially his "L'évolution du thème eschatologique dans la tradition johannique," *Revue biblique* 68 (1961) 507-24.

2. Rudolf Schnackenburg, *The Gospel according to St. John 1*, translated by Kevin Smyth (New York: Herder and Herder, 1968), pp. 72-74.

3. Cf. M.-E. Boismard, review of F.-M. Braun, *Jean le théologien et son évangile dans l'Eglise ancienne* (Paris: Gabalda, 1959), in *Revue biblique* 67 (1960) 592.

4. Cf. Rudolf Bultmann, *The Gospel of John: A Commentary*, translated by G. R. Beasley-Murray, R. W. N. Hoare, and J. K. Riches (Philadelphia: Westminster, 1971), pp. 461-86.

5. Cf. Alv Kragerud, *Der Lieblingsjünger im Johannesevangelium: Ein exegetischer Versuch* (Oslo: Osloer Universitätsverlag; Hamburg: Wagner, 1959).

6. Cf. M.-E. Boismard, review of Kragerud, in *Revue biblique* 67 (1960) 405-10.

7. Cf. Kragerud, *op. cit.*, pp. 53-83.

8. Cf. especially M.-E. Boismard, "Le chapitre XXI de saint Jean: Essai de critique littéraire," *Revue biblique* 54 (1947) 473-501.

NOTES TO CHAPTER 8

1. [The *Bundeschuher* were a peasant confederation active on the Upper Rhine; their name was derived from the peasant's sandal or clog, which served as their symbol.]

NOTES TO CHAPTER 9

1. Cf. E. Nestle, "German Versions [of the Bible]," *New Schaff-Herzog Encyclopedia of Religious Knowledge* 2 (1908) 143-47; K. Galling, "Deutsche Bibelübersetzungen," *Religion in Geschichte und Gegenwart*, 3rd ed., 1 (1957) 1201-10.

2. The humanist, Jakob Wimpheling, notes in his *De integritate libellus* (Strasbourg: J. Knobloch, 1505), ch. 28, that "we now find people from the lower classes reading the Old and New Testaments in German." Johann Ulrich Surgant makes the same observation in his *Manuale curatorum* (Basel: M. Furter, 1503), fol. lxx.

3. Martin Luther, "An Open Letter to Pope Leo X," translated by W. A. Lambert and Harold J. Grimm in *Martin Luther: Three Treatises* (Philadelphia: Fortress, 1960), p. 274.

4. Of the 337 printings of Luther's German Bible, in whole or in part, which we know of from 1522 to 1546, 44 were done in Alsace; cf. *Luthers Werke* (Weimar edition), series *Deutsche Bibel* 2 (190) 201ff.

5. The copy is in the BNUS under number R. 10087.

6. Cf. Charles Frédéric Heitz, *Das Zunftwesen in Strassburg* (Strasbourg, 1856), passim; Ulrich Craemer, *Die Verfassung und Verwaltung Strassburgs von der Reformationszeit bis zum Fall der Reichstadt (1521-1681)* (Frankfurt, 1931), pp. 90ff.

7. Sebastian Münster, *Cosmographia* (1535); quotation from the reprint of 1598 (Basel: Sebastian Henripetri), p. 668.

8. Cf. Philippe Dollinger, "La tolérance à Strasbourg au XVIème siècle," in *Hommage à Lucien Febvre* (Paris, 1954), pp. 241-49.

9. Sebastian Franck, *Germaniae chronicon* (Augsburg: A. Weissenhorn and H. Steiner, 1538), fol. 282 recto: "Was man anderswo henckt, dz streicht man zu Straszburg mit ruten ausz."

10. Cf. Jean Adam, *Evangelische Kirchengeschichte der Stadt Strassburg bis zur französischen Revolution* (Strassburg, 1922), pp. 67ff.; Henri Strohl, *Le protestantisme en Alsace* (Strassburg, 1950), pp. 37ff.; Miriam Usher Chrisman, *Strasbourg and the Reform: A Study in the Process of Change* (New Haven, 1967), pp. 113ff.

Notes to pp. 219-223

11. Cf. Bernd Moeller, *Reichstadt und Reformation* (Schriften des Vereins für Reformationsgeschichte 180; Gütersloh, 1962), p. 25; French translation, *Villes d'Empire et Réformation* (Geneva, 1966), pp. 32-33. Cf. also Ernst-Wilhelm Kohls, "Evangelische Bewegung und Kirchenordnung in oberdeutschen Reichsstädten," *Zeitschrift der Savigny-Stiftung für Rechtsgeschichte* 84 (1967), *Kanonistische Abteilung*, pp. 110-34.

12. Cf. the following works, among others: Camille Gerbert, *Geschichte der Strassburger Sektenbewegung zur Zeit der Reformation 1524-1534* (Strassburg, 1889), *passim*; Abraham Hulshof, *Geschiedenis van de Doopsgezinden te Straatsburg van 1525 tot 1557* (Amsterdam, 1905), *passim*; George H. Williams, *The Radical Reformation* (Philadelphia, Westminster, 1962), pp. 241ff. The chief source I have consulted, however, is the documentation assembled in *Quellen zur Geschichte der Täufer* VII: *Elsass 1: Stadt Strassburg, 1522-1532*, and VIII: *Elsass 2: Stadt Strassburg 1533-1535* (= *Quellen und Forschungen zur Reformationsgeschichte 26-27*), edited by Manfred Krebs and Jean Rott (Gütersloh, 1959-60); henceforth referred to as *Quellen*, with volume and page number. -- In the Introduction to volume 1 (i.e. *Elsass* 1), p. ix, the editors themselves suggest a classification of the non-conformists still to be found at Strassburg and add to the three categories I have proposed the anti-Trinitarians (Thomas Saltzmann and Michael Servetus), the "epicureans" (pastors Anton Engelbrecht and Wolfgang Schultheiss), and the humanists (Otto Brunfels and Johan Sapidus).

13. On these leaders, all of whom for various reasons rejected infant baptism, cf. the *Mennonite Encyclopedia*, 4 volumes (Scottdale, Pa., 1955-59).

14. For example, Fridolin Meyger, notary, and Lukas Hackfurt, superintendent of the city's charitable works; cf. *Quellen*, 1, p. 132, notes 7-8.

15. Cf. Rudolhe Peter, "Le maraîcher Clément Ziegler, l'homme et son oeuvre," *Revue d'histoire et de philosophie religieuses* 34 (1954) 255-82.

16. *Quellen* 1, p. 9.

17. *Quellen* 1, p. 15.

18. *Quellen* 1, pp. 33-34.

19. *Quellen* 1, p. 38.

Notes to pp. 223-227

20. *Quellen* 1, pp. 145ff.

21. *Quellen* 1, p. 65.

22. *Quellen* 2, pp. 296, 297, 300.

23. *Quellen* 1, p. 63.

24. These two places were about nineteen miles south of Strasbourg.

25. *Quellen* 2, p. 297.

26. Cf. Peter Kawerau, *Melchior Hofmann als religiöser Denker* (Haarlem, 1954).

27. *Quellen* 1, pp. 258-59.

28. *Quellen* 2, p. 14.

29. "Butzer habe den Strassburgern das Licht ausgeptzt"; cf. Timothée-Guillaume Roehrich, *Geschichte der Reformation im Elsass und besonders in Strassburg* (3 vols.; Strassburg, 1830-32), vol. 2, p. 100.

30. *Quellen* 2, p. 110.

31. *Quellen* 1, pp. 259, 553. Illkirch is near Strasbourg, about four miles south of the center of the city.

32. *Quellen* 2, pp. 386, 388.

33. *Quellen* 2, pp. 321ff. and 345, note 1.

34. On Schwenckfeld, cf. Alexandre Koyré, *Mystiques, spirituels, alchimistes du XVIème siècle allemand* (Paris, 1955), pp. 1-19; Gottfried Maron, *Individualismus und Gemeinschaft bei Caspar von Schwenckfeld* (Stuttgart, 1961).

35. Cf. Roland H. Bainton, *Katherine Zell* (*Medievalia et Humanistica: Studies in Medieval and Renaissance Culture*, new series, 1; Cleveland: Case Western Reserve University Press, 1970), 28 pp.

36. *Quellen* 2, p. 80.

37. *Von Christo Jesu unserem säligmacher....Christliche und trostliche Lobgesäng*, 4 parts (Strassburg: Jakob Frölich, 1534-

Notes to pp. 227-229

36); there is a photocopy of this very rare work in the Wilhelmitanum Collegium Library at Strasbourg.

38. Paul Akpers and Markus Jenny, "Es kommt ein Schiff, geladen," *Jahrbuch für Liturgik und Hymnologie* 10 (1965) 147-52.

39. On Franck cf. Koyré, *op. cit.*, pp. 21-43, and especially the writings of Doris Reiber: first, her critical study of Eberhard Teuffel's *"Landräumig"--Sebastian Franck, ein Wanderer an Donau, Rhein und Neckar* (Neustadt an der Aisch, 1954), in *Bibliothèque d'Humanisme et Renaissance* 20 (1958) 218-28; then her article, "Sébastien Franck 1499-1542," *ibid.*, 21 (1959) 190-204; finally her unpublished dissertation for the doctorate in religious studies from the Faculty of Protestant Theology in the University of Strasbourg: *La pensée religieuse de Sébastien Franck* (1970; copy in the Bibliothèque Nationale at the University of Strasbourg [BNUS]).

40. Sebastian Franck, *Chronica: Zeytbuch und geschychtbibel von anbegyn bisz inn disz gegenwertig M. D. xxxj. jar* (Strassburg: Balthasar Beck, 1531).

41. Cf. Jean Lebeau, "Erasme, Sébastien Franck et la tolérance," in *Erasme, l'Alsace et son temps* (Strasbourg: Publications de la Société Savante d'Alsace et des Régions de l'Est, 1971), pp. 117-40.

42. *Quellen* 1, pp. 342-43, 358-59, 395, 541-42.

43. *Quellen* 1, p. 136, with the references in note 33, above.

44. *Quellen* 1, p. 561.

45. *Quellen* 1, p. 563.

46. *Quellen* 2, p. 314. The printers at Strassburg who dealt mainly in such books were Johann Schott, Johann Schwan, Christian Egenolf, Johann Schwintzer, Balthasar Beck (whose stepdaughter became Sebastian Franck's second wife); at Hagenau there was Valentin Kobian. On these cf. François Ritter, *Histoire de l'imprimerie alsacienne aux XVe et XVIe siècles* (Strasbourg, 1955).

47. Cf. the basic work by François Wendel, *L'Eglise de Strasbourg: Sa constitution et son organisation, 1532-1535* (Etudes d'Histoire et de Philosophie Religieuses 38; Paris, 1942). The reader may profitably consult the unpublished dissertation (1960) of Charles Buell Mitchell, *Martin Bucer and Sectarian Dissent* (in the Yale University Library).

Notes to pp. 229-234

48. *Ordnung und Kirchengebrauch...uff gehabtem Synode fürgenommen* (Strassburg: Johann Pruss der Jünger?, 1534); a copy of this very rare book is in BNUS, under number R 10579.

49. *Kurtze schrifftliche erklärung für die kinder* (Strassburg: Matthias Apiarius, 1534); copy in BNUS, R 102399. Cf. Ernst-Wilhelm Kohls, "Martin Bucers Katechismus vom Jahre 1534 und seine Stellung innerhalb der Katechismusgeschichte," *Zeitschrift für bayerische Kirchengeschichte* 39 (1970) 83-94.

50. Cf. Wendel, *op. cit.*, pp. 179-87; Jacques Courvoisier, "Bucer et la discipline ecclésiastique," in *Mélanges offerts à Henri Meylan* (Geneva, 1970), pp. 21-29.

51. To name but a few: Mathis Pfarrer, Nicholaus Kniebs, Johann Lindenfels, and Michael Rot.

52. Cf. Werner Bellardi, *Die Geschichte der "Christlichen Gemeinden" in Strassburg, 1546-1550* (Leipzig, 1934).

53. Cf. Courvoisier, *art. cit.*, p. 25.

NOTES TO CHAPTER 10

1. We cannot be sure that the leaders of the communities we shall be studying knew of the German community established in the early eighteenth century (1732) at Ephrata in Lancaster County, Pennsylvania. They may well have been aware of it. The community was made up of Seventh-Day Baptists; they professed a community of goods, but a relative one, inasmuch as the members were not obliged to hand over all their possessions. What they held in common was, in essence, the tools and products of their labor. A monastic strictness reigned, so that in the surrounding area the place was called "the monastery". Celibacy was obligatory; men and women lived in separate buildings. Some German historians claim that the community was known to some religious circles in Germany, and, in point of fact, though it rapidly declined after the death in 1786 of its founder, Johann Konrad Beissel, it was still in existence at the beginning of the present century. A German visitor in 1911 found eleven members there, all celibates and living according to the principles of the original community. It is possible, then, that Rapp

Notes to pp. 234-267

and other community leaders knew of Ephrata, since most of them founded their own colonies in Pennsylvania and adjacent Ohio. Moreover, as Desroche observes in his study of the Shakers, there were communications between the various groups. -- We may also note that a German community called *Woman of the Desert* was in existence as early as the seventeenth century (founded by Kelpius in 1684). Beissel seems to have been a member of this community before establishing his own.

2. In addition to the studies of American scholars-- Noyer, Nordhoff, Hillquitt, Hinds, Buskee, and Infield--I have derived special help from R. Liefmann, *Die kommunistischen Gemeinden in Nordamerika* (Jena, 1922).

3. On this point cf. my essay, "Le statut de la femme dans le communisme," *Cahiers Internationaux de Sociologie*, no. 43 (July-December, 1967) 45-66.

NOTES TO CHAPTER 11

1. Cf. Rüdiger Reitz, "L'Eglise souterraine en Allemagne Fédérale," *IDOC International*, no. 21 (April 1, 1970).

2. The Meaux group, with Bishop Briçonnet and Lefèvre d'Etaples at its head, was a typical informal group. Cf. R. J. Lovy, *Les origines de la Réforme Française: Meaux (1518-1548)* (Paris: Librairie Protestante, 1959).

3. The informal groups gave a joyful welcome to the World Council of Churches' Conference on Church and Society (Geneva, 1966). But they are sure that this initiative will have no successors.

4. Since I cannot go into the question here I refer the reader to an interesting publication of the World Council of Churches, *The Church for Others: A Quest for Structures for Missionary Congregations* (Geneva: World Council of Churches, 1968), and to the report of P. Keller, "Formes nouvelles d'une Eglise pour les autres," *Foi et vie* 65, no. 6 (1966).

5. Cf. E. Trocmé, "Les eglises pauliniennes vues du dehors: Jacques 2, 1 à 3, 13," in *Studia Evangelica* 2 (Texte und Untersuchungen 87; Berlin: Akademie Verlag, 1964), pp. 660-69.

Notes to pp. 268-302

6. Dietrich Bonhoeffer, *Life Together*, translated by John W. Doberstein (New York: Harper and Row, 1954).

7. For a more detailed study of the Pentecost, 1968, Eucharist, cf. my "Vers une solution du problème eucharistique," *Revue d'histoire et de philosophie religieuses* 49 (1969) 165-75.

8. Cf. Henry Bruston, "Le problème posé par les petites communautés," *Information--Evangélisation*, no. 1 (1971).

NOTES TO CHAPTER 13

1. To refer only to French Catholic studies, there are: Henri Denis, "Les communautés de base sont-elles l'Eglise?," in *Les communautés de base = Lumière et vie*, no. 99 (1970) 103-32; P. Toulat, *Les "petits groupes" et l'Eglise*, unpublished document of the Episcopal Secretariat, Febraury, 1970; A. Liégé, O.P., "De nouvelles communautés d'Eglise," *Réponses chrétiennes*, no. 37 (April, 1971).

2. Without mentioning his own group, Marcel Légaut has sketched the ideal of such a community in his *Introduction à l'intelligence du passé et de l'avenir du christianisme* (Paris: Aubier, 1970): "Unlike religions based on authority the religion based on invitation does not take shape initially in a collectivity that develops among men by using chiefly sociological means. It grows rather by individual contact and personal influence; the other must want to respond. It grows with a circumspection that is in sharp contrast to the spectacular kind of mass manifestations and propaganda methods that are used by the religions of authority. The members of a religion of invitation are not isolated but they do continue to be solitaries. They are all the more so as they better understand the nature of the personal call involved in such a religion, as they live up to that religion more perfectly in liberty of spirit and tenacious perseverance, and as they advance further in the way of fidelity" (p. 227; cf. p. 285).

3. It seems that the term is difficult to translate into German. K. Bergner in his German translation of Jean-Paul Audet's *Le projet évangélique* (cf. note 7, below) has *Stammgemeinde*. Is this an appropriate equivalent?

4. José-Maria González-Ruiz, "Genèse des communautés de base en contexte ecclésial," *Lumière et vie*, no. 99 (1970) 43-49.

5. Dominique Barbé, *Demain les communautés de base* (Paris: Editions du Cerf, 1970).

6. Georges Casalis, "L'Eglise des 'petites communautés,'" *Parole et mission* 12 (1969) 533.

7. I do not care for this ambiguous word, which is used a good deal in Germany. In Alois Müller (ed.), *Democratization of the Church* (Concilium 63; New York: Herder and Herder, 1971), Rudolf Pesch, Karl Lehmann, and Norbert Greinacher explain in their several articles that "democracy" in this context does not refer to a political system but to a set of values which are characteristic of a certain kind of shared life. -- The idea of the Church as a brotherhood has been explained in splendid fashion by Joseph Ratzinger, *The Open Circle: The Meaning of Christian Brotherhood* (New York: Sheed and Ward, 1966), and in his article "Fraternité," *Dictionnaire de spiritualité* 5:1141-67. Above all, however, cf. Jean-Paul Audet on brotherhood as applied to our present subject in his *The Gospel Project*, translated by Edmond Bonin (New York: Paulist Press, 1969), and in his essay "Priester und Laie in der christlichen Gemeinde: Der Weg in die gegenseitige Entfremdung," in *Der priesterliche Dienst* 1 (Quaestiones Disputatae 46; Freiburg: Herder, 1970), pp. 115-75.

8. Georges Crespy, "Les impacts de notre culture sur les communautés de base," *Lumière et vie*, no. 99 (1970) 61-76, especially 64-70.

9. Cf. Winoc De Broucker, "Communautés de base pour des chrétiens des grandes villes," *Etudes* 332 (January-June, 1970) 111-20.

10. The Note of the French bishops is in *Documentation catholique*, no. 1559 (March 15, 1970) 278-83. The Note is a comment on the Instruction *Actio pastoralis Ecclesiae* issued by the Congregation for Divine Worship and dated May 15, 1969; text of the latter is in *Acta Apostolicae Sedis* 61 (1969) 806-11. Cf. R. Coffy, "La signification du phénomène 'Groupes,'" *Maison-Dieu*, no. 100 (4th quarter, 1969) 123-29; B.-D. Marliangeas, "Réflexions sur les messes de petits groupes," *ibid.*, pp. 130-38; F. Nikolesch, "Die Feier der Messe im kleinen Kreis," *Liturgisches Jahrbuch* 20 (1970) 40-52; Etienne Amory, S.J., "Reflections on the Group Mass," *Lumen vitae* 26 (1971) 263-72, who cites the text of the Belgian bishops, issued in March 1970.

Notes to pp. 311-317

11. Cf. Vatican II, *Dogmatic Constitution on the Church*, no. 32, translated in Walter M. Abbott, S.J. (editor), *The Documents of Vatican II* (New York: Herder and Herder, Association Press, 1966), pp. 58-59.

12. Karl Barth, quoted in A. Dartigues, *Que dites-vous du Christ?* (Paris: Editions du Cerf, 1969), p. 117. Compare Vatican II, *Pastoral Constitution on the Church in the Modern World*, nos. 39 and 57; Abbott, pp. 237 and 265.

13. François Biot, "Les réunions de Bourges et de Lourdes: Des signes sur notre route," *Hebdo TC*, no. 1373 (October 29, 1970) 17. Cf. also J. Guichard, "Communautés de base et contexte politique," *Lumière et vie*, no. 99 (1970) 77-102; Guichard observes: "No initiatives come from the groups themselves; *all look to political problems posed in terms set by others*" (p. 97). -- Vandalino, near Turin, is a representative and significant example; cf. *IDOC*, no. 37 (January 1, 1971) 60ff., 84.

14. James E. P. Woodruff, "Black Power vis-à-vis 'The Kingdom of God,'" in *The Underground Church*, edited by Malcolm Boyd (New York: Sheed and Ward, 1968), p. 98.

15. Mary Daly, "Dispensing with Trivia," *Commonweal*, May 31, 1968, p. 323.

16. John Pairmann Brown, "Toward a United Peace and Freedom Church," in *The Underground Church*, p. 39.

17. Paul Evdokimov, *La femme et le salut du monde* (Paris: Castermann, 1958). Bernanos again: "God does not choose the same men to watch over His Word and to fulfill it": *Letter to the Europeans*, in *Plea for Liberty*, translated by Harry Lorin Binsse (New York: Pantheon, 1944), p. 266.

18. Cf. the literature cited in note 1, above.

19. On the insertion of the small communities into the Church as a whole cf. Max Delespesse, *Révolution évangélique?* (Paris: Fleurus, 1970), pp. 34, 89, 96.

20. Cf. my *Lay People in the Church: A Study for a Theology of the Laity*, translated by Donald Atwater (rev. ed.; London: Chapman, 1965), chapter 3. But cf. also Johannes Baptist Metz, "Does Our Church Need a New Reformation? A Catholic Reply," in *Post-Ecumenical Christianity*, edited by Hans Küng (Concilium 54; New York: Herder and Herder, 1970), pp. 81-91.

Notes to pp. 317-319

21. Cf. Vatican II, *Dogmatic Constitution on the Church*, no. 48: "The final age of the world has already come upon us (cf. 1 Cor. 10:11). The renovation of the world has been irrevocably decreed and in this age is already anticipated in some real way. For even now on this earth the Church is marked with a genuine though imperfect holiness. However, until there is a new heaven and a new earth where justice dwells (cf. 2 Pet. 3:13), the pilgrim Church in her sacraments and institutions, which pertain to this present time, takes on the appearance of this passing world. She herself dwells among creatures who groan and travail in pain until now and await the revelation of the sons of God (cf. Rom. 8:19-22)" (Abbott, p. 79).

22. A. Liégé, *op. cit.*, p. 21.

23. In relation to our theme cf. M.-D. Chenu, "Carismi e gruppi spontanei," *Sacra doctrina* 15 (1970) 431-45.

24. Louis Lochet speaks as follows of the revision of life; we quote his words because they are relevant to what we shall be saying in a moment about the Christian man. "There is, I think, a kind of 'discovery' that is specific to our age and lies in the line of the Incarnation; it is the discovery of the Christian values that are involved in daily life, in events, even in 'profane' history. The discovery brings with it an invitation to acknowledge these values by faith so that we may become sharers in God's plan as it is being brought to fulfillment in the entire life of the human community. Here we have a new and undeniable aspect of fidelity to the basic thrust of life in Christ and in the Church....A new dimension of personal and communal life forces us to take another look at everything and by faith to see God coming to us from below, as it were, that is, in the midst of everyday life, of our encounters with others, and of events. We must learn eventually that life according to the Gospel means a twofold fidelity to God's Word: as it comes down from heaven and as it arises from the earth" (*Vie Spirituelle Supplément*, no. 66 [September, 1963] 445, 447).

25. Cf. the interesting remarks of Testis [= Maurice Blondel], *Le Semaine Sociale de Brodeaux et le monophorisme*, a reprint from *Annales de philosophie chrétienne* (Paris, 1910); Lucien Laberthonnière, *La notion chrétienne de l'autorité* (Paris, 1955).

26. Cf. Karl Delahaye, *Ecclesia Mater chez les Pères des trois premiers siècles: Pour une renouvellement de la pastorale aujourd'hui* (Unam sanctam 46; Paris: Editions du Cerf, 1964).

Notes to pp. 320-325

27. Marcel Légaut, "La passion de l'Eglise," *Etudes* 333 (July-December, 1970.) 426; cf. note 2, above.

28. There are some remarks on this point in my paper at the Brussels Congress of September, 1970; cf. *Concilium* (French edition) no. 60, Supplement for 1970, pp. 153-54.

29. See J. Robert, "Des prophètes pour aujourd'hui," *Parole et mission* 12 (1969) 564-74.

30. In *L'Eglise souterraine* (Gembloux: Duculot, 1970), p. 52.

31. A. Nesti, "Le phénomène des communautés de base en marge des institutions de l'Eglise en Italie," *IDOC*, no. 22 (April 15, 1970) 45.

32. Richard McBrien, "The Underground Church in the United States," in *Secularization and Spirituality*, edited by Christian Duquoc, O.P. (Concilium 49; New York: Paulist Press, 1969), p. 117.

33. Theodor M. Steeman, "L'Eglise souterraine: Aspects et dynamisme du changement dans le catholicisme contemporaine," *IDOC*, no. 3 (June 1, 1969) 74.

34. *Art. cit.*, p. 88.

35. *Art. cit.*, pp. 68ff., 88-89.

36. "Schism of Consciousness," *Commonweal*, May 31, 1968, p. 331.

37. Benjamin Charles Milner, Jr., *Calvin's Doctrine of the Church* (Leiden: Brill, 1970).

38. Cf. notes 13 and 16, above.

39. Cf. note 30, above, and corresponding text.

40. *Notre combat* (Groupes T. C.), nos. 39-40, p. 23, quoted in J. Guichard, *art. cit.*, p. 97. Cf. the same author's *Hommes nouveaux, nouveaux Chrétiens?* (Paris: Editions du Chalet, 1971).

41. J. Cardonnel, interview in the *Nouvel Observateur*, November 4, 1968, quoted by J. de Fabregues, *L'Eglise, esclave ou espoir du monde* (Paris: Aubier, 1971), p. 186; the author provides numerous other quotations of a similar tenor on pp. 186ff., 194-95, 208ff.

Notes to pp. 325-337

42. *Art. cit.*, p. 86.

43. Cf. A. Nesti, *art. cit.*, pp. 45ff.

44. Cf., e.g., J. Flamand, *Monde et réalités terrestres* (Paris: Desclée De Brouwer, 1969), pp. 269ff., where he is summarizing E. Doens de Lambert, "Qui le Christ a-t-il épousé: L'Eglise ou...le monde?" *Etudes franciscaines* 16 (June, 1966). -- On the question of a secularized liturgy and on the other points mentioned there is a vast literature; I cannot go into developments, quotations, references, etc.

45. J. Richard, "Le problème de sécularisation," in *Le prêtre hier, aujourd'hui, demain* (Ottawa Congress, 1969; Paris: Editions du Cerf, 1970), p. 345.

46. I shall give only two references: "Avons-nous à lutter contre la construction de nouvelles églises?" *La lettre*, no. 146 (October, 1970) 16-20; "La contestation des Chantiers du Cardinal," *Notre combat*, nos. 45-46 (January-February, 1971) 22-30.

47. Quoted in *Le monde*, March 18, 1971.

NOTES TO CONCLUSION

1. I have expressed myself elsewhere on this matter: *Ministères et communion ecclésiale* (Paris: Editions du Cerf, 1971).

www.ingramcontent.com/pod-product-compliance
Lightning Source LLC
Chambersburg PA
CBHW050613300426
44112CB00012B/1478